# MISSISSIPPI MADNESS

## Canoeing the Mississippi - Missouri

**Nicholas Francis & William Butcher**

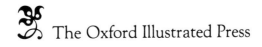

The Oxford Illustrated Press

To the memory of the Indian Nations of
North America: The Dacotahs, the Cheyennes,
the Sioux and many others without name.

The Oxford Illustrated Press

© 1990, Nicholas Francis and William Butcher

ISBN 0 946609 94 2

**Published by:**
The Oxford Illustrated Press Limited, Haynes Publishing Group,
Sparkford, Nr Yeovil, Somerset BA22 7JJ, England.

Distributed in the United States of America by Sheridan House Inc., 145 Palisade
Street, Dobbs Ferry, New York 10522, USA.

**Printed in England by:**
J.H. Haynes & Co Limited, Sparkford, Nr. Yeovil, Somerset.

**British Library Cataloguing in Publication Data**
Francis, Nicholas
    Mississippi madness: Canoeing the Mississippi –
    Missouri.
    1. United States. Mississippi River. Canoeing –
    Biographies
    I. Title    II. Butcher, William
    797.1'22'0924
    ISBN 0-946609-94-2

**Library of Congress catalog number** 89-85543

Line drawings by John Rankin.

# Contents

# *Acknowledgements*

First and foremost, I would like to offer my deep thanks to the members of the back-up team, Bill, Liam, and Tim, for it was they who shared my hardships – and on occasion saved my life – without always receiving the same recognition as I did. My warmest gratitude must also go to Professor McWhirter, whose farsightedness made it all happen, to Randal Sadleir, whose efficiency, imagination and flair led to the idea becoming a material reality, and to John Munslowe and British Airways for their great generosity. My special thanks are also due to Lord Victor Matthews and Trafalgar House Investments, to Bass Charrington, and to H.K. Furniture. I owe a special debt to my parents, my brother Robert, and my sister Louisa for their loving support. Finally my thanks to my friends back home, Roger McMahon, John Skinner, John King, Kay Butcher, and Jeannie Smith, for they were good enough to believe in it all from the beginning.

I would also like to thank: the people of America, whose incredible warmth gave me the strength to carry on through that great land; Cathy, Gerard Legrand, Ewen Macleod, Jim Landers, Anne and Jim Terleph, Ian Reid, Chris Newell, Colonel Blashford-Snell, Graham Butcher, Irving Rymer, Ian Brett, Everett and Terri Hicks, Joe and Ethel Watson, Mr Carey, Bob Singer, Jack Ayres, the Wrights, their generous friend the pilot, Leah Grant, Freddie Morton, Mr Haddlerland, the Chamber of Commerce of Bismarck, Jim and Cindy, Ben Innes, Albert, Jim and Laura, Bob Hatfield, Myron and Mrs Four-Bears, Charles, Mr and Mrs 'Driftwood' Saltman, 'Rattlesnake' and 'Granny Claws', Dan Murphy, Randy of CBS, Ron and Diane Carson, Gordon Brown, Phenix Kayaks, The Outdoor Store, Mayor Conway, Colonel Moran, Mr and Mrs Garnett, Debbie Matkin, George, Jack, Sam, Earl, Grey Hammett, and A. Maxwell Wright of New Orleans; Graham Butcher, Evelyn Ross, Valerie

Murray, Dr Andy Martin, and Bernard Bouchard; Tim Eley, Scott Dine and Bernard Vaillant for the photographs. And lastly, my special thanks to Stéphane for all her help and support.

To those whose names I have omitted, I offer my deepest apologies. Forgotten by my pen, they are not forgotten in my heart.

N.F.

NOTE ON AUTHORSHIP: This book was written by Nicholas Francis and William Butcher together. We both consider it such a joint work that it would be invidious to attempt to ascribe individual authorship to particular parts.

N.F. and W.B.

NOTE ON TERMINOLOGY: In this book the terms 'kayak' and 'canoe' will often be used interchangeably. More precisely, 'kayaks' (covered canoes, of Eskimo origin) and 'Indian canoes' (normally open) will frequently be considered as both belonging to the general class of 'canoes'.

# *Foreword*

I have long had a passionate desire, hitherto unpublicised, to sail down the Mississippi. Once, a few years ago, I almost achieved my ambition. Everything was arranged for me to set off from St Louis and head for New Orleans. But, as has so often happened, official engagements suddenly intervened and it came to naught.

In my wildest dreams, however, I never visualised anything like the venture so brilliantly described in this book. For a start, I never thought of throwing in the Missouri as well. For me it was to be the Mississippi, on a comfortable steam packer for the inside of a week. I had booked a splendid cabin. I made sure the food was good and accompanied by a plentiful supply of mint juleps and other forms of refreshment popular in the southern states.

Why this hidden passion? Perhaps it was because just after ceasing to be an undergraduate at Oxford I visited New Orleans on the way to Mobile whilst taking part in a debating tour of the United States. I was fascinated by the city, especially by the older part and its superb French restaurants. Perhaps because having seen the great breadth of the Mississippi I was curious about whence it came and how it had broadened out. Perhaps because on a later occasion I went on an expedition in the Gulf of Mexico to an oil rig and saw the effect of this river flowing into the sea. Perhaps because of always associating the Mississippi with negro spirituals and genuine jazz. Whatever the cause it has deepened with the years.

This very readable book describes how four young men satisfied their desire to find a purpose in life at a critical time of their careers. How they made the preparations for their expedition and overcame the difficulties they encountered on the way. How, in the process, they substantially helped the worthy cause of cancer research. And how, as a result of all this, they have established several world records.

Congratulations to them on their achievements and good luck in the future. I shall go on waiting—and hoping—for a pleasant spring cruise down the Mississippi.

The Rt Hon Edward Heath MBE MP
August 1989

# *Mississippi Dreaming*

## I

I had wormed my way, inch by inch, out of the treacherous mud. I had survived one cold night without protection. By drinking the silty water of the inland sea, I had dulled my hunger.

But now every stroke was an effort, and the first house still lay three days ahead. Also, my canoe had developed a leak, and the sun was going down. I was just starting my 25,000th stroke since the taste of food, when I heard a sound rather like distant thunder. Seconds later, a plane hopped over the hills, seemed to hesitate, then banked steeply. I wondered if I was dreaming when I saw Bill's curly hair and lopsided grin. But the Mars Bars that bounced off the shore tasted wonderfully real . . . .

The bridge that had brought me to that surprising rendezvous spanned not only two continents but also a large part of my youth. To understand where I was and what I was trying to do, it is perhaps best to go back a little.

It was raining when it all began, and it felt cold. A decade would pass before it finished, and it would be raining again; but the drops would be warm and fall from a translucent sky. It started in the darkened library of a boarding school in Scotland, and it would all end when a mighty river flooded gratefully into the gleaming blue of a tropical sea.

The intervening period was a time of great years and of wasted years; from meetings with irate professors appalled at my lack of progress to meetings with a president and a future king apparently impressed by my progress. It would above all be a time of searching and of growing, while I groped my way towards a distant and elusive goal.

This book, then, is the account of the first recorded kayak conquest of a primordial American dream. The journey was the age-old one of

9

self-discovery; but it was also one where a British boy who once smoked forty cigarettes a day used the longest single canoe trip on the globe to alert the world to the dangers of a terrible scourge. In short, to aid the fight against cancer, I attempted to canoe the 3810 miles of the Mississippi-Missouri. This is the story of my Journey to New Orleans.

II

My interest in canoes started early. Walking back from school one day, I saw a beautiful covered canoe in a shop-window. Sixpence pocket-money a week seemed reasonable credit to me, so I took my school-cap off, put a deep voice on, and bought the £42 kayak, 'to be delivered to Mr Nicholas Francis's residence in a fortnight's time'. Two weeks later, my mother answered the phone. 'Yes . . . Do you not mean Doctor Francis . . . it was a young man who made the order – a schoolboy?' Then the reckoning came. My parents eventually located my hiding place, and demonstrated in no uncertain terms that any remaining canoeing plans would have to be postponed indefinitely!

At thirteen, I was sent away to boarding school. Most of the boys had been at prep. school, and were used to public-school life; but I hadn't, and wasn't. What didn't help either was that I was also the only Roman Catholic in a staunchly Church of England establishment; half-French (when de Gaulle had just kept Britain out of the EEC); and the only boy to have thin black gym-shoes. I was socially dead. I became a loner, rejecting all forms of sport and taking long walks in the bleak Highland landscape.

I did have one friend, though. David Combe and I used to go to the musty school library together and pore over Britain's imperial past: Livingstone, Scott, Lawrence, Hillary and Tenzing; the winning of India, the saving of Canada, and the losing of the United States. One especially dreich afternoon, David asked 'And you, Nick?' Without hesitation, I replied: 'Some day, I will attempt something worthy of this glorious past.' The starting-point of the circle, if indeed there was one, had finally been found.

As I drifted and rebelled my way through school, my mind was mainly elsewhere. The rest of my family had set a standard of excellence in most of the things they had done, and I was searching for some way of living up to their achievements. When I left school, this search had produced no practical result at all, but I had at least found a number of well-defined aims for myself. To experience life as quickly as possible; to earn some money of my own; and to climb a ladder towards a plateau at fifty-five that is customarily called success. My real ambition, however, was to go far beyond this plateau, if necessary by going round it, and to experience

10

adventure like my heroes – to find my other self by taking paths not already worn down by thousands of previous feet.

The first two aims were achieved by means of a tree-felling job, which shocked society and worried my parents but did wonders for my physique and self-confidence. All in all, it took more than eight months to get the school out of my system. But then, when I went to Aberdeen to study languages, all the side effects came flooding back. The University and I gave each other up, and, on the spur of the moment, I went to sea.

Travelling the lower deck of the Merchant Navy had further effects on my development. I grew up quickly; and I discovered the lure of the sea. After a hectic day's work, I used to walk along to the fo'c'sle and stare out into the dark abyss all around. I would try to imagine what it would be like to be in a tiny vessel amongst the raging elements, instead of being protected by thousands of tons of machinery. I had still never been within spitting distance of a canoe, but I slowly acquired a belief, perhaps irrational, that I would be able to handle one when the time came. At this stage there seemed no particular hurry.

After five months, I decided to have one last go at fitting in. At the grand old age of twenty-one, I signed on for a degree in 'Hotel and Catering Management' at Strathclyde University. I had no idea what it entailed; but I was encouraged by my Uncle Gerard, who worked in that line of business himself, and that was enough.

I felt very relieved to find that I could stick it – just! In my spare time, I found myself concentrating on fencing, table tennis, and mountaineering. Only slowly did I realise that perversely all three were activities I had rejected at school, and that, like the tree-felling, all three depended on well-developed arms. The future would bring these ideas together again with a vengeance . . . .

The future began to happen, almost by chance, a couple of years later. Strathclyde students were required to gain work experience in the long vacation before their final year. My intention had been to work in Argyllshire for a while with a friend called Ewen Macleod, and then to go to Paris and work there. But as soon as I got to the Glenborrowdale Hotel, Ewen showed me the magnificent sea loch stretching out behind the back door. Loch Sunart freed the dreams and pangs that had been battened down in me for half a decade. I decided to buy a covered canoe and to stay in Argyll all summer long.

Ewen and I hitched into Fort William and ordered a superb 'Kester Torridon'. A week later a phone call came for a Mr Nick Francis – who answered 'present' this time – and soon a gleaming plastic-wrapped doll was delivered: a hair under 16 ft long, 1½ ft wide, and less than 40 lb in weight. At last I had found a sphere in which I really wanted to test myself.

11

After an interminable day, we carried the kayak down to the moonlit sea loch. In a state of great excitement, we nearly cracked her wide open with a half-bottle of Moet & Chandon. After an age of trying, something finally gave, champagne gushed, and Ewen slipped *Lady Midnight* lightly into the water. She fitted like a new glove. But she also felt extremely sensitive, and I felt terribly awkward. Then, very slowly, we moved off together . . . .

I measured one of the islands at the mouth of the loch: exactly 10 miles right round. Then, at two in the morning, I paddled round it myself, taking ninety minutes' – an average of $6^2/3$ miles an hour. Further nocturnal experiments taught me that I could 'cruise' at 5 mph almost indefinitely.

A few weeks later, I read that somebody had just broken the cross-Channel record. He had canoed the 22 miles in 3 hours 36 minutes: 'only' 6 mph. With intense training, I thought, I might have a chance of breaking that record myself. Once the idea was in my head, I couldn't get it out. Every night, I used to go round that island, working at my speed and stamina, until in the end I knew every pebble and blade of grass on it.

Once or twice I capsized in choppy water. Each time, I tried to get back into the canoe while still on the water, but each time I was thrown off the bucking stern. In the end I gave up, and simply swam to the shore. A decision I was to regret some years later.

To reduce the boredom, I started counting. Five hundred strokes, I found, covered one mile. After 5 miles, I would have some chocolate and a cigarette. Then, exactly on the hour, I would set off again. If I dawdled, the rest period disappeared; if I rushed, my upper arm muscles gave me hell. In the end, I had it finely tuned down to the nearest minute.

Only too soon, the long hot summer of '75 came to an end. I had however become a happier and more confident young man. I had also acquired a new set of priorities. First, to try and get my degree. Second, to carry out a medium-distance sea journey. Third, to have a go at the Channel. And fourth – provided these last two forays went well – to attempt some supreme challenge – though at this stage I wasn't quite sure exactly what.


### III

All through that year, I waited and dreamed. With my mind on other things, I took my finals and then a job as a hotel-porter. Very soon I had £200 in my pocket and bulging muscles on my arms. Then I decided to canoe round Ireland.

The full story of my shoestring Irish trip, with its disappointments and disasters, but also its triumphs and highly comic moments, would almost take a book in itself. Here I will simply record that, starting from Carnlough in Northern Ireland, I in the end reached Hookhead, near Waterford. One of the reasons I had to stop was money; and the other was that I had failed one of my finals. Liam O'Neill, a very good friend from Strathclyde and a native of Carnlough, kindly drove down to fetch me. Tanned but still uninspired, I resat the exam, before taking the high road down to Dover.

My second canoe venture was not without its problems either. Again, I will only record that I paddled as fast as I could, and managed to average $5^3/4$ mph. But this was not fast enough, and in the end I was left with a handful of shattered dreams. I went despondently home, to discover a consolation prize. I had passed my final final and was now a Bachelor of Arts! On the rebound from this shock, I found a managerial post at a three-star hotel in Edinburgh. The job itself was pretty awful, but it did at least afford some breathing space to think about what I should, or could, do with the rest of my life.

My mind wandered inconsequently back to my early heroes. Many of them had been soldiers, but the military life now seemed much too stifling. The others had been explorers; but every last corner of the globe had been mapped out long ago – even the moon had been done. In any case, I wanted to be a backwoodsman rather than a technician/administrator. I wanted to be able to plunge myself completely into what I was going to do. I had already followed through two canoe journeys, one with some success, but one with the bitter after-taste of failure – which can be just as much of a spur. Now finally, I had to make some sort of choice between the material satisfactions of having a regular job and the less tangible ones of pursuing self-fulfilment. I dithered for weeks, and then gave in. I would go for the challenge.

Eventually my thinking became clearer. It would have to be a canoe journey, either across a major sea or down a very long river; and it would have to be something that had not been done before. From there, my vagabond spirit made a quantum leap. My pocket atlas showed me that the distances were not that great. In my innocence, I decided to try – quite simply – for the longest single canoe trip in recorded history.

That was settled, then. But where did the record stand? I hurried to the Scottish National Library and carried out mountains of research on every conceivable waterway.

First, the North Atlantic. I soon discovered that two different people had already attempted it, but that both had used sails, and that neither had been totally successful. In 1938, Franz Romer reached the West Indies in a Klepper canoe, but had died before setting foot on the American mainland. Hannes Lindemann repeated his compatriot's feat in a double canoe in 1956, but he had also drowned, while island-hopping towards Florida in a hurricane (he couldn't swim!). As a result it wasn't really clear whether the Atlantic could be considered canoed.

Next there was the Nile. My atlas showed that the longest branch, the White Nile, came down from a country called Burundi. The river had been attempted in 1953–4 by a Franco-American canoe team under Jean Laporte. They did reach the Mediterranean safely, but had had to miss out about 800 miles of the most dangerous or inaccessible sections. Not bad going, I thought, but hardly conclusive.

What about the Blue Nile? It started in Ethiopia and had exacted, I soon found, a terrible toll. The first attempt to even navigate it had been in 1903, using steel boats. But these had been wrecked after only five miles, and, as the men trekked back to Addis Ababa, natives castrated one of them. In 1962, two canoeists had been killed by local bandits. Other expeditions had lost their boats, been shot at, or been attacked by crocodiles. Only in 1968 had the river even been navigated, by Colonel Blashford-Snell's team in huge rubber boats. The cost was again extremely heavy, however, as they lost a man through drowning. Since then no attempts had been made. Aha – an uncanoed river at last?

Then came the Amazon. Despite all my searches, there seemed to be no record of any sort of navigation of the whole length. All I could discover was that about 3400 miles of it had been canoed by an American team in 1970 and that Helen and Frank Schreider did 3845 miles in a powered boat in 1969. H'm . . . .

That left the Mississippi-Missouri. But here, my most exhaustive researches produced an almost complete blank. Certainly, early explorers had navigated most of the Missouri from the Rockies down to the confluence at St Louis; but it seemed pretty clear that the whole of the Mississippi-Missouri had never been canoed. Very interesting . . . .

I turned with great relief to the actual lengths of these stretches of water. The Atlantic was the easiest as I could measure it on my pocket atlas. It was about 1900 miles across the shortest bit (Ireland-Newfoundland); or 3300 for a slightly warmer route (Portugal-Florida). Not bad for a start. Now for the rivers!

I hauled down dozens of dusty encyclopedias and even a few theses on the hydrological systems of the world. (If only my geography teacher could have seen me.) Most authorities gave the Nile or the Amazon as the longest river – but some independent souls preferred the Mississippi-Missouri. I delved deeper, and at last began to understand why. The length of a river isn't that simple. There are a number of embarrassing problems.

Where, for instance, there is a river that splits into two, you clearly take

14

the longer stretch; similarly, when two branches come together. But what do you do if both happen in succession (a geographer's description of an island)? Again, if a river 'crosses' a lake, you take the crow's-flight distance, but what do you do if there's a kink – or two – in the middle? Do you measure the shortest route down the river? The route along the middle? Along the current? What do you count as the beginning? The drop on a tree that fights its way along to other drops and hence down to the ocean? And as the end? The point on the river 'opposite' the point where dry land stops? Where the marsh stops? Where the fresh water stops? What happens if there are tidal or seasonal variations? Or if the river has been artificially lengthened or shortened?

If I could answer all these questions, I realised, I would be better off applying for a Professorship in Hydrology than planning a canoe expedition. I decided to take all distances with a large pinch of salt – which gave more constructive results. Until about 1960, the Mississippi-Missouri did apparently reign supreme as the longest river in the world. The effort had shrunk it considerably however. From an amazing 4500 miles in the eighteenth century and 4300 when Mark Twain was writing, it had shrivelled first to 4200, and then to a mere shadow of itself. Current estimates ranged from about 3600 to 4200 miles.

The White Nile was obviously a very strong contender, unlike its Blue brother. It had undergone a period of juvenile growth, well into the twentieth century, when one just wasn't an explorer if one didn't lengthen it by another 50 miles. But it was now generally reckoned to be between 3900 and 4200, though getting shorter all the time (having reached senility without ever really being mature).

The Amazon also weighed in, like an ageing boxer, at various figures. Since 1960, most of these had been between 3800 and 4100 miles, although some authorities muttered darkly that it cheated by leaping from its own bed into its neighbour's. The dirty beast!

As for the others, even I could see that the Yangtze-Kiang, the Yenisey, or the Ob (the *what?*) were mere also-rans, just wet trickles. In sum, there were two and a half runners, but still no clear winner. I girded my loins, and set off for the library again.

Only then did I realise that in any case it didn't really matter. The Nile and Amazon expeditions had each 'only' done about 3400 miles; and so nothing was easier than finding something longer. Any of the terrible trio would do. I accordingly plumped for the one that hadn't been canoed at all. With tremendous relief, I chose the Mississippi-Missouri.

Rushing back home, I proudly told my parents, in a single breath, that the Mississippi-Missouri was by far 'the longest river in the *history* of the world', that a few authorities thought it still remained the longest, that it

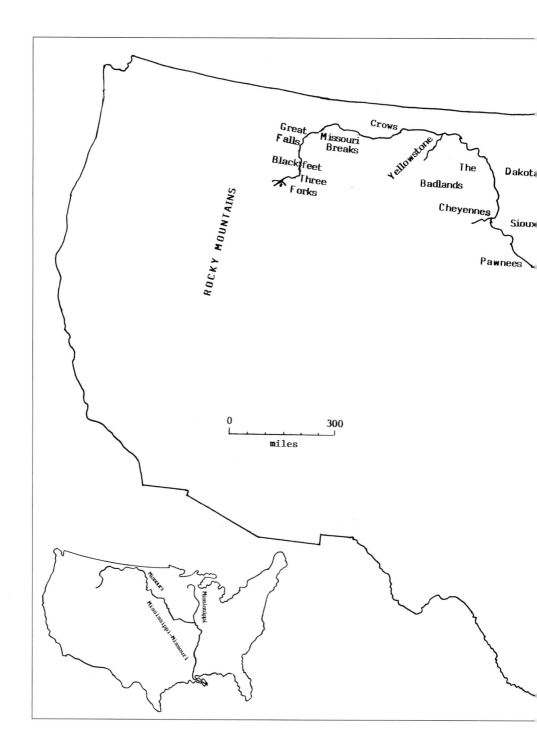

The Mississippi-Missouri.

City

ha

Mississippi

as City

St Louis

Cairo

Ohio

Memphis

Vicksburg

Natchez

Baton Rouge

New
Orleans

Fort Jackson

Gulf of Mexico

was definitely the longest uncanoed river in the world, and that a successful navigation would be the longest continuous canoe journey ever.

In response, my mother popped a proverbial thermometer under my tongue, and my father started looking at me less like a father and more like a doctor!


## IV

I was terrified, when I began to think seriously about it. I bought a road-map of North America, and shakily traced the course of the Mississippi-Missouri River, from the source of the Missouri up in the Rocky Mountains, over the Great Plains, and on to St Louis, where the Mississippi came in; then down across the sweltering cotton-fields of Mississippi and Tennessee; and finally through the subtropical swamps of Louisiana, and out into the Gulf of Mexico. Taking her length to be 3800 miles, she was almost the distance from Britain to India. If I wanted a challenge, here was challenge enough!

In my own private language, I began to call the river the 'M-M'. She was the lifeblood of America – she *was* America! She went regally past Three Forks, Great Falls and the Dakotas, Sioux City, Omaha and Kansas City, Cairo, Memphis, Vicksburg, and Fort Jackson. On her banks were the Missouri Breaks and the Badlands; the hunting-grounds of the Crows, the Cheyennes, the Sioux, and the Pawnees; the battle-sites of the Civil War; the birthplaces of jazz and the blues. She was eminently and exotically French; it was my ancestors who, under Louis XIV and XV, Napoleon, and others, had explored the river system, and who had owned it all for about 100 years. The names Pierre, St Louis, Natchez, Baton Rouge, New Orleans were living witness of this heroic age; and French, of a sort, was still spoken on the banks. As I paced the cold, hard streets of Stevenson's Edinburgh, I madly chanted these glowing litanies of history to myself. In a final paroxysm of self-induced excitement, I realised that canoeing the M-M had a unique resonance. The canoe was invented by the North American Indians. I would be approaching their heritage in a vessel they could clearly recognise as their own.

Then I came back down to earth. I had £40 a week and an overdraft. The only person I had met who was even remotely connected with this area was Robin Knox-Johnstone, the round-the-world yachtsman. This was when he autographed his book for me – and for a hundred other people.

I sought advice everywhere and anywhere. A captain at Army-Headquarters (Scotland) wanted to send half a company down the river with me. A director of the Scottish Tourist Board whose canoeing experience consisted of a technically perfect descent of the Water of Leith, told me it was all just a ploy to avoid getting a 'real', i.e. office job. The most travelled of my friends, William Butcher, argued that the project was impossible on financial, physical, and psychological grounds.

The only person totally in favour from the beginning was a girl called Jean Smith. Week after week, she used to come over from Glasgow to see me, when I was up and when I was down. As the weeks dragged by, she gave me all her strength. I will always be grateful to her.

Only with Jeannie's help did I manage to survive, to resist all the eminently sensible opinions thrust upon me. Only by repeating, again and again, 'The M-M has never been done, I can do it', could I begin to take the first steps towards planning such a crazy venture.

# The Ruin of Many a Poor Boy

I

I knew I would be passing through very sparsely inhabited regions for many hundreds of miles. With an estimated speed of 70 miles a day (including the current), I would be out of touch with civilisation for several days at a stretch. From bitter experience, I also knew that, if you do get caught up in a storm, you need the knowledge of some sort of haven to pull you through, rather than just a wet and miserable sleeping-bag. Otherwise, you find yourself doing all sorts of stupid things. A back-up team, I decided, was an absolute necessity, for both practical and mental reasons.

In the meantime I had to keep my body and soul together, but I couldn't spare the time I needed while I was doing my managerial job. Feeling a bit silly, I stepped off the career ladder I had just clambered onto; found work as a night-porter; and began to plan the expedition during the day.

My mind wandered off to the why and wherefore. Hillary's famous 'Because it is there' remains a vital inspiration; but in my view is no longer enough. The man who scales the North Face of Everest or rows the Atlantic must have skill and courage and luck, but what if one of those ingredients is lacking? What if appalling weather conditions result in a rescue, costing thousands of taxpayers' money? Does he have the right to expect that rescue when it was he who put himself at risk? I knew that the answer was no. I would have to devote my efforts to a constructive cause. The solution came quickly to me: I would raise funds for a medical charity.

Soon after, I was delighted to get a hearing with Mr Colin MacKenzie, who worked for the Cancer Research Campaign. Once in his office, I quickly described my earlier ventures, spread the multi-coloured map of North America over his telephone and blotter, and passionately propounded my project. I presented the expedition as a response to the appeal which the Prince of Wales had made for the coming Jubilee Year. He had called on the youth of Britain to get off their backsides and do something constructive in the field of physical endeavour. I went on to say that the C.R.C. could make huge amounts of money by inviting firms and private individuals to sponsor the expedition on a mileage basis. I also pointed out that it could be a huge publicity venture.

Colin MacKenzie listened to the end. Then he said, in his broad Scots accent 'That's all moost inter-r-esting, Mr Fr-r-ancis. But how much wull it all *cost?*' My dream came down to earth with a crash. I muttered something about the need for a detailed breakdown, based on the most recent prices; and beat an undistinguished retreat to the door.

Very early the following morning, I was carrying twenty-three man-sized rubbish-bags out to the back of the hotel. I had to hold my breath with each one, but was glad to feel a ray from the rising sun. There was still a handful of people having yet another last drink at the bar. For the first time, I could contemplate such a scene with a semblance of serenity. The guests' complacency and easy money represented in my mind the considerable benefits of the managing career I had given up. They had attractive wives in the double living-rooms and beautiful cars in the double garages. But now, at last, I realised that their lives encompassed a great deal of reality, but not very much dream; and that man must live by trying to bring the two together. At the same time, I knew very well that the road to dreams was paved with well-intentioned misfits – that the chances were stacked very high indeed against me.

So it was that a curiously bitter-sweet feeling came over me as I waited for the 24 bus, singing quietly to myself 'Mothers, tell your children, not to do what I have done':

> There is a house in New Orleans
> They call the Rising Sun
> An' it's been the ruin of many a poor boy
> And me oh God I'm one.
> Now the only thing a gambler needs
> Is a suitcase and a trunk;
> And the only time that he is satisfied
> Is when he's all drunk.

## II

Despite the rigours of my education, I knew nothing about living in the wild. Fortunately, Liam did, having spent three years in the Royal Navy Reserve, travelling extensively and finishing up as President of the Strathclyde section. His leadership qualities were also clearly strong, since he was working as an Assistant Manager at the Royal George Hotel in Perth; he had an excellent knowledge of mechanics; and he was a straightforward sort of person. My mind was made up – I would ask him to be back-up leader.

Next, I had to decide the actual size of the back-up team. Its members would be responsible for such varied tasks as: driving, photography, camp-duties, paperwork, and the all-important media liaison. I knew I would have to plan on having two further members.

Five minutes before going back to the C.R.C., I finished typing out the following (not very professional) estimate:

| | |
|---|---:|
| Transport to and from the USA for four persons ................... | £640 |
| Main back-up vehicle: probably a Dodge or Range-Rover, bought second-hand ...................................... | £5000 |
| All-terrain vehicle with short wheel-base and four-wheel drive: Austin Champ or Jeep, second-hand ........................ | £1000 |
| Food for four persons at an average outlay of £3 per person per day over eighty days ............................................... | £960 |
| Fuel for the two vehicles ...................................... | £600 |
| Canoes: two sea-kayaks (Kester Torridons) ........................... | £180 |
| Tent ................................................................ | £80 |
| Catering equipment: stoves, butane gas, pots, pans, etc. ......... | £30 |
| Four sleeping bags: £20 each .................................. | £80 |
| Four sets of clothing: anoraks, boots, wetsuits, etc. ............... | £200 |
| Tool-kit, two spare tyres ....................................... | £90 |
| Life jackets, flares, glass-fibre repair-kit ............................ | £100 |
| Ropes ............................................................. | £80 |
| Maps ............................................................. | £30 |
| Second-hand power-saw and axes ............................... | £60 |
| Miscellaneous ................................................... | £150 |
| Insurance ......................................................... | £200 |
| **Total** ............................................................ | **£9660** |

As Colin MacKenzie slowly read, my mind was racing. The list was in fact very incomplete. There was no allowance for a support boat, cameras, firearms, or radio equipment. But against that, the total came – somehow – to less than £10,000. This had to be good news – expeditions like power-boating the Congo or going up Everest backwards normally cost hundreds of thousands of pounds.

This time, the Appeals Secretary was more forthcoming. He emphasised that the Cancer Research Campaign were held to a very tight budget. Of every pound they raised, 93p had to go towards research, which left very little money indeed for ventures such as mine. I underlined once again what the C.R.C. could get out of it. At last, MacKenzie said that he was prepared to discuss the matter further with London.

I waited for weeks and weeks – and then weeks more. I realised that I had now burned all my boats. Maybe I would have been better listening to the Tourist Board director's advice after all?


## III

My brother Robert reminded me that we had relations in Katonah and in Nebraska, and that Uncle Gerard was now living in Arkansas. These relatives, some of whom I had thought of as rather distant ones, came a whole lot closer when I realised that Katonah was in New York State and that Nebraska and Arkansas were both 'on' the river. Encouraged by Robert's support, I finally started to read about the lands I hoped to be passing through.

I found out that the English language carries within it the traces of the mighty Mississippi. 'Touch and go' came from frenetic coal-stops during steamboat races; a 'carpetbagger' was an adventurer with a flimsy hold-all who shifted south to exploit the new Black voters after the Civil War; and 'selling a man down the river' was probably, in the slave-era, to prevent him from ever seeing his wife and children again.

I began to read Mark Twain. *Tom Sawyer*, I quickly discovered, was pretty childish, and in any case hardly featured the Mississippi at all. But then I tried *Life on the Mississippi*, Twain's true-life experience as a steamboat pilot between 1857 and 1861 – and was totally and irremediably hooked. Twain had known the joys of the river – and its rages, for his brother had drowned in it.

It had all started when he left Hannibal, his home town on the Mississippi, in search of adventure. His original idea was to join an expedition exploring the Amazon, so he headed down towards New Orleans and Brazil. He might have got there – and hit posterity with *Life on the Amazon, Huckleberrio Finno*, and *Thomaso Charpentiero*. But it was not to be. Down to his last $30, he persuaded the pilot to teach him 'all' the secrets of the Lower Mississippi, for the sum of $500 . . . 'which I'll, er, pay you out of my first wages'. I supposed that all a pilot had to do was to keep his boat on the river, and I did not consider that that could be much of a trick, since it was so wide.' But he soon realised the dangers of a river that can change its course in a single night. He even took his pseudonym from it, for 'mark twain' means '2 fathoms (12 feet)'. It implied that the boat could squeeze by, but only just – perhaps a sardonic comment on the writer's life . . . .

Twain claims that a steamboat pilot was the only unfettered and independent human being on earth. With time, however, he found that the Mississippi no longer excited him: 'All the grace, the beauty, the poetry, had gone out of the majestic river.' He himself thought it was because he knew the river too well; but it may be that the coming of the railways destroyed the very *raison d'être* of the steamboats.

Then I glanced at *Huckleberry Finn* – and for twelve hours was dead to the world. It spoke of caving banks and Spanish moss, of bullfrogs and water-mocassins, of leaning river-shacks and one-horse towns on sleepy creeks. But it above all talked of Huck and Jim rafting down a river where 'you feel mighty free and easy and comfortable', of 'floating' a 'monstrous big river'. The words reverberated in my head: 'the great Mississippi, the majestic, the magnificent Mississippi, rolling its mile-wide tide along'. It was everything I wanted to do, it was freedom, adventure, escape, it was the American way of life written in universal terms.

Twain had inflamed my imagination. I wanted to relive the adventurous spirit of America from before the railways. I wanted to rediscover Huck and Jim's life. But I wanted to be part of the river, not just 'floating' on its surface. I wanted to put the magic back into the Mississippi.

Liam told me that a close friend of his, called Timothy Eley, was very interested in the trip. He was just finishing a degree in geography at Strathclyde, and had followed a training course as a reserve sublieutenant on the *Captain Scott*, where he had been named 'best all-round cadet'. I met Tim, was impressed by his determination and resourcefulness, and decided to invite him to join us. He would be our geographical expert, but above all carry out the camp-duties.

For the fourth member, I did think of William Butcher. But I was really looking for a professional photographer. After interviewing a fair number of candidates, I finally chose Rick Beattie, who was about to finish a three-year diploma in photography. He seemed easy-going, but not afraid of expressing his opinion. I just had to hope he wasn't *too* laid-back.

As May 1977 budded, the C.R.C. continued to make encouraging noises, but insisted that there had to be some financial commitment on my part. Playing my very last card, I phoned my Uncle Gerard in Arkansas, and invited him to be associated with our venture. Very kindly, he put his 'mobile home' at our disposal.

So then when I announced to the C.R.C. that the main-vehicle part of the budget was covered, Colin MacKenzie's bluff was called! I went to see Professor McWhirter – the man really in charge – and put my case to this most understanding person. Two days later, the Mississippi-Missouri Cancer Research Solo Kayak Expedition (MMCRSKE for short) came into the world, with a silver spoon of £3500 in its mouth. Now the game was definitely afoot!

IV

We started by ordering four glass-fibre kayaks from Chris Newell of Inverness: two 16-ft sea-boats with directional stability, for use on the Lower Missouri and Mississippi, and two shorter slalom-boats, for the 1000 miles of white water I had read about at the top. The two sea-boats, especially, caught my imagination, with their simple, streamlined shapes. I named them *Cameron of Lochiel* and *Lochinvar*. Identical they were, and yet how different their fates – for one, a cruel end on a distant shore, for the other, a proud place in a national museum.

Scottish Television wanted to film me in action. Dutifully paddling up and down, I executed a smart telemark turn as I came into shore. I moved my lips to answer the first question, but heard only the sound of the camera. I thought of the half-million spectactors out there, but this time the question didn't sound quite the same. 'Nick Francis, will you be the first man to piddle 4000 miles to New Orleans?' I caught an incontinent twinkle in his eye, the cameras whirred again, and I was finally able to produce the flow of words required.

On the last day of May, Liam and I drove down to London. We were lucky to be able to limit expenses through the generosity of well-wishers: Tim and Rick stayed with college friends, and Liam and I stayed with William Butcher. In the morning, we had our first meeting with Randal Sadleir, the Chief Public Relations Officer at the Cancer Research Campaign. With his enthusiastic help, the Mississippi snowball soon began to roll. I found myself in the British Airways Head Office, asking for sponsorship. We would be flying the flag in America, just like them. Could they help? They did, with a magnificent gift of £2000. Lord Matthews of Trafalgar House Investments (Cunard) offered to transport our equipment to the United States free of charge. Alders Furniture of London gave the funds a boost.

Rick joined us on 13 June. I gave him £380 as a separate photographic fund, and he assembled an impressive-looking kit, using his own camera-body as a base. On the 14th, we went to look at a second-hand

Avon inflatable with outboard engine, price £300. Anxiously eyeing the patches, which seemed to have totally replaced the original rubber, I enquired if the boat hadn't seen action as an advance craft at Gallipoli. The owner told me rubber boats weren't invented till after the Second World War. I gave up at that point, but wondered to myself who would be rescuing whom.

On 15 June, we packed the car with the four kayaks, two sets of paddles, shell-shocked Avon, outboard engine, two tents, assorted camping gear, and other bits and pieces. We set off, groaning, to Southampton and the *Atlantic Cognac*. Then full-steam back to the London office again, where Randal bounded in. Bass Charrington had offered us their nineteenth-century ship, the *Old Caledonia*, as a venue for a send-off press-conference. It was on the Embankment, just along from Fleet Street. Definitely an offer that the press couldn't refuse.

On the 16th, we went to talk with Colonel John Blashford-Snell in his nuclear-bomb-proof lair, somewhere below Whitehall (more I cannot say!). We insured the equipment. We went to the American Embassy to fill 'out' forms. Suddenly, we had a panic. The *Old Caledonia* was all organised, but the four kayaks were sailing drunkenly across the Atlantic. A frantic phone-call to the British Canoe Union, and one of their members generously offered to bring his sea-kayak the whole way down from Derby.

Tuesday 21 June arrived and, with it, butterflies in my stomach. Then everything started happening at once. My parents arrived, and hugged me warmly. Tim showed up, having finished his finals the day before. The star of the show, the kayak, arrived (thank God!). The butterflies became a flock of geese and started trampling around. Liam and Tim carried the Baidarka to the shore and I slid her sleek length into the current. Then I got in. She was unfamiliar, and I unsteady. A barge passed and I waited for a while. I was just starting a short sequence for the BBC, when the wash hit me. Only by savage side-paddling did I avert an ignominious capsize. That evening, the London *Evening News* wrote: 'Crowds hung fascinated as a small canoe bobbed like orange-peel upon the murky waters of the Thames.' Had they but realised!

The following day passed quickly with media meetings. I phoned MacKenzie, and emphasised that if we were going to plug cancer research across America, the home-based publicity and fundraising would have to be totally his responsibility.

On Thursday 23 June, four hours before the flight, I realised that there might be problems taking money out of the UK. A hectic race with William ensued through rainy streets to the Bank of England herself; then another sprint to the departure lounge at Heathrow, where I breathlessly rendezvoused with the back-up team. Flight **BA** 609 to New York was soon announced and William wistfully wished us the very best of British luck.

We looked at each other, and took a deep breath. Then we walked across the shining tarmac and towards the greatest adventure of our young lives.

# *All Gone to Look for America*

I

Tim and I walked down to Katonah Lake, New York State. Beside a jetty, we saw the dim outline of a two-man open canoe. Hesitantly, we climbed in and paddled away towards the centre. A full moon came out and then was gone behind the clouds. It was very warm and unnaturally still. A snapper turtle came up and looked over his powerful hooked jaws at these strange humanoids with accents from far to the east of Long Island. We rested on the paddles and felt very close. That lunch time, we had been watching the pouring rain. Now we had finally made it to America: we were ready to take anything on.

But in the morning, stepping down from the early commuter train, we felt a bit lost. The soaring acres of plate-glass looked magnificent from a distance, but when we were actually amongst them, the claustrophobia and humidity felt overpowering. In desperation, I decided to ask a police-officer for directions. He was wearing dark glasses, chewing a piece of gum, and methodically hitting his palm with a dented baton. His teeth and baton maintained their perfect rhythm as he answered: 'Get-a-f...in'-map-Mac'.

We eventually walked into a café and found Liam and Rick with their host Jim Landers. Aged 25, he had already been working as a journalist for five years. Not long before, he had met Liam while based in Belfast, from where some of his despatches had appeared in the *Washington Post*. He knew Woodward and Bernstein. He was now working for *The Trenton Times*, but looking for something new. My mind was racing. Jim had a Plymouth Duster, which he offered to put at our disposal. On the spot, I invited him to join the expedition. Jim accepted, provided only that he could come and go as he pleased. We shook hands on it.

I started talking to a very pretty girl who was standing in the bus queue

28

in front of me. She seemed quite interested in our trip. I groped for my cigarettes but the packet was empty. 'I could really do with a fag,' I said invitingly.

'You're into fags, are you?' she replied, her eyes narrowing attractively.

'Not all the time!'

'Will you please excuse me?' She had gone and Jim stood there, grinning at me: 'In the States, a "fag" means a homosexual, you idiot!' How embarrassing!

I had a meeting with the directors of the American Cancer Society. They began by telling me that they could do nothing to help, as they had had no prior notice.

'What about my Uncle Gerard?'

'Do you mean the blind gentleman in Arkansas?'

'?'

(Apparently, when asked what date we were arriving, he'd said 'I'm running blind.') After further useless sparring, I realised that the A.C.S. were afraid the expedition would draw funds out of their own coffers.

'Surely we are on the same side?' I argued, but without effect. Knowing that foreigners were forbidden from doing any fundraising at all on their own, I offered the A.C.S. half of the funds we might raise, pointing out that they would be getting the full benefit of the publicity. Still no. I finally offered them *all* moneys raised in the US. They said that each state branch of the A.C.S. was autonomous, and would therefore resent any directive from New York. In any case, there wasn't time. There ensued a long, fraught silence.

At that moment, the Public Affairs President walked in. The director at the end explained: 'This young guy, Nick, has just come over from England, funded by the British Cancer Society. He and his buddies think they'll kayak all the way down the Mississippi and the Missouri. He says this trip might raise a bundle.'

Another silence, and then the newcomer replied: 'It's great! The first descent of America's longest river. "A canoe for cancer." "A man against a monster." It's a copywriter's dream. I'll pull out every small-town Rotary Club and every bigshot state-governor. From the Rockies down to the Gulf. Across thirteen states. Just imagine. This could become the biggest thing since the selling of the President!'

There was an even longer silence. Then the end gentleman got slowly to his feet. 'Irv,' he said, 'you blew it!' With these words, I knew that my fundraising dream had taken a lethal blow. I was tempted to say that this was not the way to fight a terrible killer; but realised that they didn't think I could possibly do the river. And I still hoped to win them round by doing a reasonable stretch of it.

So it was that we said goodbye as if nothing had happened. But I was seething inside as I walked out through the huge marbled lobby.

## II

Jim introduced us to a tough friend of his called 'Tilt'. He had gained this strange name when he lost part of one leg while covering his helicopter gunship's take-off from a jungle clearing in Vietnam. Tilt asked me where we were going. So as to avoid all mistakes, I slowly got the map out, carefully unfolded it, and then confidently pointed to the top left-hand corner – thank God my finger found the thin blue line straight away. A heavy silence hung as Tilt studied the Badlands and the Missouri Breaks. Then, very softly, so softly I had to lean forward to hear, he intoned 'You's headed into bad country, boy.' I knew that some of it was for effect, but even so I could feel gooseflesh prickling down my back. The room temperature had suddenly dropped twenty degrees.

Having wound up the East-Coast business, Jim, Rick, and I caught the night-train for St Louis. At 8 am, Jim woke us up, and pointed down at the biggest and brownest river I had ever seen. We rushed to get our things together. But Jim just laughed and said 'I'd like to see your reactions when we get to the Father of Waters himself. Gentlemen, meet the Ohio.' We smiled sheepishly, put our cases up again, and went back to sleep.

We eventually rolled into St Louis at 10 pm, climbing down into a temperature of 95°. Setting off in search of the Mississippi-Missouri, we came to the end of the street, and there she was, lying in front of us. At first I was a bit disappointed. She was as big as you could imagine – about half a mile across – but she seemed very flat.

As a brown splash wet my feet, however, my feelings slowly changed. I tried to visualise a solo kayak in the midst of that sombre swell and a seed of awful fear grew deep inside me. In a very short time, I would be canoeing off into the unknown. I really couldn't believe that that icy river-course could ever be made to join up with this brown sea whose perspiring bosom now seemed much too large. I tried to follow the river down – Montana, North Dakota, South Dakota – but my brain was just a seething blank, I couldn't recall any of the other states. I couldn't even remember what state I was in.

After a while, we went back to the hotel and I fell into a hot and troubled sleep. I dreamed I was pulling on a muddy blue pullover three sizes too big for me, but I couldn't get into it, the sleeves just kept on getting tangled up.

To go from St Louis to Rogers, Arkansas, on Independence Day, you take three buses, losing air-conditioning on the second and suspension on the third. We were very glad indeed to be met by Gerard, Liam, and Tim brandishing ice-cold beers.

It was obvious that Gerard was hoping to come with us; but it was equally obvious that it just wouldn't work. Gerard was over twice our age, and he operated in a highly-organised, almost military, manner. We, in contrast, were already using a distinctly bits-of-string style. There was just no way that we could work together over a long and gruelling expedition. Feeling very guilty, I tried to bring Gerard round to the idea that there were important character differences and that this would cause problems; and he eventually accepted the idea with very good grace.

My uncle then made two extremely generous offers. The first was a gleaming white palace on wheels, with full-size fridge and cooker, six beds, carpets, power-steering, stereo, television, and air-conditioning. Total value, £11,000. I looked in the wall-to-wall mirror at the grisly gang: we were afraid to even sit down. I knew we would wreck it if we took it over the rough terrain of thirteen states. I thanked Gerard, but said I just had to decline it, with real regret.

His other offer was a magnificent set of maps, drawn up by the US Army Corps of Engineers, and covering the whole 3810 miles of the Mississippi-Missouri. Their scale was one inch to a mile, and they were based on surveys done only three years before. Tim and I started gleefully fitting the individual sheets together. But then we stopped. Gerard had told us that the result would reach out of the living room, over the front lawn, across the main road, through the neighbour's house, and into his swimming pool: 317 feet in all! We looked again at my tired road-map; and solemnly tore it into bits. It had seen sterling service with MacKenzie and Tilt, but its time had finally come.

Alone in bed that night, I studied the crisp white pages with their blue band that just grew and grew. Suddenly I remembered some notes that Bill had put together in his university library. Uncrumpling the serried sheets, I read some incredible facts: altogether, the river has 100,000 affluents. It is so long that the water takes three months to get to the end. The catchment area includes two Canadian provinces and thirty-three American states: every state east of the Rockies except Florida and those silly little ones in the Northeast. Plus one that is west of the Rockies. Total area: $1^1/4$ million square miles, or eleven times the size of the British Isles. Mark Twain called the basin the body of the nation: 'all the other parts are but members'. Jules Verne said the United States were just two mountain ranges with a river in between. Smiling at Bill's résumé, I thought about

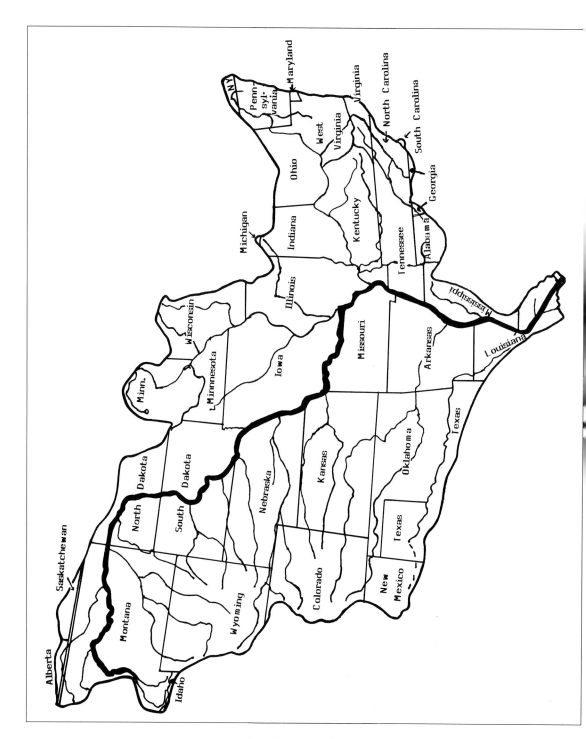

The Catchment Area.

the help he had given in London. Perhaps I should have invited him after all?

Three o'clock chimed, but still I couldn't get to sleep. I idly leafed through the maps again, curious to see what the rapids on the Upper Missouri looked like. I searched – and searched. I couldn't find them. There was no sign of the 1000 miles of white water I'd told everybody in New York about. They had been almost totally replaced by 1000 miles of *still* water – six huge reservoirs, up to 7 miles wide and 230 miles long, each one a veritable inland sea.

My sleep was again agitated. At breakfast, I felt really awful. Then, straight after, Jim took me aside, and said he was very worried about how disorganised the expedition was. I said I agreed, but could we leave it for a few more days until we all got into our stride? He agreed we could, apart from one problem: money . . . .

My original manoeuvring was rebounding on me. My costing had included £5000 for a main vehicle – and then I had told the Cancer Research Campaign that this part of the budget was covered by Gerard's mobile home. Without that home, there was now a big hole.

'You've simply been switching the hole back and forth across the Atlantic,' Jim said.

'Like a three-card trickster?' I prompted, and then pointed out that there had to be at least the *promise* of money for me to operate.

'That's what they said about the Mississippi Bubble.'

Guessing wildly, I argued that the Bubble was just an investment scheme that got off the ground too quickly. I pointed out that if I hadn't acted as a go-between, there wouldn't have been a hole at all for the two of us to be arguing about.

Jim did have a very good point though. I told him that, while waiting for the two final £500 cheques that the C.R.C. had promised 'further down the river', I would split the big hole into a large number of little ones, try to tie some of them down with pieces of string, and hope that some of the others would just float away. But were we ever going to get to the Missouri? I began to wonder.

IV

Early the following morning, Liam and Gerard went out to study the used-vehicle market of Rogers County, Arkansas. At lunch time, I glanced at the top of their list and gasped. But the second from bottom vehicle looked interesting: a six-year-old Dodge pick-up with 90,000 miles on the clock, price $1600. What we really needed was a newish four-wheel-drive, but with our total resources now down to $1100, we decided to buy the

33

Dodge. The proprietor accepted $600 down-payment, plus the promise of five monthly instalments of $200. I hoped to resell what was left of the truck long before the last three were due – I was back in the business of pyramid-selling!

I also wanted to buy a firearm. 'For animal or human predators?' said Jim. I held my ground, saying that I wanted a .44 magnum powerful enough to blow an alligator out of the Mississippi if he decided he wanted my kayak for breakfast. 'If you used a .44,' riposted Liam, 'you'd blow *yourself* out of the water!' In the end, we met at exactly halfway, the old lady who ran the laundromat lending me a .22!

One final question still remained to be settled. There was already a mounting pile of urgent correspondence (the C.R.C., for instance, might be wondering where we had got to . . .). Also, I began to realise, we needed an advance-man: someone prepared to travel alone into unknown towns and arrange contacts 'from cold'. I could think of only one person who fitted the requirements: William. He had also worked as a lifeguard, and you never knew . . . .

Liam drew up a long list of items that we'd forgotten to bring, and I phoned Bill. Although it was three in the morning, he was overjoyed, and promised to set out the day his librarian contract finished. I explained that he would have to pay his own way out, as the expedition coffers were in such a desperate state. He just replied 'I'll hitch the land bit.' Brave words, I thought, knowing the 3000 miles involved.


# V

At last, on 9 July, we were nearly ready. Tim screwed a freshly-painted board onto the back of the pick-up, announcing MISSISSIPPI-MISSOURI CANCER RESEARCH SOLO KAYAK EXPEDITION. As a last contribution, Gerard gave us a light rifle. Then we said a sad goodbye, and the little convoy started out.

Through a blanket of CB static came an inimitable Midwestern drawl: 'Ten-four. Your handle?' More static, and then 'Do you have a copy on me? . . . Two bears on the Interstate, 8 miles, moving.' This was too much. All we could manage was: 'Wallflower, calling Daisychain, are you receiving me? Over.' A long pause. Then, very clipped and very British: 'Daisychain receiving Wallflower, loud and clear. Your message please. Over.' Those coast-to-coast truckers must have blanched!

Our new toy made the time pass quickly. Soon we were at Omaha, and overlooking the Missouri River. She looked very brown and very turbulent. This terrible creature would be my companion and foe for the weeks ahead. Who would win? I remembered the Thames and felt more than a little queasy.

We headed up through the treeless wastes of Nebraska and South Dakota. Well after darkness, we stopped in 'Mobridge' and set up camp, together with a fine crackling fire. Our senses crawled as Jim told us about wolves, coyotes, bobcats, bears, eagles, and vultures. This was real pioneering stuff. After all those months of dreaming and scheming, we were finally getting there.

Awake with the dawn, we eventually arrived at the parched plains of Montana. Jim told us that it was the last state to be seen by White men – François and Louis-Joseph de la Vérendrye in the middle of the eighteenth century. Even now, he said, it has only a few hundred thousand people in an area the size of England.

We saw what he meant as hour after hour passed on the dead-straight road, and only the occasional lonely farmstead rushed by. As we drove into the first foothills of the Rocky Mountains, the sky lowered in preparation for a violent electric storm. Still the road stretched interminably ahead, and the whole of humanity seemed to have been wiped from the face of the earth.

Then the rain started to lash down. Awed by this savage display of nature's magnificence, we switched the radio on, seeking respite from the desolate world enveloping us. The Abba song 'Knowing Me, Knowing You' was blasting out. As night came down, the storm got worse and the wind buffeted against the two-ton pick-up, howling between the kayaks like a stricken banshee. Each flash of lightning silhouetted a new jagged peak, rising out of a blasted landscape, incandescent for a moment and then dying as swiftly as it had been born. Somewhere above us, the stars were glowing across a myriad miles of empty space but they were invisible through the shifting curtain of darkened cloud and driving rain. Pressed together in our fragile cockpit, we felt that we were driving into hell itself, with only the wipers and the music holding out that terrible night.

But tomorrow we would be there, and I could finally begin my Journey to New Orleans.

# A Bad Start in an Alien Land

If you come down to the River
Bet you gonna find some people who live
You don't have to worry if you have no money
People on the River are happy to give.
(Creedence Clearwater Revival, 'Proud Mary')

I

Three Forks is a tiny hamlet situated a mere 600 miles from the Pacific – as far west as Salt Lake City, the Grand Canyon, and Phoenix, Arizona. Its altitude is only 4000 feet, but on all four sides are mountains over 10,000

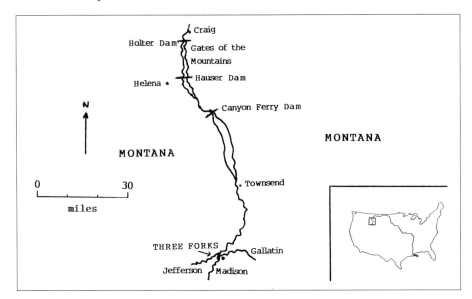

Three Forks to Craig.

feet high – part of the range that stretches from Alaska to Tierra del Fuego, by far the longest in the world. The hamlet itself might easily pass unnoticed. But a traveller would be blind indeed if he didn't see the significance of the only bar. It is called the Headwaters Café; and it is here that three small rivers, the Jefferson, the Madison, and the Gallatin, meet to form the longest river in the Northern Hemisphere.

After a slow breakfast and a dilatory wash, I had yet another cigarette. I studied the charts. I mentioned that it was the thirteenth of the month. At this point Tim enthusiastically asked 'But what made you decide to start *here*, Nick? At university, we always talked about the Mississippi-Missouri-Jefferson-Beaverhead-Red Rock Complex.' I took a deep breath, and said that the simplest answer was that I wanted to canoe the Mississippi-Missouri, and not any other river, however elegant a name it might have. The M-M, I considered, was already more than enough on my plate.

Everything ship-shape (before the start).

Tim and Rick carried one of the slalom-boats down to the water. Everybody wished me the best of luck, and Liam gave me a gigantic shove. I had set off.

As I moved out of sight, I felt more than a little awed by the malevolent snow-capped mountains hemming me in on all sides. I stopped paddling, took a deep breath (again) and started counting each stroke: one-two-three-four, five-six-seven-eight . . . . The canoe shot forward.

There was no sign at all of any human presence except my own, just the steep, gravelly slopes of the mountains falling into the dark water. Only the thin ranks of severe fir trees maintained a puritanical verticality, as if saying 'ü' in disdainful unison. It all made me think I was in some kind of Teutonic folk tale. I was just looking for the sombre shapes of starving wolves slinking slyly along the silent shore, when the sun came dazzlingly out: I was immediately transported 2000 miles further east and the gently unwinding river was now leading Hiawatha towards his Minnehaha. She was combing her long black hair on a sunlit rock just around the corner. Then a glimpse of a deer-trail changed me into a Mohican, and I was kept busy stealthily stalking for a few hundred more strokes. But after that, my repertoire of mythical archetypes became totally exhausted. I was exactly 4 miles out of Three Forks.

For the foreseeable future, I realised, I was going to be spending my waking hours sitting in a boat that was $1^1/2$ ft wide and uncomfortable to boot. Also, I had something to confess to the back-up team and I wanted to get it off my chest. Another problem I knew would be physical fitness. My upper arm muscles were already aching slightly, and I was now sweating. I suppose I should have expected this, as I had been rushing from pole to post for months, but not doing any real exercise, let alone kayaking. In addition, I had never quite managed to give up smoking. Admittedly, this did make it a little paradoxical to start canoeing a river for cancer. But I really couldn't help it. I reckoned it was better to help Cancer Research by whatever means I could. Who knows, I might need *them* some day! But I resolved to stop the filthy habit as soon as I possibly could.

By one o'clock I was starving, and pulled into a little bay with smooth shining sand. The water lapping at its edges was the sort of blue-green you see only in brochures. I drank some, lying face down, Robinson Crusoe-style. But then I opened the lunch-bag: peanut butter and grape jelly sandwiches. The same as yesterday, and the day before, and the day before. Hardly fare for a ravenous pioneer in virgin territory.

After a short rest, I left my own little corner of paradise. At about five o'clock, the river started to broaden out and slow down. As I rounded a right-hand bend, I saw a dam stretching across the river, and a tiny figure up amongst the mountains. It was Liam with the radio. 'Twenty-four miles down,' came his metallic brogue, 'only 3786 to go!' I heard gunshots. Tim was trying out his expertise. So far so good.

## II

I rested for a while, enjoying my exhaustion. And then Tim suggested I might make for the village of Townsend, 'not far downriver'. I groaned, but dutifully set off. After a few more miles, I made out the silhouette of a bridge and an old truck with three kayaks perched precariously on top. As I came closer I was surprised to discover a bottle of Schlitz swinging on the end of a rope – a touch of Liam's genius. But access was clearly impossible, so I shouted my thanks and paddled beerily on into the night.

I paddled for another 6 miles without seeing any sign of Townsend. Over the last hour, the air had become much colder. There was no moon, and visibility had dropped to about 20 feet. All I could see was the unnatural glow of the kayak against the inky river, as smooth as a black billiard-ball. Whenever I stopped paddling, it became deathly quiet, with the kayak just drifting through a sea of dark nothingness.

All of a sudden, there was a tremendous splash. I nearly jumped out of the boat with fright. Some bastard's throwing rocks at me, I thought – but then I realised I was too far from the bank. Another loud splash, this time behind my right shoulder. Then I saw something small, furry, and floating. I tried to twist away, but too late, and the bow brushed against it. In a flurry of water, it came alive. It was a beaver, and seemingly a very angry one, for his tail crashed down again. The noise was just as bad, but this time I got drenched as well. Pushing his tail up in the air, he wiggled naughtily, and disappeared from view.

So much for my idea of being in a vessel that forms part of the river, I mused. I'm at the mercy of any smart-arsed little beaver. Give me the poetry of a warm Scottish bed any time. I realised that it would be folly to go on; and therefore decided to stop. As the greyish outline of an isolated sandbank drifted into view, I eased the bow gently towards it. It would be colder there than on shore, I knew, but at least the creepy-crawlies wouldn't be able to get to me.

I huddled against the fibreglass trying futilely to fight the cold. To save weight, I had brought no extra clothing or sleeping bag, and the temperature had fallen to about 40°. Where the hell *was* Townsend? What the hell was I doing, frozen and miserable, on a sandbank in the middle of the Missouri?

Hour after hour crawled by, and an icy mist came down, coating the kayak with a shiny veil. Just before five, the cold slivers of dawn crept into the sky. I climbed stiffly into the kayak. Soon there came a muffled whine, and the grey slouched shape of the inflatable came storming into view, with Liam at the helm. He kindly explained to me that the beavers had been slapping their tails to warn their downstream friends. It was Bastille Day (14 July), and in honour of my ancestors, breakfast was *oeufs sur le*

39

*plat* washed down by a vintage Nescafé. Twelve years in the dreaded prison wouldn't have taken as much out of me as that one night!

I grabbed a few hours sleep, and then a young reporter arrived fom the Helena *Sunday Independent Record*. As I hastily pulled on my British Airways jacket, he said 'Hi! I'm Randy' (!), and enquired enthusiastically if I could put my thing through its paces. Whatever turns one on . . . I thought, starting some fairly complicated combinations, but he said he couldn't see what was going on. 'Take him out in the inflatable, could you Tim, for some close-ups?'

As the boat scudded by, I telemarked strongly and ploughed impressively through the deep wake. The reporter was in ecstasy. 'Come a tiny bit closer, Tim.'

The snub-nose slewed round, and then her bow lifted out of the water as she came hurtling across the full width of the Missouri. 'Finely judged', I thought, starting to get ready for the wash – but she just kept on crashing. I gesticulated madly and after another fateful second, Tim wrestled with the rudder and the grey nose started to turn. I was back-paddling with all my force, but knew that it was much too late.

A confused image of foam and rubber as my arms swung instinctively upwards. Then an elephant sitting on my chest. Next, water, water everywhere, the taste of Missouri mud in my mouth, and a burning pain in my ribs. Liam's face leaning over and pulling me from the river.

In the darkened tent, Liam was probing my ribs. I took over the delicate task, and could feel that the end bits of two of them weren't quite right. In unison we diagnosed: cracked ribs! I groaned. Liam tried to reassure me by saying that the kayak had taken the full brunt of the impact. In fact, just where my right knee had been, there was now a ragged four-inch hole. Also, the propeller had gone right over my head.

Randy went away, and I took stock. After less than 40 miles of my assault on the Mississippi-Missouri, the tally was as follows: no confession; one missed rendezvous; one freezing-cold night in the open; one damaged kayak; and two cracked ribs. Or, as the front page of the *Sunday Independent Record* proclaimed: 'A Bad Start in an Alien Land!'


III

The next morning, the pain was too bad for me to even consider paddling. As I made this announcement, the different reactions gave me the opportunity to think about what I had wanted to discuss anyway. Rick, I felt, was not fully involved in the expedition and I was worried that he might be concentrating on the wrong sort of photographs. It was also obvious that camp duties were not being evenly distributed.

40

I had a talk with him. He said he was disappointed by the trip, he hadn't expected it to be like this. In addition, what was left of the £380 wasn't enough to buy film with: in college, they had been taught to take large numbers of shots of the same object and use only a few of them. I asked if he could try to adapt his methods but I could see our conversation was going nowhere.

The problem with Tim was almost the opposite: more than enough motivation, but applied in all the wrong places. Led by his enthusiasm he had already encouraged me twice to canoe further – when it was beginning to get dark, and when I was injured. I took him aside, and he argued that the expedition lacked coherence, and that everything was moving too slowly. I agreed, but pointed out the reasons for some of the problems we had had. As we talked, Tim quickly adopted a more constructive attitude. He offered to repair the slalom-canoe with the fibreglass kit. I took Liam aside in turn and asked him to assert his authority more fully, assuring him of my support.

On the 16th, things started to feel, and go, a bit better. The team met me for a hot lunch; and by dusk the day after, I had beaten Canyon Ferry and Hauser Dams. Ninety miles in five days was much slower than I'd imagined. I just had to hope my average would pick up.

After dinner, we heard the sound of wolves baying in the distance. It must have made some connection in my brain, for I started rummaging through my battered suitcase. Finally, I pulled out William's 'Dossier No. 2', 'Early Explorers on the Missouri'. Liam threw another couple of logs on the fire, and by the flickering light I read out the closely-spaced lines.

It was the French who had first claimed this area, in 1682. Never a people to do things by halves, they had in fact claimed possession of the whole Mississippi-Missouri basin. What they called 'Louisiana' (after Louis XIV, the Sun-King) included therefore about two-thirds of the modern United States, plus bits of Canada – quite an empire. Their claim was admittedly a bit tenuous at this stage, as they hardly knew where the Missouri ended – let alone began! But explorers had then worked their way up most of the river valley, followed by the fur-trappers. Settlements were made, and the claim was just beginning to be a bit firmer, when France ran into problems back home. In the end, she was forced to give up her North American Empire altogether. That part of Louisiana west of the Mississippi went to Spain (hence the name Montana, 'Mountain' in Spanish) and most of the rest, to the British. In 1800, both parts came back to the French. But in 1803, Napoleon came under pressure in the New World, and only had enough troops to defend either Louisiana or Haiti. Had he made the right decision, it is just possible that the language of North America today would have been French. As it was, he decided to save Haiti (where they do still speak French). At the knock-down price of three cents an acre, the United States took possession of the Mississippi-Missouri basin – and more than doubled their surface area.

Parts of the purchase were still unexplored. President Jefferson wanted to see what he was getting, and, even before the deal was arranged, had issued orders to Captains Lewis and Clark to reconnoitre. Their mission was to head up the Missouri to its source, and then down to the Pacific. At that time, Britain still claimed most of the land west of the Rockies and north of the Spanish colonies. Lewis and Clark were accordingly issued with passports, and instructed to keep a low profile and to come back the safest way – probably, Jefferson wrote, via Cape Horn.

The expedition finally set off from St Louis in May 1804, with a 55-ft keelboat and two pirogues. They had several guide-interpreters with them, including a fur-trapper called Toussaint Charbonneau and his Snake-Indian wife, Sacajawea ('Bird-Woman'), a native of Three Forks. The crew pushed, pulled, rowed, and towed the boats up against the current. They passed the town of Saint Charles and then, about 60 miles out, the last White establishment on the river. With multiple interchanges in French, English, Minnetaree, Snake, and Sioux, friendly contact was made, as instructed. Amongst the Ricaras, the laws of hospitality dictated that women had to be offered to male visitors, normally by the husband or brother. ('When do we get to Injun country?' asked Tim, with a wicked gleam.) The one Black in the expedition got special attention, wrote Lewis, for the Indians 'desired to preserve among them some memorial of this wonderful stranger'. ('Would a blue-eyed Irishman do?' said Liam.)

An encouraged expedition struggled on. After about a year, they came to the Rockies, and then to a place where the river split into three. Sacajawea had come home.

They sat on the Pacific shore for a long while, but couldn't find any ships to pick them up. They decided, consequently, to come back the same way, and this is where their problems started. A wolf bit through the hand of one of the men while he was sleeping. They were attacked by Indians, and had to kill two of them. And Lewis was shot in the thigh at 40 yards' distance by one of his own party, who claimed he thought he was an elk.

The expedition got back to St Louis looking like the Swiss Family Robinson. They were thus not only the first White men to cross what was to become the United States, but the first to navigate the whole of the Missouri. This last fact is all the more remarkable given that the source of the Mississippi, 8000 feet lower and 1000 miles closer to civilisation, had not yet been discovered.

Subdued by the memory of these great men, we carefully refolded the sheets, and went to bed in virtual silence. Much later, I heard something moving near the pick-up. I slipped the safety-catch off my gun and crawled out Indian-style, with Liam and the rifle hot on my heels. Silhouetted against the moving river-blackness was a stationary black form. We froze. If baby bear was there, mother bear was as well. The grizzlies in this region, Jim had said, weighed as much as a third of a ton and occasionally grabbed people from their tents and ate them. We crouched until our bones ached. Still it didn't move. Finally Liam picked up a small piece of wood and threw it nervously at the immobile intruder. Its only reaction was a strange rustling noise. I boldly lit a match and saw a shiny rubbish-bag. We clearly had something to learn about wilderness survival: Lewis and Clark wouldn't have had this problem!


## IV

Early next morning, with my ribs now just a mild ache, I paddled into some of the most beautiful scenery in America. First there were bare grey rocks, sloping gracefully down into the sparkling blue water. Then the rocks grew red patches and adopted a more aggressive stance. At the next bend, two skyscrapers conspired together to crush the river out of existence. Only at the last possible moment did a small crack appear – the beginning of the famous Gates of the Mountains.

The sheer sides of the Rockies groped 1200 feet above me. Against the sun I could see fantastic shapes – ledges, pinnacles, caves, holes right through the rock. Further on were forbidding mountain passes, shrouded in coniferous forest. All this stark desolation made me think again of the Norwegian fiords, but here there was something still more grandiose and inhuman. Even Lewis and Clark – very rarely affected by natural beauty – had been struck with awe at this point. As I thought back to their tremendous exploit, I finally realised the full enormity of my own attempt. I was trying to take on the Missouri with my dwarf-sized kayak and my bare hands. I felt extremely vulnerable, as the cold of the terrible overhanging cliffs crept into my bones.

As suddenly as they had started, the Gates stopped, and projected me into a wall of blazing hot sunshine. I was both relieved and saddened it had been so short. But soon, with the help of a slight current, I was swallowing up the distance to Holter Dam. Two worries filled my mind over the last 10 miles. We had used up virtually all the money, and were down to $30. I was also thinking again about the back-up team. I was having more hot meals than the others. I really felt I needed that amount of protein – as it was, I was 9 stone, and sinking fast. But we couldn't afford it for everybody. The resultant tensions and jealousies disrupted organisation and motivation. Longer-term goals were being totally neglected . . . .

Jim contemplates a passing kayak.

It became a lovely paddle. The scenery was now decidedly Alpine – high mountains, but relieved with greenery, and even the occasional chalet perched against the clear blue sky. Just after passing *Prickly Pear Creek*, I spotted something moving on the left bank. It was a baby deer. A week's fresh and succulent venison. I slipped the paddles inboard and aimed my gun. The kayak drifted until we were only 20 feet apart. I looked into the face of the little creature with its splayed legs, and knew then that I could never pull the trigger. I slowly got the paddles out again.

Half a mile later, there was a choice of routes. I took the left-hand one, but then it became narrower and narrower, and the current slower and slower. My way was finally barred by a tree-trunk, with a dome-shaped structure at the far end – my dozy friends the beavers taking their revenge for my sleep-paddling. Undeterred, I climbed out of the canoe as heavy-footedly as I could, lifted it over, and dropped it down the other side. A nifty foot to stop it drifting shiftily away, and soon I was sitting on top of it, holding on to a projecting branch, and wondering how I'd got myself into such a situation. I'd never gone from sitting on the kayak to sitting in it before. Keeping hold with my hand, I slipped my weight backwards until the whole kayak was sticking rudely upwards. Then I curled my right leg into position. But just as I was twisting my bottom on the hull, something happened, and I was rolled into the water. It was absolutely freezing. Mr and Mrs Toothy Beaver must have been chortling away all the time!

At dusk, I came into Craig, admiring the tiny village nestling below the steep mountains, and soon hit camp. Tim had a piece of good news: someone in the local bar was interested in buying part of our radio equipment. We climbed into the pick-up and drove there. With a heavy heart, we sold our two base-units for $150. The expedition was solvent again, but for how long?

At that moment a huge cattle-rancher came in. He was wearing all the appropriate gear, and looked very hard but very honest. Tim got up, introducing him to us: it was Everett Hicks who had set up the radio deal. Everett seemed to like our story, and invited us up to his ranch the following day. I quickly decided I needed a day off.


V

A little after midnight, we were woken by a high-powered pick-up grinding and slithering over the gravel track. It was Everett, with one of his cowhands, two bottles of bourbon, and forty cans of beer. We threw some wood on the embers and had ourselves a party. As the beer started to dwindle, Everett led me over to his pick-up and proudly showed me his armoury. He had a pump-action shotgun, a .44 magnum and enough weapons to take on a small army. Unclipping the magnum, he challenged me to a marksman competition. With my miserable pea-shooter, I felt distinctly outgunned but felt I had no choice. After half a dozen cans had been dangerously demolished (by Everett), his companion stood up. He shouted that we were both plumb crazy, and stalked off into the night.

We had another beer, and Everett talked about his 3000-head ranch. The rugged face flickering in the shadows belonged, I realised, to the last of a pioneering breed. His kind had won this savage terrain, no matter what the cost in Indian lives – or their own. He would share the last of his wordly possessions with you; but never try to steal his cattle or his women: he would kill you without blinking. There was a long, contemplative silence, and then he was gone, leaving us with our thoughts in the calm of the night.

After breakfast, we had a tidy-out. The bottom layer of the pick-up was just a mass of half-closed suitcases, half-open plastic bags, soggy bits of paper, and mud-caked socks. Liam threw it all out, remarking *en passant* that my pile was by far the biggest and dirtiest. While brushing out the cab, he made another discovery. In the space behind the seat, there was a neatly-pressed green kilt. Tim's initiative was voted intelligent but undemocratic. His toilet bag and shirts were ceremoniously dumped in the back, and three bulky suits joined the kilt, virtually crushing the sporran out of existence. Such, I suppose, is the painful price paid by innovators.

Spick and span, we pulled up at a sign marked: L.Y. RANCH. TRESPASSERS WILL BE SHOT. There was a skull to prove the point – a bull's I think. We had steak after delicious steak. Everett asked if we would like to spot some bears. We jumped at the idea and, accompanied by his beautiful young daughter Terri, into the back of his pick-up. Then it began to pour. We huddled under an old tarpaulin. Further and further we drove, climbing over the barest of tracks. Suddenly Everett killed the engine and the four corners lifted slightly. Ahead of us appeared about fifteen elk, each animal cantering gracefully and easily across the track. And then they saw us. The little ones and the hinds continued, more urgently now, sensing the danger. Two magnificent stags stopped as if in mutual understanding – both knowing what they had to do – waiting for their young to pass. Then slowly they turned towards us, lowered their antlered heads and froze. After long seconds, Everett gently released the handbrake and we freewheeled back down the ravine, leaving them alone with their hinds and their victory.

As we arrived back at the cold campsite, each of us was silent with his memories of the day. I thought back again to the disastrous beginning of the week, and realised that the land didn't seem quite so alien now as before. Although I couldn't bear to look at the maps, the Mississippi-Missouri hadn't beaten me yet – I was still moving.

We said a warm goodnight, and then slept like dead people.

# The Patient Mariner

I'm the captain and the owner, and the mate, and the pilot, and watch-man, and head-deck-hand; and sometimes I'm the freight and passengers.

*(Huckleberry Finn)*

## I

The next day was Thursday 20 July, and I set off towards lunch at a village called Ulm. The wind, I noticed, was in my favour for the very first time. My mind seized this pretext to wander off to Romer's amazing Atlantic crossing. From there, a thought came to me: why not hoist a sail myself? Even jamming a couple of branches behind the seat and stretching a pullover across would help. Nobody need ever know.

But then my conscience crept back. I was trying to canoe the river, not sail it. Any artificial help would spoil the whole idea – otherwise I wouldn't be able to look at myself in a mirror in ten years' time. To compensate, I pulled my British Airways jacket into a looser position, and sat up straight. After a few miles I realised that it didn't seem to be making any difference, so I pulled my jacket tight and slouched down again. Once you've let yourself in for a masochistic thing like pulling some paddles through a river a couple of hundred thousand times, you might as well go the whole hog.

Then I tried to calculate exactly how many strokes were in fact needed to get to New Orleans. Three thousand eight hundred and ten miles, 5000 strokes a mile, call it around two million. Deduct a quarter for the current. That made $1\frac{1}{2}$ million. 'One and a half million?' I'd go off the clock about fifteen times before I got there. Some river . . . .

Liam was suddenly on the shore, shouting and waving me in. While I ate, we got talking about Bill. He ought to be somewhere past the Great Lakes by now. I sneaked a look at a meticulous schedule Tim had drawn

47

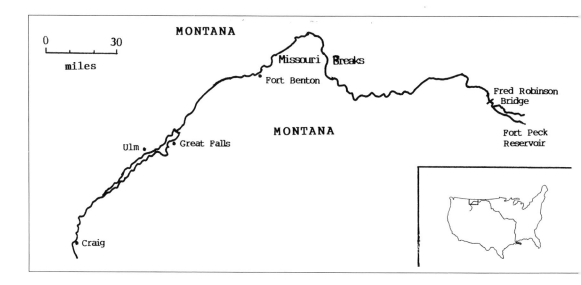

Craig to Fred Robinson Bridge.

up for me at base-camp. It showed me as 600 miles further on. He'd be doing well to find me.

Next day, after a hard slog under the hot sun, I rendezvoused with the team at 2 pm. Exactly thirty minutes later they told me I just had time to get to Great Falls, where Jim had arranged a press-conference for five o'clock. I groaned but paddled off again. It was now hotter than ever, and I had to keep pouring the cool Missouri water over my head.

I arrived at 5.05 and was impressed to see about a dozen men with cameras assembled on the bank. As we mutually surveyed each other, I though that the figure at the end looked vaguely familiar. I looked again, and realised with a shock that it was Bill!

We had a joyful reunion, until the press clustered round. In great form, I told them about our various adventures and emphasised the charity aspect. 'Where can our readers send contributions?' I muttered something about sending it to the C.R.C. in London, but I knew that for most Montanans, England was about as far away as the fifth dimension. In any case, the currency regulations probably prevented you sending money out. Once again, I cursed the A.C.S.'s selfish attitude.

At last it was over, and beers all round. As we drank the lukewarm liquid, Bill told us about his trip.

## II

His problems had started, he said, at Kennedy. Immigration had grilled him in teams for hours, asking him again and again why he had only $300 in his pocket for two months and where he was going to stay. At long last he had escaped. It was 90°, and there was a black-out covering the whole of New York. Bill had hitched through miles of riot-torn suburbs and three o'clock in the morning he was standing, Dylan-like, on Highway 80.

Two thousand seven hundred miles later, he walked into a newspaper office in Northwestern Montana. He put down his rucksack and asked the pressmen if they had any idea where a British kayaker was. 'We're meeting him in five minutes. Want a lift?' came the cool reply.

We examined with delight the equipment Bill had lugged up into the scores of lorries: a 40-ft strip of rubber to reinforce the inflatable, a brand-new tape recorder with dozens of music cassettes, and lots of other goodies, all paid for out of his own pocket. 'How's your diary going, Nick?' My splendid hard-backed notebook was empty bar four lines at Three Forks. 'No matter', said Bill mysteriously. 'The wonders of science.' By this time, it was too late to do any more canoeing. The team set up camp while I sat in the cab of the pick-up playing with the recorder. Once Bill had shown me how to operate it, I thought back to New York. The first thing I discovered was that it was very hard to just speak into an inanimate machine. Bill was excused camp-duties and promoted tape-recorder operator. By bedtime I had recorded two weeks – at this rate I'd soon catch up, I told him. I'd be just about in the year 2000 by the end of the trip.

Next morning, I was raring to go. I knew that the day's schedule included Great Falls, one of the most impressive sights on the whole Mississippi-Missouri complex. Lewis and Clark had written about the water falling 'in one smooth sheet over the precipice' and forming 'a perfectly white foam 200 yards in length', with spray 20 feet high displaying all the colours of the rainbow. I was just setting off, dreaming, when a Scottish voice sounded: 'Make sure you don't go over the edge, Nicky. It's quite a drop.'

As if to make sure, there they all were. But anybody save a myopic midget on a sinking surfboard would have seen the rough strata of stone curving away on both sides. After a quick portage, we looked at the falls from below. There was just a narrow curtain of water dropping tamely into a large pool. Only the battered and ravaged rock formations helped us imagine the awesome destructive beauty the place must have once had.

I amused myself paddling behind the curtain – let nobody say I had left any stretch uncanoed – and then we discussed the next bit. The map showed half a mile of rapids, and I was worried that the lowness of the water would make it worse. After a reconnaissance on foot, I set off in one of the slalom-boats. I wasn't used to its manoeuvrability and found myself

Canoeing the *whole* river: Great Falls.

oversteering. But with the sun blasting down and the water spraying everywhere, I soon began to enjoy myself. I had to do a long sequence of savage back- and side-paddling to just scrape past rock after rock that seemed to be groping and lunging at me. Only too soon I came to the end, breathless and shaken up, but exhilarated.

Somehow, Rick hadn't managed to take any action photographs at all. I told him I was extremely disappointed as the Cancer Research Campaign desperately needed dramatic shots. 'Do you want to do it again?' asked Liam.

I then made a bad mistake. I asked Liam to tie a rope round the bow of the kayak and tow me part of the way upstream. Near the bank lay a stretch of smooth water, and I thought my idea would be easier than climbing out of the canoe. But even before we got moving, there was a hitch. The rope tightened, then went completely slack, and the 6-knot current grabbed the bow of the kayak and spun us bodily sideways. I started to telemark to keep my balance but the rope snapped tight again at the worst moment, and the stern jammed against a rock. All of a sudden the whole wanton destructive power of the Missouri was rushing against me.

We stayed there for a couple of seconds, but then the equilibrium started slipping away. Liam had to let go completely, and I quickly tried to bring the canoe parallel to the current again. But the water was much too strong. The kayak, out of control, turned over completely.

I was suddenly upside-down under the cold, savage water, fighting for my very life. Instinctively, I tried to kick myself free from the tiny cockpit. But something was jamming on the right. I remembered the handgun and cursed. Again I pushed as hard as I could with my arms, but it was no good. Clawing sideways, I desperately lunged towards a split-second of air. I was inches away, when the canoe twisted me back under.

I heard later what happened next. The team had watched with horror as the smooth orange bottom of the kayak moved wildly back and forth. With each movement, they expected to see me emerging from the water. Rick had apparently been too surprised to take any pictures. But something had clicked in Bill's head. He did a quick calculation, bounded over the shore, pushed off with all his strength, and arced over the inshore rocks. His arms, head, and chest made it to the deeper water, but his left hip hit a submerged rock.

At about the same moment, a combination of desperation and self-preservation pushed me deeper into the cockpit, and then outwards again with all my might. My legs snapped tight, my muscles trembled with the strain, and something finally gave. With my head twice its normal size, I was wriggling out of the hole and then I was breaking the surface drinking in the cool air. The water was pure glitter, and the colour control of the sky and grass had gone haywire. To my amazement, I saw Bill as well, treading water only a few feet away. Still swept along by the current, we slowly worked our way together into shore.

Bill's flesh showed a nasty-looking jagged cut that was bleeding badly but the hip bone had absorbed much of the impact and he assured us it didn't need medical treatment. I myself was in one piece, but shaken, and with a splitting headache. I had lost my leather hat, jersey, bottle, and knife. The canoe itself had been washed up further down.

'Does this sort of thing happen often?' Bill enquired, one eyebrow slightly raised.


## III

In the afternoon, I changed kayaks again and headed off towards a series of dams. At each one, the team portaged the canoe round and raced on to the next one. The dam-keepers kept telling us it would be much easier to simply relaunch at the bottom. But the boys persevered. First it was Black Eagle Dam, then Rainbow, Cochrane, Ryan, and finally Morony.

Somewhere on this stretch my crotch and matches were definitively

51

A hot portage (Bill and Tim).

doused by an incoming wave. Coming up to a 5-mile and 2500-stroke break, I beached my boat and walked through the 'garden' of a riverboat shack. Halfway through the arid scrub, a window opened and a head filled the frame.

'Wherethehell you going?'

'Have you got a match?'

'That land's full of rattlers. Nothin' is getting me in there', and the head disappeared.

I looked down at my paralysed feet, my smile congealing. Minutes or aeons later, stone-weighted matches came sailing through the air. I crashed back to the fence as noisily as I could.

Somewhere also on this stretch, Lewis and Clark had described an island perched above some falls. On the island was a single cottonwood tree, and on it the proud nest of a solitary eagle. For my part, I couldn't find the island, and certainly didn't see any eagles – just a couple of vultures, looking very down at heel and miserable.

As I rounded a bend I heard the characteristic zip of high-velocity bullets. They were producing little spurts of dust on the sun-baked bluff on my left – but I had no idea where they were coming from. I pulled in and waited for them to stop, but they didn't! In the end I decided to risk it. I moved boldly across the wide expanse of water, wincing maniacally with each ricochet.

Relieved when they ended, I paddled on through a dappled paradise of cool pools and glorious meadows – just like England in 1950s technicolour. Late that evening, I saw thousands of small white stones spelling out 'Fort Benton', together with the statue of a dog. It was 'Shep', immortalised by Elvis Presley, and arguably the most famous dog in the world. When his shepherd master died, the body was sent east for burial and Shep began a long and tragic vigil which was to last for five years, waiting for his master who would never return. He dug himself a rudimentary shelter beside the railway track. In conditions of minus 20° or plus 90°, the dog waited for each train, scanning the passengers, searching for the familiar smell. It was always the same . . . the last passenger left . . . the train drawing away into the night. The end came tragically when a passing train ran over his body. One can only hope that Shep rejoined his master and Maker.

Beside the superb old-style railway bridge, there appeared a blue tent, plus a roaring fire and a pan of mince and tatties. As Tim ladled, Liam told us about the history of Fort Benton. When the first steamboat had set off for here in 1860, the crew and passengers had had to stop the boat every couple of days to chop wood and hunt game. With the crazy Montana gold-rush of the 1860s, things began to get organised. For a start, the mountain-boats, as they were optimistically called, were made arrow-proof, as the Pawnees and Sioux had come to resent the puffing intruders. In the 1870s and 1880s Fort Benton became a major port – the only one in the world 4000 miles from the ocean. Liam then told us that some of the boats came here 'directly' from New York State. 'Yeah, via New Orleans!' came our sceptical chorus.

'Not at all. Via the Allegheny, the Ohio, the Mississippi, and the Missouri. Just make sure, Nick, you don't end up in Manhattan!'

Liam had found a list of steamboat wrecks on the Missouri, and it made horrifying listening as he emphasised the disasters. Up to 1897, the US Corps of Engineers had classified them as follows: whirlpool 1;

overloading 1; collision 1; ran into bank 1; storm and wind 2; sandbars 4; explosion of boiler 6; bridges 10; rocks 11; fire 25; ice 26; snags 193. 'The snags are the ones to watch.' We gave a round of applause; but he hadn't finished yet.

Fort Benton had also been the main staging-post for the Northern Overland Pony Express from Missouri to Oregon. The N.O.P.E. was set up as a rival to the Pony Express to California, but with two major differences. It blazed its own trails; and it operated in totally hostile territory – at that time there wasn't an American military outpost in the whole of Montana. Its riders were often beaten or killed, and the service had to be stopped after only a few months. Then in 1885, concluded Liam, the Northern Pacific railroad arrived, and a whole heroic era in the winning of the West came to a sudden end.

Next on the agenda was money. After only 250 miles, we were virtually broke again. What made matters worse was that some of the members had brought their own money. I understood the problem perfectly since I myself was without a penny to my name. Finally Liam came out with an idea that had been in all our minds for a while. 'What do you do? Why, you go out and get a job!' I said I could see huge problems: legal ones, time ones, and expedition-coherence ones.

I had a sudden desire to be back on the river. It was a beautiful evening as I headed off through the bare, dry hills. As the sky turned red and then blue-black, however, the water began to run out. The encyclopedias, I decided, had been dead right to call the Upper River unnavigable. As my boat began to slide, I cursed the dams and the two-year drought.

Twain reports that he would calmly cruise in until he touched, apply full power – and just scrape over. It worked twice; but then we were well and truly stuck. I reluctantly placed my hands on the warm, smooth slime. Having checked that the kayak's draught was, as advertised, exactly 4 inches, I wriggled my bottom. Her bottom wriggled. I swung the whole boat forward excruciatingly slowly. Then I brought my hands quickly back into position before she could get comfortable again. I manhandled that boat until my shoulders ached with pain. Tim had told us stories about 'gumbo' mud: about the Missouri being too thick to drink, but too thin to plough; or so sticky it has problems going round bends; or so muddy that if you throw a man in, he just breaks his leg. Now I knew that some of them might be true.

Then the river came back. I slowly paddled another 10 miles, came into the dark shore, and lit a fire. For a while, I sat and appreciated the gentle sounds of nature. Only too soon an engine whined and a snub-nose came threading its moonlit way. In the boat were Liam, Bill, and some unwanted male groupie. We started back upstream, but there was a wet whirring noise as the propeller dug itself deep into the mud. Liam cut the motor and we jumped out of the boat and pushed. Only after minutes of sweating and swearing, did we notice that our passenger hadn't lifted a finger.

We'd go up one channel for a hundred yards, only to get stuck in the invisible cloying mud. Back we'd come. And so it went on, blind-man's-bluff in a moving labyrinth. We kept going only by inventing a system to get us through that crazy night. Bill found himself a position with one foot hanging over the side. Out of the darkness came 'One leg – full stern ahead, Mr Bosun!' or 'mark twain – go easy!'. Co-ordinating the information more efficiently than a 32-bit microprocessor, Liam nursed the boat along, alternately caressing and cajoling it. I was leaping in and out like a Chinese coolie. 'Three quarters of a leg – one knee – half a shin!' I leapt out as clumsily as I could, and swamped the groupie. Then an arched silhouette was looming up. We were home at last.

Jim and Tim had been working their way through Fort Benton. At their fifth plastic-covered musak-drenched old saloon-bar, they had found a small silo-building firm that was looking for heavy labourers. If we were caught, we would be put on the first plane out. Also, the wage offered of $2.50 (£1.04) was an insult, especially for Liam and Bill who had given up jobs paying four times as much. But it was either work or starve. We decided that the members making such a sacrifice should have the unheard-of right to one square meal in a café each day, together with one glass of beer.

Thus it was that, the following morning, Liam and I loaded the inflatable down, said a guilty goodbye, and roared off. Fifteen miles on, I pulled *Lochinvar* from her hiding-place. Then, with Liam in convoy, I canoed into the Missouri Breaks, and back through time itself. As the river cut through a succession of geological faults, we left the last traces of human activity, the last scraps of vegetation, and soon we had nothing but the bones of the Breaks for company. All we could see was an occasional etched rock, surging effortlessly out of the water, plus a stony wall swept smooth by aeons of waves with regular rock layers, chiselled in three-D by some divine architect.

The blue sky, grey stone, and green river went on and on. Finally it was time for lunch. Afterwards, I scrambled up the cliff, and was amazed by the change. With the sweat drying on my brow, I could see the Missouri literally breaking through the countryside, violating hollows, slicing through hillocks, shouldering off rivals. Only in the cactus-strewn distance did it apparently exchange force for guile, working its weary way up until it could survey the high, rolling plains of Montana. I knew, however, that this was just an illusion. The Missouri would never see what I could see:

Kirk Douglas coming over the dusty horizon with a thousand longhorn all the way from Texas. But then again, it had its own secret visions, its own cherished memories: gold prospectors panning, buffalo drinking, coyotes swimming, coloured canoes paddling, painted Indians whooping, shy long-haired girls bathing.

By nightfall we had covered 32 miles. At a little bay, Liam showed me how to build a makeshift tent out of our tarpaulin and sundry sticks. As the food started sizzling, I looked out across the ghostly drifting river, towards bluffs and 'buttes' that hadn't changed for 10,000 years. Captains Lewis and Clark had camped on the same spot, I knew, and gazed out on the same primeval cliffs.

Early next morning, we came back to civilisation with a shock. There was an abandoned chain-ferry and a ramshackle bar. Four hatted cowhands were lounging against the counter. As Liam went to the 'restroom', eight eyes descended on me, and stayed there. I ordered two coffees, feeling as though I had just arrived from another planet. A loud voice cut through the silence: 'Maybe he thinks a handgun makes him look more virile!'

The sugar-lump softened in my hand. (HURRY UP L-I-A-M!) 'I've been canoeing through the Breaks,' I said quickly. 'We're hoping to make it through to New Orleans.' A hint of interest dawned in two of the eyes.

'Hey, you the guys kayaking for cancer, or sump'n?' All was well. I decided, however, never to wear my gun in public again.

Then it was back to the untamed wilderness. Back in Fort Benton, I had overruled Liam, and chosen tea that was twenty cents cheaper. That night, we discovered that it was 'green (ie Japanese) tea', and didn't taste the same. We had forgotten the sugar, and in fact it tasted absolutely awful!

We saw a narrow hole in the side of a sheer bluff. This was meant to be one of the hide-outs of Butch Cassidy and his 'Hole-in-the-Wall Gang'. I gleefully remembered Tom Sawyer's wet attempts to reconstruct his own hole-in-the-wall and Huck Finn's corrosive comments. At our lunch halt, I again felt restless. I'd read about some amazing fossils that had been found near here: one of only two egg-bound dinosaur embryos in existence; the body of an Akylosaurus – a 24-ft long club-tailed horned toad; and a 47-ft skeleton of Tyrannosaurus Rex. But all I could see was bare rock.

That night I had a dream. There was a sort of a path leading up to the plateau, and I began idly following it, but it just petered out halfway. As I started to work my way back to the river, I spotted some lumps lying in the sand, and casually turned them over with my foot. Then I was kneeling on the ground examining them more closely. They had angular bits on the sides, and there was a slight indentation on the bottom: primitive arrowheads! I quickly looked up, expecting to see a ring of white head-dresses; but cliff, sky, and Missouri were the same as ever. I smoothed the hot sand over, hoping that nobody would disturb the site for at least another 100 years, and returned to the lonely shore. Then I awoke with a pain in my right side. I'd been lying on a very sharp, very angular but exceedingly ordinary stone.

Two days later, we arrived at the brand-new Fred Robinson Bridge, having covered 130 miles in four and a half days. The desolation of the place had got to both Liam and me, and we felt totally exhausted. The sun was burning hot and however many pints we drank we still felt thirsty. I tried some water from the Missouri and felt even more parched. Ahead of us lay Fort Peck Reservoir: 150 miles of still water, up to 7 miles wide, with only two very rough access tracks – one on each side. And not a single house. We were down to $10, and had very little petrol or food left. We decided it would be folly to continue. Our only choice was to get in touch with the gang.

We hitch-hiked 4 miles along a tar-blistered road and came to a little farmhouse. The owners kindly said we could use their phone. We had forgotten to note the number of the bar in Fort Benton and the bar wasn't in the book. Feeling very despondent, we walked back to the furnace at the bridge. Then we sat and vacantly watched the Missouri – even its force seemed to be subdued, as though unable to drift in that terrible heat. The MMCRSKE was in a total fix.

At that moment, a three-man open canoe came into sight. We waved, and they pulled in. By sheerest luck, one of them was going back to Fort Benton that night. Yes, he'd be very happy to carry a message for us. Thank God for the Montanans!

We settled down to wait. Only three incidents broke the monotony. A dog had to have a fight with a skunk right beside our tent. Unable to breathe, we abandoned camp for the afternoon. At our new chosen spot, we discovered a 'prairie-dog': a squirrel-like creature that kept popping out of his hole to examine us before darting incredulously back in. Then, just at dusk, we heard a melancholy sound wafting upstream. We found a beautiful girl playing a bagpipe lament. For a moment, time wavered and I was back on a Scottish sea loch. But the music stopped only too soon; and it was back to camp and a hot peanut butter dinner.

Late the following afternoon, a blue car arrived. Jim brought $50. Liam and I were a bit disappointed as we had wanted to see the boys again. Our note had however been a bit brief ('Stuck at Fred Robinson Bridge. No money, no food, and no fuel'), so I suppose we got what we deserved. But in fact, we still didn't know where to go from here. Liam just wasn't enjoying the wilderness. We finally decided to wait till the boys' first day off, and then perhaps change the team round.

We read and we slept. We slept and we read. Some of the time, I worked on the tape-recorder. Two days later, the boys arrived, exhausted by their marathon of laying concrete and hoisting aluminium sheets.

We cooked a massive dinner and invented a policy. I suggested that Liam could return to the (relative) comfort of Fort Benton and that Bill could accompany me through the reservoir. Everybody seemed pleased, and I announced a celebratory round of beer. The closest bar was 20 miles away; but Jim had a six-pack in his boot. Once again he had saved the day.

On Monday 1 August, we spent ages consulting maps, arranging for extra fuel, repairing the inflatable, and loading supplies. By late afternoon we were ready. It was nineteen days since Three Forks, and I had covered 399 miles – 1 inch on my pocket atlas, and an average of 21 miles a day.

But now I had a burning determination to paddle on as fast as was humanly possible. Fort Peck here we come!

# In Which We Lose the Missouri

A boat that cannot, on occasion, climb a steep clay bank, go across a cornfield and corner a river that is trying to get away, has little excuse for trying to navigate the Missouri.

(George Fitch)

## I

At 6 pm, Bill and I moved out into the Missouri River. It was still 90° in the shade and the current barely reached ¹/₂ mph. We left the last track behind, soon the last tree, and then we were entirely on our own. Looking round at the austere ruggedness, we shared a mood of mad exhilaration and some trepidation.

On the third day, I set off early, leaving Bill with the task of striking camp at 'Soda Creek Bay'. We had arranged to rendezvous for a late lunch at Devil's Creek, 20 miles on. My morale was high, as the wind was for once behind me and, curiously, I detected a slight current. I headed straight on for about 10 miles, counting my strokes as usual, and humming – which was less so. Beginning to suffer from the sun, I decided to come ashore for a few minutes. I canoed into a dusty, drought-cracked creek.

I was halfway towards the cool shadow of a cliff when my foot seemed to slip and the surface suddenly gave away beneath me. To my absolute horror, I felt my body sinking.

Within a second, I was up to my waist in cloying, stinking gumbo mud. My legs couldn't move, and the brittle surface kept breaking beneath my hands, exactly like a nightmare. Then I was really frightened. There just didn't seem any way out. But then I had an idea. I pulled my lifejacket off – thank God I was wearing it today. I could now feel myself slowly sinking again, but with huge breaths I blew it up hard and placed it carefully in front of me. Using my elbows and wrists to distribute my weight, I pushed

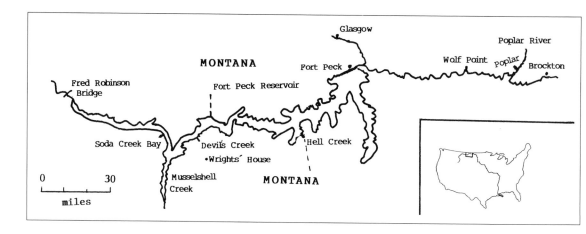

Fred Robinson Bridge to Brockton.

down on the rigid rubber. It held! I pushed harder, trying not to jerk it. With relief, I could feel my whole body pulling at the sticky mud. I arched my ankles, and felt less resistance in my feet miles below. Sweat was stinging my eyes, but I was now halfway out.

I leant forward, putting even more weight onto the jacket, and began to swim in slow-motion with my lead-heavy legs. Progress was desperately slow, but eventually my right foot emerged and then I was completely free, apart from a whole mound of malevolent mud on the middle of my back. Still not trusting the treacherous surface, I pushed the jacket forward a few inches and then moved after it. I slid onto a harder patch and continued to crawl forward as slowly as my nerves would permit. Eventually my hand reached *Lochinvar's* hull. Leaning on the hot fibreglass, I stood up, very glad to hear the mud dropping off, and feeling a bit like the first Neanderthal to stagger to an upright position. And then I was in the boat, moving away from that terrible place as fast as I could go.

What surprised me after a few minutes was the gradual convergence of the two shores. I went another 200 yards to make certain, but there wasn't the shadow of a doubt: in front was just a dried-up creek. I got the map out, and deduced that I was $3^1/2$ miles into Musselshell Bay. This isn't the Missouri at all, I angrily muttered, it's Shit Creek, and I'm up it. But at least I've still got my paddles.

As I paddled those $3^1/2$ miles back, I realised that it was the wind on the surface that had simulated a current. I also understood why the name Musselshell seemed so familiar: Lewis and Clark had also had problems here. They had been virtually eaten alive by horse-flies; they had been attacked by a grizzly weighing 500 lb and measuring 8 ft $7^1/2$ in from head

60

to foot (they had had to kill it to obtain this information); and they had been obliged to thread their way through the putrid carcasses of over 100 buffalo chased over the cliffs by Indians disguised in wolf-skins. As I looked round at the dry landscape, I realised how much it had changed. The mountains didn't look now as if they would support a single prairie-dog.

I got back to the junction, checked the maps, and carefully turned right. I was getting pretty hungry, as I hadn't even finished my breakfast. At 4.30, I calculated that I had done the 20 miles. Dead on schedule, a beautiful lagoon of unspoilt white sand came into view. I started to wait for Bill. I reasoned that he was probably only a mile or two ahead and would surely come back to look for me. By 7 pm I was very, very hungry and finally admitting to myself that something had gone wrong. I climbed up a hill and scanned the horizon. Nothing but desolation. There seemed little else I could do, so I lit two huge driftwood fires as signals. I was carrying no equipment, not even a packet of biscuits. Maybe Bill's been bitten by a snake, I thought. In this hellish place they'll take a week to find him. Mercifully, my exhaustion at last caught up with me.

Dawn came up and I had to decide what to do. Basically, I could stay put, paddle on, or paddle back. I looked at the maps again. Something must have happened to the power-boat or to Bill – otherwise he would surely have come looking for me. Reluctantly, I decided to paddle back.

As I rounded each headland, I confidently expected to see him – but each time there were merely miles of nothing. Famished and depressed, I started to cross the expanse of water opposite Musselshell. Soon *Lochinvar* was caught by a side-wind which brought 6-ft waves crashing angrily over the hull. Twice I almost capsized, and twice my heart came into my mouth.

I arrived at Soda Creek Bay at 2.30 pm to find the carefully-dispersed remains of the camp-fire. Now extremely weak, and wondering whether the nightmare was ever going to end, I headed 'downstream' once more, trying to ignore the racking pains in my shoulders. Water started seeping into the rear compartment, making steering very difficult indeed. Once again I crossed the bay opposite Musselshell. Once again the huge waves crashed viciously over me. Coming into the end of the crossing, I pulled in and baled out nearly a gallon of water. I began to wonder whether God existed and whose side He was meant to be on.

I was just on the 25,000th stroke since the last taste of food when I heard a sound like distant thunder. I tried to ignore it but suddenly a tiny plane hopped over the hills and after a moment turned towards me. Through a haze a package dropped and at the same moment I recognised Bill at the window. Feelings of relief and affection for my faithful friend flooded through me, but my shouts just stuck in my throat. All I could manage was a feeble wave. I sprinted to the shore, grabbed the package, and found two Mars Bars inside. A message read: 'Camp is 12 miles ahead, on right bank. Will wait for you there with hot dinner. *Bon voyage!*'

As the plane banked steeply out of view, I pulled in once more. I scooped up some of the gumbo mud that had nearly killed me the day before, and carefully covered the inside of the hairline crack. Now we would see just how sticky it really was.

The burning fireball of the sun moved closer and closer to the varnished horizon. It began to get dark, and still camp was nowhere to be found. At last I rounded a point and saw a yellow fire in the distance. Ten minutes later, Bill was helping me out.

We were very, very pleased to see each other. He give me a large tot of rum ('for medicinal purposes') followed by a whole plateful of barbecued chicken. It was nectar and ambrosia, and for a long moment I was in the land of the gods.


# II

Bill threw some more driftwood on the fire, and explained where he had been. He had stopped after exactly 18 miles. He tried the radio set, 'on the hour, every hour,' as we had agreed in cases of emergency. In the late afternoon, he had decided to look for me. Just in case I had made superhuman speed, he started to go the 2 miles 'downstream' to the rendezvous point, but after only a mile, the engine had made a terrible noise and broken down. He paddled anxiously into shore, and walked quickly along to Devil's Creek. No luck, so he had walked four or five miles back 'upstream', and climbed up to a high vantage point. Still nothing.

The distance back to Soda Creek Bay by foot was about 25 miles, and would involve being out of sight of the lake much of the time (thank you again, Musselshell). So he waited, until he was worried sick. At 2 pm the following day, he left a note on the inflatable, and half-ran the 10 miles up into the burning mountains to the nearest house. Nobody there – so he went on to the next one, another 5 miles. In it, a Mr and Mrs Wright had let him telephone the US Coastguard at the dam but they were too far away to do anything. Finally he had phoned an old pilot friend of the Wrights'. For $10, the pilot landed in a field, hauled Bill aboard, and headed full throttle for the Missouri. Finally they saw something long and orange moving painfully over the surface of the sea.

My getting lost had been a terrible mistake, of course, but all the rest seemed to follow on automatically, as in a Greek tragedy. The situation had been saved by the pilot's amazingly efficient and generous action. The spirit of America is alive and well, and is to be found in Central Montana. I just hope that a copy of this book will reach him.

On the Thursday morning, we found ourselves with a difficult decision. The inflatable was dead. We were stranded in the exact middle of the hostile reservoir, and opposite the Fort Peck Indian Reservation – half a million acres of nothingness, where the once-mighty Crow Nation huddled in a handful of hamlets and drank itself to death. But we were also 1850 miles from the end of the Missouri. Very reluctantly, I decided to canoe to the end of the terrible reservoir on my own.

My shoulders were still aching, so I put off starting. The morning seemed to pass very quickly, as I sat and daydreamed. Just before lunch, I spotted a whitish bird standing idly on the shore. I gestured silently to Bill, and went to fetch the rifle. The deer had got away, but this time I was really hungry. I took one pot-shot at it, then another. It just kept on standing there, pretending hard nothing had happened. Bill reloaded, and took two more shots. I crawled towards it. When I was about 30 feet away, I took careful aim. Shot number six finally saved our honour, and I strolled casually over. I showed the bird to Bill but now it seemed much smaller than before. To be frank, there was hardly a scrap of flesh on its miserable frame – even if we'd known how to pluck and gut it. But it did get a decent burial . . . .

After lunch, we made a rendezvous for 10 pm on Saturday. Then I set cautiously off, loaded with $2^1/2$ days of provisions. My friend the headwind was soon back, sending a lot of water crashing over the foredeck. After only 16 miles, I felt very weary. I cracked three eggs over some corned-beef. Settling down beside the glowing branches, I was soon sleeping like a log.

In the morning there was a moment when the blue unspoiled beauty of the lake was all mine. I lit a cigarette but then brusquely stubbed it out. I looked at the map: the lake was absolutely featureless until Hell Creek, 34 miles away – a hunting cabin tenuously connected to the rest of the world by a rough track. Still, it looked better than the competition.

I arrived at dusk. With surprise, I discovered several large power-boats together with, of all things, an ancient and dust-covered bus. Were even these infernal regions invaded by pleasure-trippers? Which should I choose – devil or deep blue sea? I decided company would do me good. Clutching the empty water bottle as a pretext, I knocked and walked in. It was full of singing and drinking. 'Water? What the hell's that? There's plenty of beer though!' A throng of people were pushing food forward. I was in luck, they told me, as they only came out here once a month. I sang and danced with the best of them. Then, at twelve, my legs began to tremble.

After a good night's sleep on the back seat of the bus, my friends offered to carry me out to the mouth of the creek. Five deep-throated roars as five times a 100 horsepower leaped into action; and then we were off, bouncing over the waves in the crystal-clear air. This is the life, I thought – why can't it always be like this? For two minutes we ruled the world. Then, without warning, we sluiced through 90°. *Lochinvar* and I were offloaded, I shouted out my thanks, and very soon was plodding on alone.

By 8 pm, the lights of the dam had finally come over the horizon – a wall 4 miles long and an inch high. I forced the kayak over the waves that night, driving it on and on. Even with all my bits and pieces, we were moving faster than on the Channel, but this time I knew we were going to win. I forgot about the counting, and went through my whole horrible repertoire of Edith Piaf songs.

Half-hidden behind a rocky outcrop were a jetty, boats, cars, and houses. With a shock, I realised that there were even trees and grass. I brought *Lochinvar* in, slowly now, trying to hold onto the precious moments. But only too soon we were there, and I had to pull the canoe out of the water. It was exactly ten.

III

At five past, Bill and Liam walked in. As we ordered drinks all round and talked together, I opened my heart to my two friends. Ever since my sleepless night at Rogers, Arkansas, I had had a terrible fear, the fear that the miles and miles of still water would prove too much for me. But now I felt that I'd somehow gained my spurs. Even if I broke my leg or something and had to stop, I would have at least proved that my spirit was willing.

My friends understood my confession. Liam pointed out that the altitude of the river was now only about 2000 feet – and so logically I had covered half of the difficult water down to the Gulf. Emboldened by their sympathy, I went further, much further, in unloading my conscience. I took a big breath, and said that, when I started, up in the Rockies, I had never gone kayaking on a river before.

There was a shocked silence. Maybe I *had* gone too far this time. At least in a confessional you can always walk out. But now I was trapped. I repeated that, apart from a certain two minutes on the Thames, I had never previously launched a canoe on fresh water. 'I couldn't tell you before, as you mightn't have let me out on the river.'

'Damned right, we wouldn't have let you out of the loonie asylum!'

'Only old Nick could do this to us. He sets off on the longest river trip in recorded history, and then calmly says he's never been on a river before.'

'Why didn't you water-ski the Atlantic on the way over? You'd had as much experience.'

'I always did wonder what he was doing, 3.81 thousand miles from the ocean in a sea-going kayak – now I think I understand.'

'I suppose, since he's got this far, we might as well let him carry on . . . .'

The storm had passed, and I deftly changed the subject to the silo-gang. Liam valiantly told me they could stick it for about another ten days. I said I felt awful that they should have to go on working but there seemed to be no other way. As it was, they had had to borrow $200 from Jim for the first instalment on the pick-up.

Monday morning was declared a rest period, but there was no getting away from the monster that overshadowed the whole town, as tall as a twenty-five storey building. Going for a walk along the top, we were cornered by a man and a dog. It was in fact the biggest earth-filled dam in the world! At full capacity its area was 250,000 acres! Did we know that it held back 150 miles of still water? Bill and I exchanged amazed glances. 'It certainly doesn't look that big.' We gave him the slip, and resumed our walk in peace.

Driving back into town, we stopped at a petrol station. A flash of blue, then a large estate car had gone past. It's the same as my cousins', I thought, *and* it had a New York plate. By this time, Jim and Anne were running towards me. They told us they had spent ten solid days looking for the expedition – we were meant to have been in Southern Kansas by now. I apologised for my tardiness, and quickly told them about the Musselshell episode, feeling pretty stupid. But Jim just said 'Remember Meriwether Lewis in 1805? He went *200* miles up the wrong bit. Keep a cool head and you'll make it to the Gulf.' With Bill and Liam chipping in, we talked about everything and nothing. We visited a herd of buffalo, shaggy and brown-eyed. 'A bit like Highland cattle,' I ruminated.

'Yeahoo,' said Liam. 'All the cows in Scotland are 6 feet tall and weigh 2000 lb . . . .'

Then Jim told us about the early explorers' descriptions of puzzled buffalo floating down the Missouri on springtime ice-floes. (Thank God I had chosen the summer!) Round the campfire we told Jim and Anne our adventures in full, while devouring a superb pioneer-style dinner; pioneer, except for the heady Nuits-Saint-Georges washing it down. Never did wine taste so good.

On Tuesday, I waved a very sad goodbye to Jim and Anne, and launched below the dam. They had given me more support than they perhaps realised.

A 'River Ranger' in Glasgow had told me that I could count on a five-knot current after the next bend. My maps confirmed that the

Missouri flowed at speeds of up to 7 mph. I had therefore promised to make for Oswego, about 45 miles downstream. But when I got round that first bend, there was just a grudging 2 mph. I cursed the drought then, and the Ranger's ignorance of 'his' river.

A few miles on, I was due to hit the Milk River. I was expecting rushing water, for various reasons. First, because the Milk came down from the Lewis Range of the Rockies, on the same longitude as California; but also because its tributaries included the 'Frenchman' from Saskatchewan and it had itself zipped into Alberta before deciding where its true loyalties lay; and finally because it became the highest point reached by a steamboat (the rather inappropriately named *El Paso* in 1850). But where *was* the Milk? I kept looking out for it. After an unhappy while, I decided that it must have been that dried-up creek a couple of miles back. Anything less milky or cosmopolitan I had never seen.

All day, I paddled as hard as I could. Just before ten, with my progress down to a depressed crawl, I was wondering if I should pull in. It was one of those nights Twain had talked about, when the river 'hadn't any shape at all'. But in the distance there appeared the tiny glow of a fire. I confidently yelled Bill's name, and received a loud howl from a coyote in reply. My senses crawled. But I got to the fire, clambered up the bluff, and was very glad to find Bill there, writing hard.

I was surprised, however, not to see the pick-up; nor even the two-man tent; and there was a terrible burnt smell. Bill admitted that yes, he *had* had a couple of problems. First of all, he had carelessly driven the pick-up into some sand on the way back from Fort Benton. The sand – fortunately – was only 50 yards away. Also an important piece of equipment had caught fire. It wasn't the rubber boat; it wasn't the tent; it was . . . his yellow sleeping-mat. Showing me a shrivelled black ball the size of a clenched fist, he told me that it was worth it just for the colour of the flames. What with all this excitement, he added, he hadn't had time to put up the tent. That night, I slept on the front seat of the pick-up, which was 4 inches shorter than me. Bill slept out under the stars.

In the morning, the current flowed much faster but it was raining hard. Reaching Wolf Point, I was very relieved to see that Bill had got the pick-up out of the mud. He told me that he was taking me out for lunch, but as we were on an Indian reservation, the hamburgers would be made from dog and snakemeat! Sure enough the faces were all bronzed and the hair long. But the food tasted good – if a bit tangy – and I never did know whether or not he was joking. In the afternoon, the rain was coming down more heavily than ever. Sitting in the pattering improvised recording studio with my coat on, I stared at the microphone and tried to recreate the sun-baked atmosphere at Fred Robinson Bridge. I couldn't.

## IV

I was away by 8 am. Thirty miles later, I arrived at a little town called Poplar. For once, I was in the right place at the right time. But for once, Bill wasn't. I rowed on a few hundred yards, to a point that was more accessible from the road. *Ancora niente.*

By 6 pm he still hadn't arrived. It was a fine evening, so I decided to carry on. I came to a bridge, but still there was no sign of Bill. I should have left a note – but I didn't have a pen . . . . As I rowed on, I expected at every moment to see the flames of a campfire glowing wanly against the brilliant sky. But soon it got completely dark and I reluctantly pulled up on a rather damp sandbar.

I woke next morning with bad cramp in my legs and a beautiful butterfly in my kayak. At 1 pm I arrived at a little Indian town with the peculiarly Anglo-Saxon name of Brockton. It had an all-pervading atmosphere of decay, with only two modern buildings: the petrol-station and the bar – about all that the Indians had ever got out of White civilisation. Without a cent on me, I plucked up my forage cap and courage, and went into the bar. Thronged on every side by friendly questions, and soon by delicious dishes, I was struck again by the hospitality of all the Montana people, whatever their ethnic origin.

A young man called Myron Four-Bears invited me home. I really didn't know what to do about Bill, so accepted. As we walked in, I saw a very old lady gazing at me from her refuge in another room. His grandmother, Myron told me, who had lost her father at the Battle of Little Big Horn. She was now reduced to weaving the colours of the Sioux war emblem onto blankets which she would then sell on the pavement outside to tourists like me who would never understand. In her eyes I read a mixture of sadness and hostility – I must have been the first White person to enter her house and she probably had too many memories. Perhaps to compensate, Myron gave me a jacket with 'WARRIORS' printed on the back. I was very aware then of the contrast of cultures. The lady making the blanket, the petrol-station advertising Pepsi; the proud old customs and the plastic baseball jacket. My hosts were neither fully Indian nor authentically American but just American Indians – a protected species.

At five, Myron drove me through the Reservation and back to Poplar. No one had seen Bill. At 8.30, we went to the security office. I tried to give no hint of my surprise, but the red skin and hooded eyes had so often fought against uniforms that a sense of incongruity never quite left me. The sergeant put out a radio message to all cars: a green Dodge pick-up with three orange kayaks should be located and picked up. We then drove back to Wolf Point, where I had last seen Bill. The security office there told us he had been located and was now heading for Poplar.

We found him. I introduced him to Myron, Bill opened his mouth and a deafening wailing noise erupted. We mimed to the police: had the Russians landed? They pointed to a huge notice: 'All children under the age of eighteen must be at their regular domicile by 10 pm. Officers have strict instructions to arrest offenders.' A curfew in America, the haven of civil liberties? Washington must be turning in his grave.

The sirens stopped and Bill was able to tell his story. He had driven straight along to Poplar, and straight down to the water. Lunch time passed, and then dinner time. In the morning, he went to explore: downstream he found . . . another river! He'd been waiting on the wrong one!

I thanked Myron for his tremendous help, and he revved noisily off. As Bill made some grape jelly sandwiches, I took stock. It was now the 12th of August and we were still in Montana. But we were 665 river-miles from Three Forks and my average had edged up to $21^{1}/_{2}$ miles a day – in spite of all the still water. In fact, as I gleefully pointed out to Bill, we were now quits, at one lost river each. Remarks about shooting up dry creeks could be countered with ones about waiting at muddy trickles. In other words, I could always count on a warm welcome when I arrived at camp.

And that, for me, was essential.

# A Monstrous Big River

Unwinding rivers, through shifting glades to fall,
Down through glorious meadows to the sea.

(Bryan Ferry)

## I

In the morning, the bow started slipping to the left and soon *Lochinvar* was slewing drunkenly over the waves. Squelching ashore, I opened the forward hatch and found a pin-prick hole, together with about two gallons of water. I cursed my careless launching, while searching round for 'quick-fix' mud. There wasn't any. I thought of chipping some off the rear repair job and remixing it but decided to leave well alone. By the time I arrived at the bridge it was very late; but my friend was there with a blazing fire; and after six eggs and six sausages, I felt much better.

We switched my equipment into *Cameron of Lochiel*. After several further hours of rain, it became a lovely evening. The sky went from orange to ochre to purple, and the water from pink to blue to black, with the paddles just slipping through the river like quicksilver. Suddenly I realised two large deer were staring intently at me, as if having never seen such a sight in all their lives. I drifted towards them, staring hard back. With an inimitable snuffling sound and a disdainful turn of the head, they cantered elegantly off.

I saw smoke floating over the reeds and knew I had arrived. I was at peace that night. For some reason, the purple sky and limpid water I shared with Bill were to remain engraved in my memory for ever.

On Monday morning, I phoned the American Cancer Society in New York. I gave some of our news and they asked if I could get to New Orleans by 17 November, 'Great American Smoke-Out Day'. I told them we still had over 3000 miles to go but that we would keep the date in mind.

69

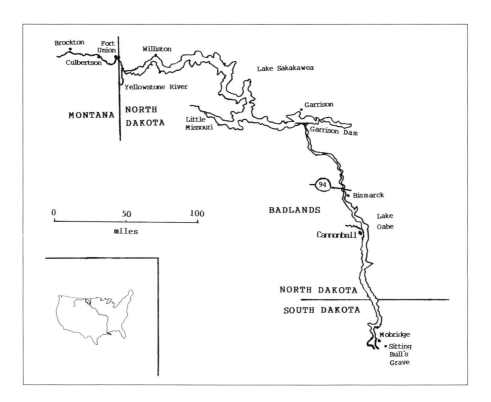

Brockton to Mobridge.

I set off – and immediately arrived at the North Dakota border. Still recovering from the shock, I saw another landmark ahead, the mouth of the Yellowstone River, down from the National Park of Yogi Bear fame. Sitting on a hummock, I contemplated the confluence.

The Yellowstone was bringing water from a 14,000-ft source in Wyoming, like its tributary, the Big Horn, and like *its* tributary, the infamous Little Big Horn. This spot was also chosen – wisely – by Lewis and Clark as the one unmistakable meeting-point on their separate ways back from the Rockies. After them, the French fur-trappers started moving into the valley of the 'Roche Jaune', undeterred that more than half of them were being killed by Indians or wild animals. Next rafts, flatboats, and keelboats crawled up the Missouri, powered by sweating horses and men and complicated combinations of ropes, oars, and poles.

Then, in 1832, the first steamboat struggled up. (The successive navigation records were clearly going to give me a countdown all the way to St Louis and the sixteenth century.) This epic trip changed history. There had been a long-standing border dispute between (British) Canada and the US, with everything swinging on the Indians. The chiefs dithered.

70

King or President? Crown or Bald Eagle? Then the Missouri came alive with the big-thunder-canoe, the fireboat-that-walks-on-water. In vain did the British swear that they had canoes that were ten times as big, and others that walked on land. The Indians just didn't believe a word. The West had been won – and lost – for ever more.

Feeling a bit humbled, I climbed into my very-little-thunder-canoe and headed out towards the line. A little tug, and soon both of us were moving on in great style.

That night I slept badly, for I knew that immediately ahead lay the second of the inland seas, called Sakakawea, after Lewis and Clark's guide. At 178 miles, it was even longer than the first.

The approaches were marked 'Hazard Area', and I soon discovered why. Man had replaced a dense green forest with rows of severed tree-trunks – a withered maze without a single bird. Several times I got lost following drowned footpaths leading into convoluted tangles of reeds. When finally I got out into an open stretch of water, a cross-wind chose this moment to blow up. Soon 5-ft waves were crashing aggressively over my bows. I couldn't even get into shore to rest because the reeds were in the way. At times like this I felt like dynamiting every single dam on the Missouri.

That evening, I had been nine hours in the kayak. I was soaked through and freezing cold, I had cramps in my shoulders and my legs felt like bars of lifeless rubber. Having beached the canoe, I tried to climb the sandy bluff in the darkness. I couldn't! But Bill was there, helping me to the fireside.

Soon I was ready for the town. The only problem was that Bill wasn't. He missed out, because I got talking to a dark-haired girl called Barb. I chatted to her for a while, and then popped the question. 'May I invite you to dinner tomorrow?'

'Can I bring a girlfriend?'

'Of course.'

'OK then.'

Perhaps Bill was in luck after all?

The following day I really flew through the water. I arrived to find Bill writing a press release of the trip so far. It was a beautiful evening, and we profited from the clear water to bathe for the first time since Fort Benton. Beating off the myriad horse-flies, we climbed up the high butte. In both directions the Missouri River snaked away, clothed only in a little sparse vegetation. On top of each butte there was nothing but parched grass, cropped very short, with reproductions of the same set-up stretching irregularly away like newly-enrolled recruits. We drove through the dusk and over a complicated route.

Barb and her friend were already there. Nervously fingering our last two ten-dollar bills, I said I wasn't really feeling very hungry, and after a short silence Bill said he wasn't either. But our two friends were, and ordered the full works, while Bill and I shared a can of root beer. There ensued a period of steady chomping. Then Barb and Cal's stomachs proved to be smaller than their eyes, for with a sigh they pushed their meals away. Not ours though. We attacked the cooling debris, and soon not a single scrap was left. At nine o'clock, the conversation started up again. 'Well . . . . It's getting kinda late . . . I guess we'll have to be going . . . but thanks, anyway, for a lovely evening.' Cracking concrete, our faces creased into crooked smiles. Then they were gone, leaving just a crumpled paper napkin and a hint of cruel crimson.

It was too dangerous to try and drive back to the river; and so the two hoboes dossed down in a filthy layby.

We felt very lonesome and far from home that night.


## II

In the morning we found ourselves on a thousand bare tracks, all of which led nowhere in particular. Soon we were driving up a gravelly neck of land. The pick-up started skidding – and then refused to go any further. We got out and spent ages burrowing away under the back wheels. It was no good. We were stuck.

'Fibreglass is tougher than steel,' Chris Newell had told me when he delivered the canoes. Taking the footrests out of the slalom-boats, we jammed them in under the wheels of the two-ton truck, and started the engine. The footrests oscillated like minnows, but then suddenly Bill was clear, with me rushing madly after him.

We realised that we were on the wrong path anyway, and started to head back. We soon came to another steep neck, with a sheer 200-ft drop on each side this time. Bill began to steer slowly between the ruts. He got halfway up, and then the pick-up started sliding. He braked to a halt, and reversed cautiously down. He tried again – with exactly the same result. We cleared all the pebbles away, and he gave it one last go, heading powerfully along the top edge. But he didn't even get as far as the last time before skidding to within a couple of feet of the lower precipice. We were stuck again. We needed outside help.

I set off and reached a little house. There was nobody there except a most unfriendly mongrel who seemed to want to take his problems of social acceptance out on me. After another two hours, I began to get cramps in my calves – the price of five and a half weeks in a kayak. But against the glare of the sun I caught sight of something small and red crawling like a fly across a painted picture. Twenty minutes later, it had become a combine harvester, with a baby fly beside it. Soon I was standing beside a shining red pick-up.

The owner's name was Haddlerland. At first, my story seemed to bore him completely; but he finally conceded that he knew the spot in question, declaring roundly that he wouldn't take his bloody four-wheel drive down there in a month of bloody Sundays. I pointed out that since it was Friday it was maybe worth a try. 'You're a facetious bastard,' came the reply as he climbed in.

As we drove over the last butte, the much-abused pick-up came into view, lying stricken on the other side of the neck. 'No bloody way am I taking my new Chrysler down there.'

'But with your four-wheel drive . . . .'

'Give me the bloody keys!'

Bill tried to tell him that the handbrake didn't work, but Haddlerland just brushed past.

Kicking the engine into life and swearing like a trooper, he built up revolutions till the five-litre engine was screaming like a castrated pig. 'He's got guts,' Bill shouted.

'Either that, or he's lost his marbles,' I cried joyfully back.

At last he reached for the automatic gear lever. It crunched into 'drive', the truck leaped forward with a vicious snarl, and then it started boisterously bumping over the ruts, like an escaped Jack Nicholson skiing stick-less on sloping sheet-ice. It continued making fast and noisy progress – both forwards and sideways. The bonnet was at a crazy angle – the driver couldn't possibly see a thing in front. The revs began to sound positively hysterical.

Just as the offside rear wheel got to the last ridge before the drop – heaven knows where the front one was – the engine slid down an octave. So did the bonnet; and the back of the truck began to fight its winnowy way along the points of no return. Another bad-tempered rumbling and crumbling, as the pick-up headed, grumbling, directly for a big hole. Somehow, it managed to bluff its way over. And then it was skidding to a grassy halt.

Without a word, Bill and I climbed the hill. Haddlerland was sitting in the cab, smoking a cigarette. We thanked him and shook him warmly by the hand. It was my hand, I noticed, that was trembling and sweating, not his. He told us to send $15 when we could.

And then he was gone, driving his red truck over the rocky plateau as if in the fast lane of the New Jersey Turnpike and two hours late for dinner. We awarded him the medal of the Spirit of America, first class.

It was early evening before we got back to the Missouri. I started lighting the fire, and then the fire lit itself, as well as some of the surrounding countryside. Bill helped me beat it out but each time we got one big bit beaten, another flared insolently up. After a minute of frantic ineffectuality, the ring of flame was getting steadily bigger; and I could imagine the dry grassland on fire for miles and miles. That would please Mr Haddlerland! Just at the moment of no return – at least the second of the day – I had a brilliant brainwave, also the second of the day. I took our ice-box, and placed it squarely on the closest patch of flame. It worked like a miracle. Bill grabbed the lid, and soon things were back to normal – except we had no fire. I started again using the burnt-out patches, but keeping a gallon of water handy this time.

It had been quite a day and the time lost was annoying. But over the fried chicken, we declared ourselves lucky all the same to be in the American West. We had had one or two problems, but we were surviving and learning. And that was what counted.


## III

I soon came to a bay where the 'Little Missouri' came in. She *must* be little, judging by the current, I decided, as I paddled gloomily on. It was Pascal who said 'Rivers are roads that work on their own, and carry you wherever you want to go.' This might apply to the Seine, but the Missouri was definitely not working here, and nor was she carrying me where I wanted to go.

Ten tired hours later, I noticed that the six-man tent was there. I gave a great shout of joy, and Liam and Tim appeared. They showed me their callouses and blisters and told me all about their back-breaking toil. Then Liam handed over the precious pay, together with seventeen letters, which he fed to me one by one. The fourth missive contained £500 from the C.R.C. We would be able to pay Haddlerland and Jim back. We were a going concern again.

The following day, the scenery had hardly changed, and I felt I'd been fighting against still water and headwinds for all eternity. Thirty hard miles later, I thought Garrison Dam just had to be somewhere close. After the sixth negative headland, I paddled wearily ashore and asked a young fisherman if he knew where we were. He didn't – a bad sign. I sat back down in the icy pool. Suddenly I heard an engine far out in the lake. Hope blocked out reason: 'Bill, Liam, Tim – whoever it is! It's me, Nick. I'm over here.' The sound died away and I was left feeling a little stupid, with the wind howling and the waves slapping against the canoe. After a couple of minutes of dismayed despair, I gave myself a good talking to. I rounded yet another headland – and saw what I had been working towards for as long as I could remember: a huge dam.

The wind changed direction (why now?), and started pushing me over the waves. I was surfing over one, cutting through the next: then, just as the third one arrived, making me hold my breath in icy anticipation, the kayak would burst up and over it. A symphony in three-four time.

Something caught my attention on the other side of the lake. I twisted round, saw headlights flashing on and off, and turned through 130°. Beaching the kayak, I started boldly crashing through the creepy-looking undergrowth. An anxious shout emerged: 'Is that you Nicky?' Wickedly, I kept my mouth shut and my legs going. Then I suddenly leaped out with with a dramatic roar, probably risking a shotgun wedding with a full-frontal destiny. A guy-rope converted me into a spastic spider. But Tim was helping me to my feet: 'What kept you Nick?' I had made it.

I noticed that Liam hadn't. Bill told me that he was in Bismarck, searching for Jim and Rick, who were meant to have been here the day before. At 5 am, we heard him returning exhausted after scouring the banks for miles. He hadn't found them.

At 7 am I ate six eggs, six sausages, and six slices of wholemeal bread. Then Tim and Bill deposited me below the huge dam, and I set off like a lovesick rabbit. I was determined to show everybody, including myself, that I hadn't been slacking.

Very soon I came within site of Fort Mandan, where Lewis and Clark spent the long winter on their way back to St Louis, and where they received a surprise visit from a certain François Larocque, a fur-trapper all the way from Quebec. He spent a year travelling round Montana, the Dakotas, and Wyoming, and then went back to Canada. He told the authorities that he had visited a wonderful new land, and that much of it was still up for grabs. But his report simply got filed in a big, dusty heap, and the United States were again able to expand unhindered.

The following morning the rain was lashing down, so Bill pointed the tape-recorder at me. At 11 am, the downpour slackened slightly and I set off with great relief, leaving Liam and Tim doing sterling work on a hole in the silencer which was rapidly becoming bigger than the one in our finances. In the afternoon, I paddled under Interstate 94, and into the outskirts of Bismarck. Two more bridges on, I noticed a crowd of people on the bank, including most of the North Dakota press corps – old Bill had clearly been busy. Jim and Rick were also there, but our photographer did not look happy. He did not give any explanation as to where they had been, or what photographs he had taken – if any.

Bill told us that the Chamber of Commerce had put the YMCA at our disposal. Remembering pathetic dances for pimply teenagers from our misspent youth, we were all a bit dubious. But when we got to the oak door, we were given six computerised cards describing us, not totally inaccurately, as 'traveling salesmen'. Then we found hot baths, saunas, and a sunken pool with a sexy Jacuzzi.

Feeling as though we'd bought new skins, we drove to the Village Inn, and devoured steak after steak – again courtesy of the Chamber of Commerce. Over dessert, Bill told us that Bismarck *was* named after the German Chancellor, in recognition for the help given with the building of the North Pacific Railroad. From there, the discussion came back, as it always did, to the dams. Bill pointed out that in 1943 an uncontrollable flood had done $65,000,000 worth of damage in the area. In 1952, more than 2,000,000 acres were again flooded by the violent might of the Missouri, with this time $180,000,000 worth of destruction. The dams, he said, meant that floods on that scale were now unlikely; each one also generated a few hundred megawatts; and finally, one of the encyclopedias he had read claimed that they 'help navigation on the river'. Some help! The next morning, I knew only too well, was dam number 3. 'New Orleans in two months!' I had promised in the halcyon days before Three Forks. Now, six weeks later, I was still only in my second state. With 230 miles of dead water – Lake Oahe – stretching menacingly in front of me, I couldn't begin to estimate how long it was all going to take.

Soon after dawn, Tim pointed at the current which, admittedly, was flowing. He got the maps out and indicated a large and unmissable memorial near the village of Cannonball – about 40 miles away. By eight, *Lochinvar* was in the water, with sandwiches and water-bottle tucked in behind the seat, and 'Nicky-cup' freshly washed. By nine, the helmsman himself was reluctantly inside, and the cool morning was moving . . . .

I must explain the 'Nicky-cup' and, with it, my toilet arrangements. (The squeamish reader is invited to skip the next few lines.) The essential problem is that it is impossible to relieve yourself normally while sitting in a kayak. It wasn't always possible to come into shore, so I had invented the system of the cup. But one day the team had somehow guessed what was going on – and from then on, the 'Nicky-cup' had become a constant source of ribald comment.

I didn't need it for the moment, so I paddled on through a fantastic Badland succession of ravines and cliffs. (You can come back now!) Soon the running water began to run out as the shorelines drifted wider apart. Oahe had arrived. By 9 pm my legs were numb and I was literally aching to come in. At long last the distant silhouette of a memorial came stiffly into view. I had had enough. I pulled the canoe well out of the water and began to walk. Almost straight away, I found myself knee-deep in muddy marsh. I ploughed on through the filth, but then came to a small river completely barring my path. Sliding down into it, I began working my way across.

Twice I missed my footing and twice I got completely drenched. After clambering up over several tree-trunks and through lots of brushwood, I hit another swamp – and then another river.

'What the hell is this?' I muttered, glaring at the distant memorial and feeling utterly miserable. Again I waded across the river. Struggling to the top, I scrambled through some bushes and then came to a drop. At the bottom lay . . . another river. I nearly wept.

I pulled my map out but it fell into soggy bits and draped itself over my hands. The moon was watching and mocking. I plunged angrily down and took the river at a raging run. At last I was through and scrambling wetly up the other side.

The first house had crumbling masonry and broken windows. Hearing movement inside, I soaked the door with an agitated knock. I was just about to go when a curtain moved. After three more minutes, the door opened, revealing an Indian face. 'Is there a police-station or a bar anywhere near here?'

'You's on a reservation. There's just a security office.' He softened a little and offered me a lift.

A young Indian dressed in a hippy-style costume was lounging with his feet on the switchboard. I thanked my friend, and asked if anything had been seen of the boys, shivering slightly. He didn't give a damn. Then another policeman walked in. I repeated my story. Charles said 'I'm going along the bank anyhow – we'll find your buddies.' I was very grateful.

Twelve minutes later, a metallic voice filled the car. 'Have picked up a green Dodge pick-up and a blue Plymouth Duster on the eastern boundary. Five Caucasian males aboard. Am holding them.' Soon we drove along an obscure dirt-track and found two familiar vehicles, blocked nose-to-tail in the blue flashing lights. They were surrounded!

## IV

I was just yawning and settling down to bed, when Bill started telling me about this fantastic girl he'd met. I congratulated him, peeling my socks off. Then he said I was invited to meet her. No thanks, I replied, thinking of the dawn start. Oh, he said, she seems to know something about Indian canoes . . . . My socks were back on, my hair was combed, and I was ready.

Bill introduced me to a charming girl called Leah Grant. She proudly showed us models and pictures of Indian life from before the White man – wooden huts with thatched roofs, elaborate stockades, and sacred burial-mounds; sturdy woven baskets, racquets, and toboggans.

She herself had been at college, and was a quarter Scottish; and felt angry at the lethargy and materialism of the village. She argued that

Indian cultural life had lost its driving wheel. The more intelligent and energetic members were forced into a certain compromise with White society. But they remained very aware of their history. I asked about the river in Sioux tradition; and from then on, could hardly get a word in edgeways.

The Sioux had originally been a river tribe. Since time immemorial, they had paddled painted war-canoes on their river – the Mississippi. The wood was birch, cedar, or white elm, and the frame was first interwoven like a basket, then covered with bark or buffalo skin, and finally sealed with resin from spruce treees. The finished product could be manoeuvred easily, had a small draught but a huge carrying capacity, could be portaged, and could also be turned upside down to serve as a temporary roof. It even carried a repair-kit in the shape of resin-balls.

But then rumours came from the rising sun of a powerful new tribe with blotchy faces. One fine day, the Sioux war-canoes were attacked by the Chippewa ones. They were used to this, but not to the stick-that-kills-at-a-distance. The subtle equilibrium of the tribes had been broken, and the Sioux Nation were driven off the Mississippi for ever.

They headed west across the endless plains to what they had heard was an even stronger river. The Missouri more than lived up to their expectations, and they settled happily on its banks, reconstructing their canoes and their lives. When the French 'explorers' arrived, said Leah, they found pigtailed and bare-breasted Sioux maidens, confidently riding the dangerous waters, just like mermaids emerging from the sunlit waves.

She led us into the backyard and, to our surprise, uncovered a painted war-canoe. She explained that her brother used it for gathering wild rice on the marshes. He usually towed it there with his twin-engined powerboat. But once amongst the tangled reeds, it came very much into its own.

I already had some vague ideas about the Indian canoe, mostly filtered from school readings of *Hiawatha*. But this was different. I had hung on every word. Now I told Leah in turn about my own repair-job with gumbo-mud and my idea of a sail. She burst into peals of laughter. We walked over to the pick-up, and I showed Leah my slalom- and sea-canoes. They couldn't be counted descendants of the Sioux ones, for they were all based on Eskimo kayaks, and used fibreglass, only introduced in 1963. But just as the Eskimos are cousins of the Indians, so my boats, we agreed, had to be related to the Sioux ones – their shared lines said all.

Leah told us about the decline of the canoe. The Europeans had imported a creature that didn't exist in America, although it seemed ready made for the rolling plains: the horse! The Sioux had adapted again. The buffalo-skins were now used for collapsible tepees, and the warriors no longer knelt in canoes, but on Spanish stallions. This way of life continued well into the second half of the nineteenth century. During the age of crinolines and ironclads, Chief Sitting Bull (?1831–1890) had been roaming free over the Land of the Dacotahs.

But the White settlers had gradually taken over the Indians' land. They needlessly massacred the bison – one steamboat load consisted of 1100 salted tongues. There had been about 60,000,000 bison running wild when the White man arrived – and not a single one left by 1895. The Indians resisted the invaders as best they could – Tocqueville, the famous analyst of the French Revolution, wrote that their courage, pride, and spirit of independence were unsurpassed by that of any European people. But they ended up taking on the fire-power of the United States itself. Four thousand Sioux and Cheyennes defeated the blustering Custer at Little Big Horn (1876). But this was to be their last victory. After being repeatedly betrayed and starved out, their last great uprising took place in 1889, and it ended when unarmed women and children were shot down at the 'Battle' of Wounded Knee. Leah's grandfather had recounted the end of the Indian dream to her with tears in his eyes – he had been there when Chief Sitting Bull was humiliated by the arrogant palefaces from the east.

We also had come from the east, virtually within living memory of these atrocities. Now even the life-giving Missouri had been dammed, and many of the hunting-grounds and burial-places were covered over with artificial lakes. A whole culture had been destroyed. No amends could possibly be made. The only way one could try to avoid adding insult to injury was to cross the Indian heartland with a degree of awe. I vowed to Leah then that I would acknowledge my debt to her forefathers.

This book is dedicated to the men and women whose canoes mastered the rivers of North America 2000 years before Christopher Columbus was born.

## V

At breakfast, it was back to the squalid reality of a modern reservation and a discouraged expedition. We had a heated discussion about my progress. Tim, in particular, said that my average was only 23 miles a day, and that this was not nearly fast enough. I told him that neither he, nor anybody in the back-up team for that matter, could know what kayaking on the Missouri meant. Liam then proposed that Tim paddle with me for a couple of days, so that we could test our respective theories. We both agreed, and Liam, Bill, and Rick arranged to meet us the following night 71 miles downstream, at the unimaginatively-named Mobridge ('Mo' means Missouri).

Leah arrived to see us off, cheering us with her presence. Tim and I did the last 300 yards on foot, carrying and pushing *Cameron of Lochiel* over the mud and water. We transferred exactly half of the provisions, waved goodbye, and then the mini-fleet was on Oahe and under way.

Tim, paddling powerfully, began to open up a small distance between us. How embarrassing! I put a spurt on, and tucked in behind him, hoping for some sort of psychological slipstream effect. An hour later, the sky was completely wiped out by fast-moving clouds: big, black, and businesslike. We paddled wearily on through a world where everything had died: trees strangulated by the water, nests destroyed in flash-floods, featherless baby birds hanging upside down from the pathetic twigs. I thought of the drowned Indian villages, and felt very angry. And all the time the glowering sky was crushing the warmth from our withered world like a black blanket.

A streak of light ripped across the heavens. There was a crack like an elephant-gun, and a roar of thunder reverberated off the low, colourless bluffs. Rain began to patter casually on the fibreglass, and then effortlessly built up its force until there were a thousand heaving table-tennis balls. Lightning speared across the sky again, and then the storm really got down to it. Tim suggested going ashore but I pointed out that there was nowhere to shelter, and that at least our legs were fairly dry in the canoes.

The wind began to turn like a weathercock. We alternately battled against and surfed over the waves. At half past four, a hint of blue returned to the dreary sky: the drops became translucent and then disappeared altogether. Coming ashore, we soon had a three-candle-power fire going. 'Shall we save the last sandwich?' I asked, baffled by the joint decision-making process.

At mile 28, I realised that Tim was dropping behind. I waited for a while, and saw a face racked with effort and fingers clenched like white claws. But there was nowhere we could pull in, so I began stopping after every half-mile to let him catch up. Then I tried canoeing slowly beside him, wiping out his pain with my Piaf repertoire. Tim's courage held, somehow.

The rain came back, less heavy, but spiteful as it drove into our faces and made the dried sweat sting. After a total of 40 miles, we came ashore. Tim tripped on a hidden rock and fell headlong into 3 feet of cold water. 'Come on, come on,' I wheedled, 'pull me up, I don't want to get my socks wet.' When we opened the hatches, however, he got his own back: my sleeping bag was soaking but his was bone dry.

In next to no time, Tim had transformed the tarpaulin into a rudimentary shelter. I busied myself with the fire and soon we were eating some lukewarm corned-beef. With a boom, the heavens opened once

A three-candle-power fire and a rudimentary tent: grey thoughts in a grey wilderness.

more, and the fire went out. Crawling into the meagre protection of the 'tent', we huddled together under Tim's sleeping-bag.

The following morning we crawled on through a bleak, damp forest of upended trees; grey horizon, grey sea, grey sky, for tens of grey miles. At one stage, Tim admitted that he had no idea where we were, and the value of an honours degree in geography hit rock bottom for me. The wind found us again in the late afternoon, blowing us back every time we paused. Tim really began to suffer. We inched along an endless headland. At last, the final outcrop of rock arrived, revealing the hazy outline of a very large bridge. We began to sprint for it, but the race became an exhausted marathon as the bridge came not an inch closer. Seven miles of hell had to finish some time, however. Well after darkness, a keen-eyed observer on the bridge at Mobridge might just have been able to see the whites of four exhausted eyes coming into a hungry shore.

We ate the sandwich. That night Tim gamely wrote in his log: 'The last two days have been a gruelling experience. It's tough going, one long monotonous slog. I can see now why Nicky gets upset when he's pushed to leave camp in the morning.'

The following day was Sunday 28 August. At some grey point we had crossed the state-line into South Dakota. The MMCRSKE had covered 1100 miles, and so was nearly halfway down the Missouri. Only at that point, for some reason, did I realise why the name Mobridge seemed so familiar: it was here that we had built our very first camp-fire, and that Jim had told us about the dangerous fauna. Since then, I wryly thought, a lot of water had flowed under that bridge.

I examined the maps yet again; and decided to take a rest-day. It was spent fantasising about dry sheets and coffee and croissants. Sitting Bull's grave was only a mile away, but I'm afraid I didn't give it more than a passing thought.

For a few hours I was strolling quietly through the French Quarter of New Orleans.

# *Lost Between Two Shores*

I fear the sea, I will admit, but all the storms and other unpleasant things I have experienced did not inspire so much terror in me as the navigation of the somber and treacherous Missouri. Steam navigation on it is one of the most dangerous things a man can undertake.

(Father Pierre Jean De Smet)

## I

Tomorrow came only too soon and, with it, the beginning of the most difficult fortnight of the trip. It started badly, and was to finish even worse.

I saw Tim running across the headland. 'Are you sure you're going the right way?'

'Any river worth the name has a current,' I muttered, turning ignominiously through 180° and stabbing viciously at the uneasy water. Still grumbling, I recrossed the bay, and then hit rolling seas. Straight away, I knew that our rendezvous at a bridge 43 miles on was, once again, wildly optimistic. It was like walking from Liverpool up into Yorkshire with a one-in-seven gradient all the way . . . .

As I paddled on, I remembered what Bill had told us about the area. It was here that a certain H.M. Brackenridge had observed the customs of the 'Chiennes' (Cheyennes). He had started up the Missouri in 1811, only seven years after Lewis and Clark, and using the same two interpreters, Sacajawea and Charbonneau. He never says exactly how far he reached, writing in a distinctly second-hand manner about the 'ferocious, savage' Blackfoot tribe around Three Forks, but it was probably somewhere just past here. Marauding Indians were indeed the reason he turned round. But he got his own back by writing that 'the world would lose but little, if these people should disappear before civilised communities'. At the same time,

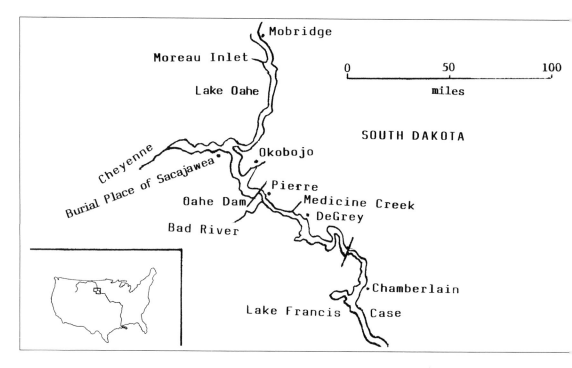

Mobridge to Lake Francis Case.

he predicted that the Indians would remain undisputed masters of the upper Missouri for at least a century – in other words until after 1911!

Brackenridge also says that, because of the wars, there were many more women than men, and polygamy and barter of women were freely practised. Some of Brackenridge's French-Canadian companions sold their shirts – and some of them ended up with no clothes on at all. His account also reveals the extent of the French influence on the Missouri (and elsewhere: he himself was brought up in Sainte-Geneviève on the French-speaking Lower Mississippi). All the settlements from Louis and Saint Charles upwards were Gallic, with romantic names like Côte Sans Dessein, Roche Jaune, Platte, Femme Osage, L'Isle à Cèdre, Roche Percée, Oeil au Fer, Rivière à Jaque, L'Eau qui Coure, Isle Bon Homme, and so on. The book itself is alleviated by such picturesque expressions from Brackenridge's companions as *'il est après ramasser des racines'* (he's after picking up roots), a little like a cross-Channel Thomas Hardy.

Bill's value-added Brackenridge kept me busy for a long time. At eight o'clock, I came to the Moreau Inlet – and reluctantly confirmed what I had suspected all along: I had only done 18 miles! I slept under my wet suit. It lived up to its name, and if I get rheumatism at an early age, I'll know why.

It was 1.30 pm the next day before I saw the long-awaited bridge stretching welcomingly across the river. I pulled up beside it: no trace of my friends. I rowed under the arches, and repeated the performance. I walked into the café, the store, and the petrol-station. No Dodge and no boys. I pushed wearily out into the lake again, and something drifted lazily into sight – a green pick-up with . . . .

As the lake broadened postprandially out again, I thought seriously about our rendezvous arrangements. When there was a bridge, the problem was of manageable size, for it was pretty hard to go a bridge too far. But often, there wasn't, and we agreed to meet at a headland or a village, frequently near a creek, stream, or river, making the situation ripe for confusion.

The main problem was that I found the Missouri a confusing sort of place. When your eyes are 2 feet from the water and bobbing up and down, and the maps are ripping into soggy pieces, promontories resemble one another and islands become indistinguishable from bluffs with creeks. So I just tried to keep a vague track of the most obvious features – bridges, sharp bends, villages – and to judge distances by means of my counting. But the Missouri was anywhere between 500 yards and 7 miles across, and my route on it kept varying, as did the speed of the current. Most of the time, in short, I had only the vaguest idea where I was.

From the team's point of view, I thought, things ought to be much simpler. Once they had found a way – any way – down to the river, our joint problem was solved – provided they got there before I rowed blissfully past. Often, however, their timing was over-optimistic. Very occasionally, I was ahead of schedule.

But most of my cold nights alone were due to rendezvous I just couldn't reach. The team craftily reckoned that they thereby made me cover the distance more quickly. They were probably right! But I was getting more and more exhausted. I just didn't know how long I could carry on.

The scenery still seemed uninspiring, so I began looking for solutions. It couldn't do any harm to agree to attach messages under the bridges. Nor could it hurt to decide on a phone number to call in case of difficulty. But I realised it would be an uphill struggle to put these ideas across. The money problems and the slowness of the trip dominated our thinking; and I felt Rick was hostile to our very aims. As a result, our discussions were about as orderly as Dali on a bad night, and slightly less uplifting than a dead dodo. Still, I gloomily concluded, I would give it a try when we were all together – whenever that was.

## II

I awoke on Wednesday 1 September to find the tent moving madly. There were white lines running across Oahe, running fast, with a gale intent on tearing them into tiny pieces.

It took me two hours to paddle 5 miles. I was just coming into the shore, wondering what to do next, when a series of side-rollers began to arrive. I was recovering my balance from one particularly vicious individual, when another swept in, and suddenly turned me right over.

Very glad that my head hadn't hit the rocks, I wriggled out of the canoe and broke the heaving, frothy surface. Retreating to the shelter of some large rocks, I waited for the wind to die down. But after an hour it became clear that it had no such intention, so I got back in and made a rather wet withdrawal from my little sanctuary.

I now had a choice. I could keep to the centre of the reservoir and be hit by the force 7 as it blew across miles and miles of open water; or else I could hug the shelter of the shore, fighting the turbulent undercurrents. I chose the latter – and soon capsized again.

Sitting on the bare shore, I wondered what I could possibly do. Deciding that the 'quitter instinct' was sometimes not altogether misplaced, I climbed the bluff in search of company. I found three beautiful bedraggled white mares, who first enticed me on, then kept shying away again with a sexy whinny at the last possible moment. Eventually, however, they led me to a cottage, where I explained my predicament to a kind old gentleman called Albert.

He pointed out through the back window, where the Missouri doubled back to within 400 yards of the cottage. I was sorely tempted to drag my canoe over, saving nearly 14 miles, as well as possibly my life, but then I thought back to the Indian canoeists on the Missouri, and resolved to try and imitate their courage. I thanked Albert again, and set off once more. But when I got to the end of the peninsula, a terrible overpowering lethargy came over me. It was all I could do to drag myself into shore and into my sleeping bag.

I woke up with a start to find water everywhere and my morale very low. I seriously felt like giving the whole trip up and going back to a 'real' job. But soon I thought of what the Tourist Board director would have said, and realised that in any case I would have to get my vessel back to port.

I paddled on like a corpse. The Cheyenne River arrived, marking the spot where Sacajawea lay buried. I was suddenly a bit touched, I must admit, remembering Bird-Woman's loyal service to Lewis and Clark and Brackenridge. Two hours later, I came back to Albert's house, and two hours after that I saw a little boat coming gamely over the waves. The occupants told me that my friends were a few miles further on. As we got talking, they showed me their day's catch: fifteen fine catfish, all fat and floundering. I asked if I could possibly have one. With a great deal of effort, we managed to stow the still-gaping fish. Two hours later I put in at Okobojo Creek. Somebody told me that the boys *had* been there, but were now 'a couple of miles downstream'. The tortoise and the hare, I thought mournfully to myself.

I opened the forward compartment. Some drops had seeped in and the crafty fish had forced his gills into them: he was still flapping, if in a near-vertical position. He had guts and soon water, for I poured two or three hatfuls into his tank, closing the hatch with a quick prayer. I now had an unstable canoe but the firmest of friends.

Four sloppy miles on, I proudly introduced 'Humpy' to Bill and Tim. They told me I was mad. 'OK, so we don't eat him, but can he be the expedition mascot?' It was useless. My two friends up-ended *Lochinvar* and poured Humpy out with a loud smack. He would never know quite how lucky he'd been.

After dinner, Rick and Jim arrived back, with something very definite on their minds. 'Let's take a walk,' suggested Rick. I felt awful, but agreed. He opened the conversation: 'The expedition was all meant to be over by "early September". Well, today is the first of the month, and you haven't even done a third! I'm sick to death. I've decided to leave.' I forgot all about giving up the trip and my total surprise gave way to a reluctant recognition that something like this had been in the air for a long time. Rick had seemed distinctly unenthusiastic about his role in the expedition and few of the photographs he *had* managed to take would be of any use to us in the future.

My mind switched to the rights and wrongs. I hadn't established any sort of expedition contract, believing the venture to be such a joint one that no one would think of leaving just because he felt like it. If only, I wryly thought, I had something approaching Lewis and Clark's powers – they had sentenced a deserter to run the gauntlet through the whole expedition, 'each man to have 9 switches', and then to be sent to Coventry for a month.

Instead, I asked Rick if he really meant it, if there was anything at all we could do to help him change his mind. He said there wasn't. I then asked him if we could have the plane ticket back. He said the ticket was in his name, and constituted his only way of getting home. I replied that the ticket belonged to the expedition, which was still in progress. He said he had stayed the allotted time.

He stalked off and I returned angrily to the dark camp. Jim told me that he too had decided to leave. I thought his decision was fair enough, and thanked him for his support. His help with transport and money, especially at the beginning, had been vital. I told Jim that I would always be grateful to him, and he wished me good paddling for the rest of the trip.

In the morning, I had another talk with Rick which ended by my asking him to leave immediately. Later that day I was still very angry and turning to Tim, I said, 'I'm going for Oahe Dam.' Tim (for once!) protested that it was getting dark, but I didn't give a damn.

Once on the water, my mind began to clear. I rowed for ages, taking a bit of a beating. But it was worth it for the view I finally got, row upon row of fairy lights, all dancing and singing. I ploughed on and as had happened twice before, the wind began belatedly to swing behind me. I paddled and counted, trying to keep my mind off all the monsters there might be in the surrounding blackness. The wind proved a fickle friend, however, and began to veer. Very soon I was on an invisible flying carpet, which sloped and slid when I least expected it to.

After a few more minutes of bedlam, an extraordinary thing began to happen. First one light, then another, flickered and went out. 'What the hell's going on?' I bellowed, imagining the end of the universe. Nobody replied, so I continued to nose *Lochinvar* through the 360° gloom, trying to remember approximately where the lights had been. Up ahead was something inkier than the rest. I paddled obliquely away from it – and the lights began to come on again. The penny dropped with a crash. The lights had been hidden by a headland . . . .

Ten minutes later, I pulled up in the lee of dazzling white concrete. Something else didn't look quite right. The dam seemed only about a twentieth of the size it should have been, and there was a slight current tugging at my bow. I wondered if I was going crazy, remembering nightmares when everything appeared through the wrong end of a telescope, moving away from me at a terrifying speed. But then another penny clanged. I *was* crazy, in a sense. Ripping off the spray-cover, I forced myself out of the canoe, and hauled it roughly up onto the concrete. This was no dam; it was a spillway. If the gates had happened to open, I would have been irresistibly sucked down into the tunnel and mangled into an orange mash by the massive turbines. Still trembling at the thought, I had to sit down.

After a while, I walked shakily along to the dam itself, where I found Bill waiting anxiously. When we got back to camp, Rick had gone, and Tim had prepared a delicious panful of stew, followed by masses of tinned pears and condensed milk. Across the ebbing light of the campfire, I could see shadows dancing on Liam's face. He came over and put his arm round my shoulder. 'Don't worry, Nicky,' he said in his soft Irish brogue. 'We'll stay with you down to New Orleans. I looked up and saw Tim nodding in agreement. At 1 am, I felt more at peace with the world. Only three 'small' reservoirs lay ahead of me.

Soon it would be running water to the end.

# III

Friday morning was a hive of activity. Liam was cleaning everything – guns, pans, and pick-up in particular. Bill was putting the final touches to his press release, making sure that there were at least twenty bits of information in every sentence, and testing it all out on anybody near earshot – but there were few takers! Tim had prepared breakfast and was poring over the maps. Because of the strain of the last few days, he 'only' wanted me to canoe 30 miles.

I left at ten, in clear, free-flowing water. Almost straight away, I went past the town of Pierre, where the French had planted a lead plate in 1743, claiming the whole area for their King. But after only 3 miles of nostalgia, I was horrified to feel the current grinding to a halt. My condition matched the name of the incoming river: Bad.

The hours seemed to pass very slowly. I was drained of energy on that infinite millpond, mute and listless under the burning heat. I felt like a sweating fly trying to climb along a sun-drenched pane. With 15 miles to go, I knew that I wasn't going to make it. Ten miles short, I was incapable of going a furlong further, and crawled dejectedly into Medicine Creek (was this some sort of Roy Rogers movie?). I waited for cars to pass. There weren't any. Two hours later a motorbike picked me up.

At DeGrey, my friends were waiting for me staring out across the lake, making me feel very guilty. Going for a walk with Liam, I confessed that I'd been beaten through lack of will-power. The slog was just going on and on, and I didn't know if I would be able to see it through. Liam was very understanding, pointing out that I'd already come 1200 miles and that there were only 240 miles of still water left.

The next day, Liam and I jointly ruled on a day of rest. And rest I did – getting up late, taking a long siesta, and retiring early to bed.

Monday arrived a day too soon, and my old tormentor Tim asked if I felt I could cover 40 miles. I groaned 'not more than 25'. I settled into my routine of counting, and something like my old confidence began to return. The sun was now scorching, making me run with sweat. I took off my hat, my life jacket, and then, breaking the unwritten rule, my shirt.

Feeling as free as a bird, I thought back to my faithful friend Humpy. He was probably old enough now to have had great-grandchildren. Why, he could easily be telling them about our fellow-travelling – about the smoky orangeness of an unidentified floating object that had come down from regions where the water was as wide as 100,000 fish and formed solid blocks, and which carried him away over two suns' distance, and left him here in this very cove; where he met a shy young damsel with the most beautiful pair of fins he had ever seen and a tail whose gentle undulation still sent quivers down his backbone . . . .

I realised I felt dizzy. Maybe I needed some sustenance? I chewed idly at a sandwich, while all the time the sun chewed insidiously at me. As I stumbled ashore, my head started turning and I lay down in a tempting piece of shade. When I tried to get up, my head spun again. I laid my head on my arms and instantly fell into a deep, drugged sleep.

Probably about an hour later, there came a familiar smell. My mind went back aeons to the last time I had smelt it. It was on the floor at home, when I was cuddling my pet tortoise. 'Yes, that's right,' I thought dreamily, 'he always smelt like that.' The hairs on my forearm were moving. I slowly opened my eyes, and found a large black snake slithering along my arm. Its flickering tongue and lidless eyes were inches away from my face.

Twisting and jerking as if I was sucking 30,000 volts I jumped bodily sideways. Then I was swaying on my feet as the 4-ft reptile coiled oilily over itself, bulging and contracting its nasty way towards the boulders. I felt a sudden heaving, and vomited copiously. Then I was paddling away as if a whole army of snakes were clutching onto the bow-rope.

The next day, my morale seemed strangely high – electric-shock treatment, I suppose. With energy renewed, I got to Big Bend Dam after a mere eleven hours in the cockpit. Only two more to go, I said gleefully to my friends.

At dawn, I felt the sudden need for the calm and security of a Catholic church, where I could maybe get everything that had been happening to me in perspective. Tim kindly drove me to a tiny whitewashed chapel a few miles away for the 8 am mass.

But there was just a coffin in the ill-lit gloom and a priest preparing the altar for a funeral service. After a moment of mutual surprise – I was in my filthy kayaking clothes, and he was an Indian – we got chatting. 'I can't give you a mass,' he said, 'but what about breakfast?' I told him about what I was doing and he told me about the Sioux and the effect that the Europeans' imported religion had had on them. Although totally committed to God himself, he didn't feel sure that his tribe were any happier in the fold of Christianity than when practising their animistic beliefs. 'The Sioux,' he sadly concluded, 'have been beaten by alcohol, the broken promise, and the Winchester.'

On the way back, I carried with me his total fairmindedness, affectionate 'Godspeed!' and the contagion of his warm humanity. We checked with the dam-keepers that I could launch directly below the outlet. But as I set off, I couldn't help wondering what would happen to me if any of the trillion cubic feet up there did come gurgling happily down.

As I paddled on, the water continued to produce a terrible sense of injustice. I had assumed that the Spirits of the River were playing fair and giving me *some* flowing water between each set of turbines. Otherwise, some of the water would be flowing uphill, wouldn't it? 'Apparently not,' said my alter ego, 'given the unshakable stillness of the water. And just look at those forests of stark, dead tree-trunks.' He was right. I was incontestably on Lake Francis Case. I began to think about the magnificent possibilities of punning. You'd have to be a case to want to canoe the lake. And what would happen if I was killed on it? Would Dick Francis agree to fictionalise it as *The Nick Francis Case: The Murder on the Francis Case*?

This innocent pastime, together with a downriver breeze, kept me happy as far as Chamberlain. I thought of 'Peace in our time'. Peace *was* with me here; and soon honour as well, in the shape of several competing newspaper and television teams. As usual, I kept a reserve of energy for a frothy surge into shore – and then fiddled around with my gear for ages, before speaking, a little breathlessly, to the cameras. Finally the last note had been taken, the last press release handed out.

As a reward, we adjourned to the local café, where I had to do it all again on cassette. Instead of Liam stirring the camp-fire and Tim chopping wood, there was Bill stirring coffee and me chopping sausages. I just hope my grandchildren will appreciate it.


## IV

Two days later, the wind turned against me again, together with the tide of our fortunes. Wind, or rather gale; and I had the paranoid impression that it kept swivelling with me, even when I turned round a headland. My speed was down to a ridiculous $1^1/2$ mph. I would have been better towing the boat along the shore – and better still waiting for the wind to abate. 'Indeed,' argued Mr A. Ego, 'the US Coastguard regulations assert that "it is dangerous to take a small boat on Lake Francis Case if the wind is more than 15 mph": the wind is three times that speed, and yours is a *very* small one'.

I told him to shut up, arched my frame resignedly forward, and dug desperately down again on the excruciating treadmill. But however quickly I worked, *Lochinvar* wobbled to a sulky halt between strokes, making the next one so much harder. At the same time, I had to tighten my grip until my hands were numb – otherwise the paddles would have flown away.

My strokes became stiffer and stiffer, and my progress slower and slower. From time to time, black clouds of soil ripped off the God-forsaken shore and descended like plagues of locusts. My eyes began flowing and my mouth got all gritty, but I didn't even have a hand free to wipe away the bits. A pain developed in my side. The only thing that kept me going was the sharp bend 3 miles ahead and my race against the wind. I began to feel it must have been sent by a spiteful God. I started swearing at a divine being who could conspire with his representative on earth to inflict this on me after 1000 miles of headwinds.

After about two hours of torment, and just as my speed was converging on zero – 3 feet forwards and 2 feet back – I reached the bend. I clawed my way round it, paddling on one side only like a wall-of-death rider. Soon I powered out of it, wobbling dangerously now like a three-wheeled Maserati. And then the windy race was on.

For several miles, I zoomed over the water as the sky got darker and darker. The wind, gusting across miles and miles of open water, knocked the life jacket against my back and flapped the hood painfully against one ear. For several more miles, I went through the motions of paddling, while *Lochinvar* bounced and scudded over the grey waves like an orange Valkyrie. Then the heavens were torn visibly asunder and went 'Bang'; and the rain came on. The rules of the game have changed, I thought to myself. All I've got to do is keep my nerve, and steer.

But the wind had still not said its last word. It was soon slapping the waves down like an irate schoolteacher. I was leaning back to try and maintain stability, but we were just going faster and faster, and starting to skid sideways.

Then the waves began to be blasted into flat black ice. I realised that if we didn't stop now, we might never stop again. Francis Case was a mile wide there and I just had to get *Lochinvar* to the shelter of the rocks. Gingerly I angled the bow towards the shore – the boat swayed dangerously as the wind tore into her side, trying to drive her over into a capsize. Side-paddling with the adrenalin of despair, I swung her back into the heaving mainstream and then sliding the bow imperceptibly to the right, I raced on and on down the centre of the lake – nudging her over – reducing the gap until finally the rocks were upon us and I floundered ashore. I dragged the boat several yards from the water, and turned her parallel to the wind. In the shelter of a sort of cave, I began to shake with cold, fright, hunger, and frustration.

The next time I looked, the canoe was dancing up and down, dying to get back. I raced out just as the bow jumped lightly into the air and the whole 16-ft canoe stepped over the shore like a dainty marionette and onto the lake. Half a second later I was in the maelstrom myself, swimming arm over arm towards her.

I nearly had the toggle when she walked again, moving another 100 feet into the reservoir. I swam even harder, and grabbed for the toggle. I missed. I made one last lunge, but the wind gusted, fibreglass lacerated my palm, and *Lochinvar* began careering like a mad ballerina over the black waters. Through the tortured sea, I caught an occasional home-movie-sequence of a thin orange shape rolling and spinning, dervish-like, before disappearing again. Then I knew it was no good.

I began to turn back – and found that I couldn't. I started to swim obliquely towards a long jutting headland. My life-jacket buoyed me up but it also restricted my movements. I swam and prayed for my very life towards that finger of rock. I knew that if I missed it, then I would stand no chance of getting back, and would have to cross the lake to the other shore, situated somewhere below the black horizon.

And then it was finished and I was retching bile and water over the shore. I'd lost one of my shoes, and my sock flapped coldly like a redundant appendage. Staggering as if drunk, I walked back along to my paddles. They'd gone as well. Giving up trying to think, I did the only thing I could do. I started walking. I walked through the driving wind and rain for two hours, and came to a small farm.

It was deserted.

After another hour, I arrived at a house with a lighted window, marked 'Saltman'. A woman came to the door. She looked startled by my haggard and half-shoeless state, but at last relented. After a hot shower and a hot coffee, I was finally in a condition to explain. Mr Saltman arrived, and I started again. But he cut in with 'Jesus Christ. You're the luckiest idiot I've ever met. Your English twisters can't be up to much!'

'I beg your pardon?'

'You rowed through the edge of a tornado. This one's just carried off my cousin's car!' I understood then why the wind had seemed so strong . . . .

We waited for a couple of hours, and it began to get a little less noisy. The Saltmans offered to drive me to my rendezvous. 'But it's a four-hour round trip to the other side of the lake.'

'No problem.'

I gave my thanks as profusely as I could, and we set off. Miracle followed miracle as my hosts used the C.B. radio to contact their 'neighbours' across the water. An hour later, 'Rattlesnake' and 'Granny-Claws' used remote control to guide 'Driftwood' and a moribund 'Wallflower' over the dirt-tracks and into a rendezvous with 'Daisychain'! We all thanked Mr Saltman again, but he wouldn't stay, and drove off on the long journey home.

As I peeled the clothes off my filthy body, I thought back again to that terrible struggle. With one sock off, I suddenly remembered that I had turned on God and cursed Him. Because of my blasphemy, it now came to me, He had thrown the wind at me and, with it, the tail-end of a tornado. I finally deciphered the message: the God that I'd met on the Missouri would not be mocked. He was on my side, but I had to believe that He was. Otherwise the Missouri River would throw everything she had at me – and on current form she had more than enough.

The other sock came off and I thought further back. The fortnight that had just finished was by far the worst of the trip – of my whole life. I began to count off the disasters that had piled up. Our photographer had abandoned the expedition. I had almost disappeared down a turbine. I had capsized near rocks. I had wanted to give up the trip altogether. I had had sunstroke and been sick. A snake had crawled over my bare arm. I had had to swim for my very life. And I had lost my canoe and paddles.

If I'd known about all this at the beginning, I don't think I would have had the courage to start off. But now, with the help of a great deal of luck, the support of the team, and the generosity of the American people, I realised that I had done 'a far better thing'. I had run away a number of times; but I had survived, and would continue, God willing, to fight the battles of better days. At this rate I wouldn't be in New Orleans until after Christmas, but I didn't care. All I wanted now was to stay in one piece.

I slept well that night, comforted by the warm presence of my three friends and dreaming of that fast-flowing water.

# Downhill All the Way

Lookin' f' [a] job in the city
Workin' for the man every night and day
But I never lost a minute of sleep
Worryin' 'bout the way things might have been.
Big wheel keeps on turnin'
*Proud Mary* keep on burnin'
Rollin', rollin' on a river.

(Creedence Clearwater Revival)

## I

Over a late breakfast of succulent fruit, we examined the huge lake, wondering how this passive and listless surface could have produced such violent effects. Eventually we gave up and Liam and Tim headed off along the shore to see if the canoe or paddles had been driven over to this side. Meanwhile I recorded my nightmarish events – not that there was any need, for they will always remain engraved in my memory.

At 2 pm, Liam arrived back, triumphantly waving a pair of paddles over his head. Minutes later, Tim rowed a lopsided *Lochinvar* into shore using a jagged piece of driftwood. There was a big hole in the front compartment, but I was extremely glad to have her back at all.

Bill drove me 5 miles 'upstream' and I got into *Cameron of Lochiel* with new resolution. Two days later, I reached the dam at the end of Francis Case. Two days after that and the river became lighter but not much clearer, for the banks were shrouded in an ethereal cloud wandering indolently over a silent world. I felt ashamed at disturbing the cosy little groups of beavers. Even their tail-splashing remained wetly muffled, as if still in the wisps of their delicious dreams. Somehow, only the orange hull splashing over the smoky drifting water seemed real – or was I an irruption into a deeper reality that only the Missouri knew?

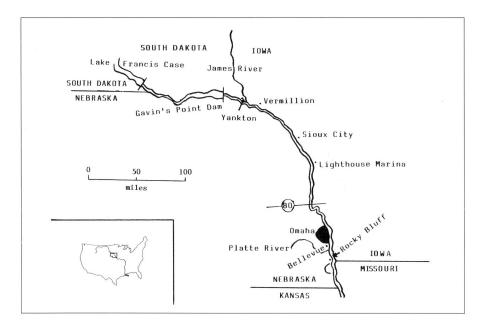

Lake Francis Case to Kansas Border.

The scene faded, and with it the current. From Wordsworth done by David Hamilton, I was switched to a hard focus of Egypt by Cecil B. de Mille, with a marshy maze of bullrushes, pestilence-struck fish, and a blazing hot sun. I slaved on for another 10 miles, going from dead-end to cul-de-sac; and then was finally able to leave this involuted world to its own devious devices.

Turning a crooked corner, I saw Yankton dam, the very last one on the river. I had made it. Never again would I have to canoe on those terrible lakes . . . .

The following day, well after lunch time, I set off towards yet another over-optimistic rendezvous, at Vermillion. Just as I was getting into my stride, I spotted a bluff where Lewis and Clark had camped in 1804. They had held a Grand Council here with the Yankton Sioux, and it was presumably the Indians who had led them to a major find just beside it: the fossilised skeleton of a 45-ft marine reptile that was completely unknown at the time. For my part, all I could see was a rusty beer-can.

A few miles later, I came to a point where the James River trickled imperceptibly in. Looking at the map, I realised that it had been so discreet as to follow the Missouri down for hundreds of diffident miles – since Bismarck in fact. Only when threatened by the Sioux River had it finally made the plunge.

At sunset, I decided to doss down where I was. I found a disused scrapyard with an old sofa. It was filthy but dry, and so was I, so the exchange was probably fair.

Conversation at the lunch-time rendezvous soon came back to money. We were once again back to our last $20, Liam told me, but Tim had efficiently found and started work as a painter (houses not pictures). Good for him!

Another piece of news was less pleasing. There was a maniac hiding out in the woods above Sioux City and shooting at people on the river. The prospect of being a sitting target worried me somewhat, so we readjusted our schedule. I paddled another 30 miles that day, and was fast asleep by nine o'clock. In the middle of the night, Liam shook me gently by the shoulder.

We carried the canoe down to the Missouri under a sky that looked unusually deep. Although I paddled as quietly as possible, I felt very conscious that the orange kayak stood starkly out against the jet-black water, and that each stroke produced a yellow shimmering trail behind the paddle. Listening to every rustle and creak in the dense forest above me, I only hoped that the maniac wasn't a sleep-walker as well.

A tense three hours later, I saw the glint of sun on metal . . . and realised that it was a statue. Just as I glided opposite, a fathomless radiating ball revealed a burning aluminium war-chief on a horse. It was the young War Eagle, who had led the Sioux to victory against Custer. Awed by the strength of the figure, I remembered what Leah had told us about the downfall of her tribe. Their leader now only existed in an alien art-form, in an unknown metal, sitting on a foreign animal. But these anomalies only added to my feeling of mysterious harmony. By now the Indians were for me such a mixture of pastoral basket-weaving and ferocious marauding, Noble Savage and coldblooded cruelty, vitality and lethargy, that this further paradox seemed somehow appropriate. Whatever the reason, that burning moment on the Great Indian River moved me tremendously. For a second, my canoe and I were close to the native spirit.

With a shock, I realised that I was coming into a low-built urban sprawl. Not all charm was broken, however, for through the calm air wafted a languorous and melancholic music, as if Fenimore Cooper had given way to Walter Scott. I rounded a corner, and saw an amazing panorama: a group of television cameramen, a man with a big golden chain round his neck, a full pipe-band – all kilted and all roundly feminine – and a small crowd of people with Liam and Bill at their head.

Once the media had had their fill, Bill introduced me to the Mayor. On the spot we were made Honorary Citizens of Sioux City, with resplendent certificates to prove it. We thanked the Mayor, and then I met Bob Hatfield of the A.C.S., the man who had helped arrange it all. Bob told us he had got us tickets for a 'football' match at the local stadium and that he was offering us beds for the night – 'Yes, with sheets'. There and then we confirmed Bill's promotion to autonomous advance-man and publicity-agent.


## II

Back in the water again on the 18th, I realised that I had touched down in my fifth state. I was at present in Iowa, capital Des Moines, pronounced Dee Moinz – enough to give the French founding fathers a heart attack! The Nebraska-Iowa line followed the centre of the river, and for a while I amused myself zigzagging across from state to state as quickly as the alternating current.

The water itself had also changed. It had been brown and silty since the last dam, but now it was smelly as well. I thought back to our bathe before the dinner-date, and to the drinkable water up in Montana. But then I remembered the terrible inland seas, and my nostalgia disappeared. I bent hard over my paddles, thinking forward to the city of Omaha, only 110 miles away now. My cousin Toni and her husband lived there, and would be sure, I knew, to lay on a good reception.

With no sign, however, of the last £500 from the C.R.C., our financial situation remained extremely precarious. Tim's artistry would keep us afloat for a couple more days, but no longer. We had decided that we ∴ould have to work again – including me this time – at least for a while. We had also come to another difficult decision. Half of any money earned would go to the individual in question. The expedition would obviously lose half of its income this way, but Tim in particular was understandably desperate to have some money – if only for postage to his girlfriend – and this had been the best arrangement we could all agree on.

For 33 miles, the farmhouses were absolutely identical – regular plank fences and aluminium silos. Finally I arrived at the Lighthouse Marina. It was pouring with rain and a waterlogged Liam and Tim hadn't really felt like putting the tent up. 'What about the toilets?' I suggested. They were at least dry. I grabbed pride of place between the wash-basin and the urinals, and barricading the door, we bedded down.

I was just telling Tim about the James, and he was just saying that it was in fact the silt deposits that kept the rivers apart, when we heard a shrill shriek of brakes. There came a hammering on the door, while we froze and listened to the drip of the tap. At last we heard a revving engine. Then he or she was gone, probably thinking that the guy inside had a real problem.

When I woke, there was a good fire going, but the Missouri looked how I felt – cold and grey. Liam and Tim wanted to drive into Omaha straight after breakfast to start black-market job hunting. I, however, preferred a midday rendezvous – both for the company and in case anything happened to me. In the end, tempted by the thought of the bright lights, I gave in.

At 7 pm, a very weary canoeist pulled in under Highway 80 (New York – San Francisco). I quickly read the mail and then Liam and Tim said what about a few more miles . . . ? Maddeningly, the current did look pretty good, and it did seem a tolerable idea, so with a well-rehearsed 'Grrr', I set off again.

After about an hour however, my arms started seizing up, reducing me to a humiliating 1 knot faster than the current. It got dark and the water was suddenly humming and vibrating as if alive. An extraordinary clanking noise was coming from the dark distance ahead. Now a long finger of light was working delicately over the surface of the river, then another, and soon half a dozen dazzling beams were criss-crossing the darkness, like an upturned blitz – only I was the target. The humming and vibrating got louder, and I was just searching my memories of Jules Verne to establish which movie I was in, when a juddering monstrous silhouette came into view. It clunked again, and I clicked. I was meeting my first towboat.

Rowboat and towboat seemed an unequal match, so I telemarked hard, and headed straight for the closest bit of shore. Minutes later the earth moved and the beast had come. It was enormous: *twelve* uncompromising-looking barges, being pushed (despite the name) against the full force of the current. Its 600 feet of metal made *Lochinvar* look like a toy. Only the tow itself seemed a bit small and overdone, with its white ornamental layers and fancy neoclassical bits, rather like a superior wedding-cake. But it resolved its inferiority complex by means of an aggressive wash of choppy waves, with compact balls of pure turbulence searching hither and thither for playmates.

Still shaking, I decided enough was enough. What luck, an overturned rowing-boat. That night I slept like a dry log. The rest of the world hadn't, though, and I had to tip gallons of water out of my canoe. A couple of miles later, a decrepit Dodge appeared. After a huge breakfast, the suburbs of Omaha came out to meet me. The Cattle City had certainly changed since the pioneer days, I decided. Instead of mooing longhorns and gun-toting cowhands, there was now just a maze of bridges, Interstates, and petroleum- and/or molasses-processing plants. It simply went on and on. The only point of interest was the left bank: one moment Nebraska, the next Iowa, and the next Nebraska again.

Four hours later, the concrete jungle gave way to timid patches of grass. Another hour, and Bellevue Bridge reluctantly appeared in the distance.

Another half-hour, and Cousins Toni and Charlie, Liam, Tim, and Bill were waiting for me – fortunately, as I could hardly climb out of the canoe.

But my tiredness was perhaps worth it, I thought, as I chatted with my friends. I had now covered 1900 miles, or exactly half of the Mississippi-Missouri. Since our last visit here, we had come a long way.


## III

We had a magnificent celebratory dinner at my cousins'. Over dessert, Bill told us about his reading on the Indian languages. The name 'Omaha' meant 'those who fight against the current' (brave souls), and 'Missouri' was the name of a tribe who lived on the banks of the river – 'lived', because the last member had long ago been wiped from the face of the earth. Then he recited the names for the river in the various Indian languages: in Hidatsa, Mati ('Navigable Stream Full of Dirt'); in Mandan, Mata ('Boundary Between Two Pieces of Land'); in Dakota, variously Minni-Shu-Shu ('Smoky Water'), Minni-So-Say ('Muddy Water'), or Wakpa-Sose-Tanka ('Stirred Up and Grandmother River'). Each name brought forth resonances in my mind, and I paid homage once more to the Indian tribes who had first canoed on the mighty river.

In the morning, Bill introduced us to a new friend, the Mayor of Omaha. For services to cancer research, four slightly hungover Britons were awarded the Freedom of the City, together with Golden Keys. Thanking him, we apologised for our unkempt appearance. Mayor Al Veys coolly replied that the early pioneers hadn't looked much better! As we chatted on about our various experiences, he proudly told us that his city was the birthplace of Gerald Ford, the former President, who was due there that very afternoon! Would the idea of meeting him interest me? I immediately replied yes, remembering Ford's commitment to the cause we were promoting (Betty Ford had suffered from cancer of the throat).

Then we had to dash to another meet-the-press, with another pipe band. The kilts were again filled with curvaceous feminine shapes, I just couldn't keep my eyes off them! During the first interview, a young journalist asked what it was like 'floating the river?' Missing the allusion to Twain I snapped back 'I wouldn't exactly call paddling a thousand miles with a wind in your teeth "floating" the river!' I was horrified to see two huge tear-drops welling up in her eyes. I felt awful! After apologising, I told her about some of our trials, and was glad to see her smiling again by the end.

Someone came running through the rain: there was a call from the Mayor's Office. Al Vey's news was all good. I would be introduced to 'the President' at 6.30 that evening. He said I should bring our photographer. We didn't have one. But Liam kindly offered his services.

At six we were there, with our exhausted exhaust announcing our presence to the world at large. We found the road completely blocked by a flotilla of shiny black Cadillacs parked side by side. Lounging against them, exactly like the guests at the Godfather's wedding, stood a bunch of strange young men. They were all dressed in exactly the same attire, alpaca suits, homburg hats, and sunglasses. This latter detail seemed most curious to me as it was still raining. The sinister band appeared hard of hearing as well, for they all wore deaf-aids. I went over to the nearest one and said in a loud voice 'Excuse me, Sir, are you a member of the Secret Service?' He gave a grunt that sounded like Marlon Brando on an off day. I took this to be an affirmative. 'My name is Nicholas Francis. I have an appointment with the President at half past six. Mr O'Neill is my photographer.' My interlocutor frowned and started to mumble into his lapel; and then he began to crackle. He listened to the left ear-lobe for a while, nodding vacantly as he did so. After a certain time, we took this to be another positive, and accordingly walked through a small gap between the motor-cars and towards the club itself. The smart entrance-hall was full of even smarter beautiful people, all suntanned with dinner-jackets and plunging necklines. But around the outside were more shiny personnel. One of them barred our passage and I repeated my implausible story. At last he gave us clearance.

We were about to go upstairs when we were thrown roughly against the wall. A man in a glossy suit, blue this time, began to put his hands in all sorts of naughty places. 'I do wish he'd stop tickling!' I said to Liam's arms, parallel to mine. Blue's colleague was wearing a worn leather shoulder-strap and a sub-machine-gun, and looked as though he'd never learned to laugh. Then I thought of Kennedy, and began to understand.

At that moment I caught sight of a familiar figure standing at the top of the stairs. It was Mayor Veys. He took me by the arm and led me over to President Ford. I was immediately impressed – both by his physical size and the aura of strength he had about him. But then I remembered that this was the man that had held America together after the Watergate debacle and given her back her self-respect. Wringing me warmly by the hand, the President said, 'We have a deep family interest in cancer research.' He wished me the best of luck in getting to New Orleans, with Liam snapping away all the time. Soon he shook Liam's hand warmly in turn, and then somebody was asking him about 'the Mayaguez Incident'. The President turned slightly; and all we could hear was 'I conferred with Secretary Kissinger . . . .'

Feeling on top of the world, we walked out of the club. With twenty shades focused hard on us, Liam turned the pick-up's ignition; it didn't backfire, thank God. We counted our money  decided to splash out, and bought ourselves a celebration dinner – peanut butter *and* jelly sandwiches!

The next day, I phoned Colin MacKenzie in Edinburgh to tell him the news. Then I rang the British newspaper offices in New York, promising them photographs of our meeting with President Ford. As soon as I put the phone down, it rang again. It was Liam. The photographs hadn't come out, and so we had no record at all of the meeting. I felt very disappointed. We were definitely not having much luck with our photography . . . .

We spent the rest of that day looking for work. Likewise on the 23rd, and then we were invited to a Ceilidh by 'our' pipe-band. I remembered the shapes inside the kilts, and accepted with breathless alacrity. When we got there, it proved a bit dull, as Ceilidhs went: but we did meet a charming gentleman called Dan Murphy. He was Irish-American, and promised us jobs in less than no time. Bill, meanwhile, had fixed himself up with an Anglo-American called Rahn-Tuttle. He was a freelance fireplace-installer. I said I just hoped next winter wasn't too cold.

On Sunday, I spent most of the day filling a tiny hole in the front of *Cameron of Lochiel*, while Liam and Tim repaired a much larger one in the pick-up's sump. On Monday, we became fully-fledged stone-masons. (We just hoped next winter wasn't too wet.) And on Tuesday, I fell in love.

It was in a smart discotheque in the centre of town. She was sitting with an older lady. I crossed the floor and asked if she would like to dance. 'I'd love to,' she replied. When the music ended, we walked slowly back to her table. Her mother smiled as I was introduced, and asked if I would like a drink.

I learned quite a lot about Cathy that evening. She had been married to an air force pilot, who can't have known how lucky he was, for they had divorced. She had two small children, aged three and five. About a year older than me, she still possessed childlike qualities of innocence and warmth. As we were leaving, I asked her if she would like to come swimming the following evening. 'I'd be delighted,' she said in all simplicity.

I met Cathy the next day. And the next, and the next. Realising that I was more proficient in a kayak than on a dance-floor, I took her canoeing on the wide Missouri. We went for meals and we went to the cinema.

Monday 2 October, arrived much too soon. I realised with tremendous sadness that Bill and I had to return to the river. The Missouri itself might have waited, but Liam and Tim, still building backbreakingly hard, wouldn't have.

Cathy drove us to draw our wages, and I celebrated with two Milky Ways. Bill had only been paid for half his work – Tuttle said he had a 'temporary liquidity problem'. Bill immediately put all the pay he had received into the expedition funds, saying he would keep the other half when it arrived.

I spent most of the day wasting time – trying to postpone the inevitable rendezvous. But eventually we drove down to Bellevue, and Cathy watched as I settled into *Cameron of Lochiel*. I felt apathetic, stiff, and very sad. Leaning on the jetty, I gave the beautiful girl a long kiss. She was crying. I set off and paddled away, but there wasn't a bend in sight. After over a mile, I turned my head and looked back. She was still standing stiffly there, but looking very small.

And then she was hidden from view, and I was wondering whether I would ever see her again.


## IV

I ploughed on through the rain, arriving after a short while at the Platte River. The weather didn't really seem appropriate. After all, the North Platte came down from sun-baked Cheyenne and Laramie, and the South Platte from dusty Denver and Colorado. Then I remembered that the Platte meant 'the flat river', and that it was regarded by the early navigators as the 'Equator' of the Missouri. After eleven weeks, I wasn't sure quite how positive this information really was, given that St Louis was meant to be just over the horizon. Undoubtedly more encouraging, I decided, was the fact that I had seen no sizable tributaries on the left since the self-effacing James – a sure sign that the Mississippi was throwing its weight around.

At Rocky Bluff there was no sign of a truck but a kindly local invited me in for coffee. Bill arrived half an hour later, accompanied by three urchin-navigators who looked as though they'd just escaped from a federal pen. His arrival cheered me up, and we chatted over a blazing fire for a long time. As usual, we spoke of plans, hopes and regrets, with the river as the centre-piece for all our dreams and fears.

We got on to what we would do after the trip, and Bill reminded me that he was going to Paris. As he talked about the bars and restaurants of the Latin Quarter, I could feel my Gallic blood moving. That night, I went to bed thinking of snails swimming in garlic and strong red wine.

In the morning, I was contemplating 'taking a left' past a rather pleasantly-wooded outcrop. A quick look at my map, and I lunged to the right, scraping under the overhanging branches. I had just missed going into a 12-mile ox-bow lake. I had dim memories of my geography teacher explaining that these originated when a river changed its mind and formed a cut-off across a loop. My other source of knowledge was Twain – but here there was information aplenty. He told stories of the farmers who owned the inaccessible and flood-prone pieces of land within the loops They used to actually encourage the river in its whims by digging unscrupulous ditches across the necks. Once a cut-off had taken, it couldn't be stopped by any means known to man. An ox-bow lake had formed, and the land had doubled in value. If Tim is in such a hurry, I thought, perhaps he could arrange something . . . .

Twain also brings his zany humour to bear on the legal consequences, which were sometimes a matter of life and death. Originally, the boundary between states had been the centre of the river. So when chunks of land switched banks, they also switched states. Given a free and a slave state, a slave could wake up one morning a free man. And vice versa. Eventually the law was admitted to be an ass, and the boundaries were fixed once and for all, no matter what happened. This now meant that bits of Iowa could be stranded on the Nebraska side. But when you're dealing with a perfidious creature like the Mississippi-Missouri, I mused, perfection is sometimes difficult to attain . . . .

Over the days that followed I tried to make up for the time 'lost' in Omaha by paddling from dawn to dusk, and often well beyond, for the nights were drawing in. On the third night, I learned about another of the hazards of paddling unseen on a waterway designed for vessels with radar and pilots familiar with every black sandbar and tree-trunk.

As was my custom, I was keeping about a quarter of the way across. I went past the flames of a huge petroleum plant, and then started cutting over to save distance on a curve. Suddenly there came the sound of rushing water. I veered away, as the bow started swinging. Then I spotted a silhouette looming right across my path – a stationary silhouette. I turned further and began paddling with all my strength but the current just swept us on.

A pile of wood and branches came into view. Since it was too late to avoid it, I swung back parallel to the current, noticing with relief a small gap. Stabbing into the water, I managed to get the front of the kayak opposite it, and immediately had to lever my vessel awkwardly round before the current twisted it and me against the barrier. The water swept us into the gap, which seemed to be only about 2 feet wide. But then the keel ground to an unstable halt, with the water agitatedly pushing the rear of the kayak up in the air. Avoiding the side-walls, I balanced the paddles obliquely against my stomach. Then I plunged my hands into the water, and lifted some of the weight off. For an eternity, the canoe was thrashing left and right, forward and aft, as I tried to anticipate the best moment to clutch onto the paddles again. But all of a sudden we were moving down a one-in-three slope of pure hell. All I could do was hold on and pray. But the faithful boat steered herself; a last nose-plunge, and we came to a heaving halt in perfect unison, like a centaur after a desperate gallop. I had met and survived my first wing-dam.

For dinner, Bill had prepared a huge plate of 'bifteck aux échalottes'. I'd been thinking hard, and now told my friend about a decision that I had come to: I was going to go and live in Paris as well. I wanted to plunge myself, unrestrainedly, into its deepest secrets.

'But what will you *do?*'

'I'll try and put down all my hopes and dreams about the river, from the difficult beginning, through our various mishaps, and on to the end.'

For the first time, all my roads seemed to be leading to a single destination. The route from Scotland to Paris, in the dream I shared with Bill, led over to an alien continent, up into its highest mountains, across its widest plains. But, whatever the risks involved, this was the shortest possible route, the safest route, the only conceivable one. If my life before this moment had seemed to be nothing but a series of disconnected episodes, now it was coming together into an organic whole. By day, then, I would be a writer in a cork-lined garret overlooking the Seine; and by night, Bill and I would drink rough red wine in the local bar.

Watching the frenetic busloads of American tourists, we would talk quietly of our own memories of the New World. The ages spent shooting at an innocent bird whose miserable flesh wouldn't have begun to fill our hungry mouths; the Ranger who wouldn't stop talking and who Bill had had to rescue me from; and the purple evening with the smoke of a huge camp-fire floating over the whispering reeds and the water full of a limpidity that you could share but never capture. A whole universe. America, our America.

Then, once the buses had loaded up and the air-conditioning had died down, we would walk slowly beside the cool flow of the Seine. We would both have the same unspoken thought, that we had seen great things together – that for us there would only ever be one river.

The Mississippi-Missouri, a world in itself, the focus of all our dreams.

# *The Missouri Breaks*

Roustabout ain't got no home
Makes his living from his shoulder bone
Break a line, borrow another
Black man die, hire his brother.

(Nineteenth century, anonymous)

## I

All through the rest of that week, I carried on as fast as I could. One of my rewards was the arrival of two new states. I told Bill that arriving in Missouri wasn't much fun – the name was already familiar. Also, I said, Kansas seemed like a step backwards after Iowa, which sounded pretty civilised (or was I confusing it with Ohio?). Indeed Kansas was positively last-frontier-like, not the sort of state you wanted to meet 1600 miles after leaving the Rockies. It had, after all, been the dumping-ground for various tribes between the 1830s and 60s, Huck Finn's 'Ingean Territory'. And so it *had* to be the back of beyond, I had convincingly concluded.

Bill reassured me that we really were making progress. He pointed out that Neil Diamond's hyper-southern drawl sang about Wichita (Kansas), and that I had arrived in Kansas *after* Missouri, which was opposite Tennessee, which was opposite Arkansas . . . . I tried to cut in, but Bill said that I should be grateful, as my shadowy, borderline existence, oscillating between states like a schizophrenic escapee or a malfunctioning transistor, would stop when Missouri occupied both banks. Then I would at least know whether inviting a twenty-year-old girl for a drink constituted an indictable offence (which it did!). What was more, Bill pursued, the Kansas capital, Kansas City, was second only to New Orleans as the home of Jazz and Boogie Woogie. It had its own style of orchestration: a swing-like beat, amazing repeating riffs, and loads of trumpets. 'Count

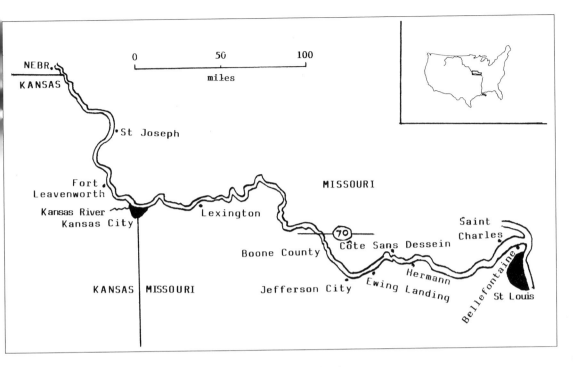

Kansas Border to St Louis.

Basie played Kansas City style. He was even Black. That sounds very southern to me, m'lud. My case rests.'

'Yeah, but where did all the jazzmen go afterwards? They went to Chicago. On the Great Lakes! And look at the Interstate numbers. After six weeks, I got to 94. But I'm still only in the mid-70s, I'm never going to get it down to 0. What sort of country is this, where even the motorways are against you?'

Looking at my watch, I realised that we were late for our own press-conference. Bill turned the ignition key, producing merely a dull clunk. After trying again, we abandoned ship. The first vehicle to pass was a film van from C.B.S.: and it stopped. The enterprising journalist stole a march on his more punctual rivals; and the MMCRSKE arrived in rather better style than usual.

Days and days of hard slogging later, I got to St Joseph, where the original Pony Express started from. Like its rival through Fort Benton, it only lasted a few months (1860–1), and it finished $200,000 in debt. But in that short period, it became something of a legend. The best-known rider was Buffalo Bill ('Colonel' William Cody), the first man in history to claim to have ridden 300 miles without a break. Another of his reported exploits was to slaughter 4280 buffalo in less than two years; and yet another was

107

to force peace on a whole Indian tribe by beating their chief in single knife combat. It all made quite a story!

St Joseph is also the point where some authorities believe the Missouri was first gazed upon by a White man. It was 1540, and Francisco Vazquez de Coronado was sailing up the Gulf of California. His expedition is then meant to have discovered, in fairly rapid succession, the Colorado, the Grand Canyon, the Rio Grande, and the Missouri. Since the Mississippi was first seen in 1541, this would presumably mean that the Missouri was discovered before its great rival, which would be quite a feat, given the relative position of the two rivers. It *would* be, if only those authorities had a leg to stand on. Unfortunately, Coronado only heard about the Missouri – and so had to be content with only three discoveries to his name. He must have died broken-hearted!

As I carried on down the river, I found myself thinking more and more about Cathy. On impulse one evening, I phoned her, reversing the charges. She sounded very glad to hear my voice, so I asked if she would like to come down for a couple of days. She hesitated, and then asked if she could bring the children. On the spot, the deal was made.

Just after passing Fort Leavenworth I was again early for a rendezvous. I got talking to a towboat captain. 'Would you like a tour?' I climbed the gangway and was shown the colour T.V., the air-conditioning, and the spotless bathrooms.

'Things have changed since Twain's day. But the boys really do need all that, because they spend a straight month on the tow, six hours on, six hours off. Then they take a month's holiday – which they need even more!' Next on the visit was the control-room, with radiotelephone, radar, fathometer, 'contraguide rudder', and automatic pilot. Again not luxuries, he told me, as they were carrying ten million gallons of petroleum – twice as much as most ocean freighters. 'My twenty barges cover more than an acre. Even with all 3000 horsepower in reverse, you can't stop in less than a mile or two. So just you keep your itty-bitty kayak out of harm's way, yeah? You don't even show up on the radar. My turbines spit out whole tree-trunks – you wouldn't give them a glassfiber hiccough. And remember, the downstream vessel *always* has right of way.' (I didn't dare ask if this stretched as far as kayaks.) 'Did you see that dirty big whirlpool thirty miles back?' (I hadn't – it must have been dark.) 'You have to steer clear even when you have 30,000 tons going for you. If a barge goes down, then the guy up front has to be bloody quick with the sledgehammer, otherwise they *all* go down, follow-my-duckling-style. D'you remember that island with the cedars on it? No? You must have been asleep. That was a steel convoy, until little Miss Missouri got hold of it. Your saltwater sailors complain if they have to work round reefs every 20 miles. Here they're every 50 yards, you have to go between them, and they won't keep still.'

I had to chip in there, as Bill had arrived. My new friend asked if we would like a trip downstream. Bill said 'Yes please,' and I, 'But how will we get back?'

'That's easy. An upstream tow. You'd best bring your boat with you.'

As we roared majestically along, we got a superb panorama of both banks, with the setting sun catching the tufts of the trees. 'If only I always had this view,' I shouted happily to Bill, 'I'd get lost much less often.'

Our friend seemed very glad to talk about his beloved Missouri. 'The old steamboat captains knew all about its tricks, baptising it variously as Great River Road, Wild Mizoo, Great Muddy, Graveyard for Steamboats, Great Common Sewer of the West, or Old Misery. Things were different in those days – you had real characters then.' (I thought we had one now.) 'When the fog came down, the whistle was the only way to find your route: you listened for the echo off the cliffs, the noise from the farms, or the chorus in the bayous. If you didn't know every log, dog, and species of frog, you were soon stuck. Often, you could just use the paddles to roll over. But sometimes you had to grasshopper instead . . . .'

Our kaleidoscopic captain suddenly pointed to the middle distance. 'The water's only ten feet there – you can see by the ripples. If the front barge gets stuck, it'll have to be hammered loose before we all get fouled up.'

'But what about the barge?' asked Bill in amazement.

'Oh that's easy. We move into the bank, tie the others up, and zip round the far side. This tow only draws 7 feet, so we use its propeller to zap the shoal clean out of existence.'

'Dead simple,' I said to Bill, 'but the errant barge?' By the time the two transatlantic numbskulls understood what he meant, we were well past the obstruction. Most disappointing, we hadn't even scraped.

'Now where was I? Ah yes, the old days: you grasshoppered over, see? You don't? Well, it meant using poles on either side to lunge the boat a few feet forward at a time.'

At last, I could show off some expertise. 'Oh yes,' I said airily, 'that's a technique I know, only I just use my hands.' This time, it was his turn to stare. He looked at the Missouri, then at the kayak, then at me. Spitting 'Chaw!' he turned his back on us.

We went under an old railway bridge, and Bill and I held our breath as the vibrating monster lumbered between the uprights with feet to spare. 'It's on purpose of course,' said our encyclopedia, who had just come back. 'The nineteenth-century bridge-builders wanted to squeeze the steamboats out of existence. The draft was already pretty small, and then with each new bridge the gap got narrower as well. In the end, one captain got so mad that he rammed one down. A young lawyer who had grown up on the banks defended the steamboat company, but apparently without conviction, and lost. His name was . . . Abraham Lincoln. In fact he went down to New Orleans on a raft: the vision of slavery so disturbed him that he . . . .' But we were never to know what Abe did, for Kansas City had already come into view.

The captain radioed a tow at the dock and we thanked our witty and informative friend, saying goodbye very reluctantly. Then back through the night to where we had started. That day *Lochinvar* had done more than 120 miles.

## II

By mid-afternoon, I was back again in Kansas City. The theory that we were getting somewhere was proved for here was a brave outpost of sherry and cucumber sandwiches. But these were just the beginnings of the welcome given by Mr Victor Studley, the British Consul. With Bill's help, he had spent the whole day arranging a huge press conference in the best hotel in town – followed immediately by an even huger dinner.

As we were tucking into the lobster, Liam and Tim arrived, exhausted from all their hard work. My joy was completed when Cathy, who had just driven 400 miles, walked in and sat down beside me. Together, the five of us devoured more meat than in the previous five states put together. Mr Studley was unanimously voted an excellent fellow, and make an honorary member of the expedition – 'Non-canoeing, I hope,' he said quickly.

Over coffee, he told us about a flash-flood that had hit the city only two weeks before: 12 inches of rain in twenty-four hours, making the Missouri rise by 40 feet. The death-toll was twenty-six people, flood damage in the City alone amounted to $100 million, and the State of Missouri was declared a Major Disaster Area. We had seen very little trace of all this (the American capacity for organisation again). But I couldn't help feeling how lucky it had been, for once, for me to be behind schedule.

After dinner, Cathy and I took the children to see the lights. We finished up in a quiet little café where John Lennon's 'Imagine' was playing. As we listened to the words 'nothing to kill, and nothing to die for', we looked into each other's eyes. I knew that I had found someone to live for. I swore to myself then that I would take no more risks on the river.

After another perfect day, Cathy and I arranged to meet for one last evening. Then I headed slowly off. Hemmed in between the high buildings, I felt very strange in my sweat-stained leather hat.

Just after passing the Kansas River, I saw an uncompromising sign reading 'Kansas City, Missouri'. This gave me a nasty shock. First of all, every schoolboy knows that Kansas City is in Kansas and, secondly, I had just left it. I got out of my canoe and asked a crisp businessman where I was. No, he carefully told me, the Missouri hadn't started flowing uphill; yes this was the way to St Louis; and yes this was a different town with the same name. I thanked my patient informer, put my hat back on, and scuttled off.

Once more I was in camp ahead of schedule. Cathy and I spent a last evening together. As the grey dawn came up, we said a sad farewell, but, this time, we promised we would meet again soon. And a moment later she was gone, on the long road back to Omaha.

My eyes clouded with emotion, I returned to where we had hidden *Cameron of Lochiel*. But when I got there, I was horrified to find only a long stretch of flattened grass. All four of us scoured the area for ages but found nothing but a few empty cartridges on the shore 50 yards away. I immediately deduced that the local hooligans must have put the kayak in the water and shot her to bits. Liam's theory, rather more prosaic, was that she had simply been stolen. Whoever was right, the boat was lost, together with my warmest pullover and only wet suit. I knew that if anything now happened to *Lochinvar*, that would probably be it: the slalom-boats were much too unstable to use, and it would be impossible to buy another sea-going kayak so far from the ocean. In that black hour, I just wished that the culprits could have some knowledge of cancer, so as to appreciate the harm they had done.

Still seething with anger, I loaded the .22 (in case Liam's theory was right and my canoe proved to be in the vicinity). The surroundings matched my mood for the water was filthier than ever, and on each bank huge concrete installations had sprouted like malignant sores, trying to force the few remaining cottonwood trees to give up and search for pastures greener.

All through the week that followed, I canoed hard and long. Amongst my few diversions were the names: Jackass Bend; Napoleon, Wellington, and Waterloo (thesis, antithesis, and synthesis?); Waverly (founded by an illiterate Scot?), Sheep Nose Bend (a gentle bend, this), Miami (!), Glasgow (again?), and Dover (strictly no comment). I was not at all surprised when I came to 'Lexington', the namesake of a major Civil War battle. Lexington was also where the stern-wheeler the *Far West* went west (cause: a snag). On a previous trip, it had been Custer's supply-boat upriver – and hospital-boat on the way back. It did the 920 miles from Little Big Horn down to Fort Lincoln in only fifty-four hours, making it possibly the most heroic feat of the whole terrible episode.

There was one final reason why Lexington had a special meaning for me: it was exactly 2000 miles from Three Forks. The tide was turning. I now had some hope of getting to the end.

A couple of days later, I arrived at Boone County, where Daniel Boone retired in 1795, on land given him by the Spanish Governor. I had hardly begun to dream of muskets, furskin-hats, and last-ditch defences, when Interstate 70 arrived. Six lanes of 50-ton juggernauts rumbled far over my head on their hurried way from New York to Los Angeles and back. They made me feel very small and exposed, and my reverie was lost for ever.

The only other incident was that my leather hat was stolen. A tough-looking man, who I'd just been talking to in a rough-looking bar, walked out wearing it. I felt very tired, and just let them both go.

Sometimes the weather was very muggy, but sometimes very cold – two or three times I had to scrape ice off the paddles. It was only the second week of October, but already a fully-fledged continental winter was lurking behind me, planning southern forays, testing its icy fingers on my neck. I mentioned to Tim that if I continued to be sweaty and numbed in equal proportions, then somehow a perfect golden mean would be reached. He agreed, pointing out that to get the same result on a mainframe would have taken weeks of work with weather statistics, contour lines, random number generation, and triple integrations (by calculus and by numerical methods). The little man, we gleefully concluded, was still holding his own.

### III

In Jefferson City, I had an unusual moment of firm resolve; I overruled Tim, and unilaterally decided on a rendezvous at mileage marker 137. As I canoed on, I thought to myself what a boon the markers had become. They simplified the rendezvous, and they also gave us a countdown to the end of the Missouri. But as 160 gave way to 159, and then to 158, I realised that the numbers were also frustrating, for a whole day's aching efforts produced only tiny changes. My 500-strokes-a-mile at least gave me some sense of personal achievement. In fact, it came to me, this very spot had to be near the million mark. I amused myself counting: one million and one, one million and two, one million and three, tum-tiddly-tum, great kayaking fun . . . . When you've just got Muddy Water for company, the simple pleasures are the best.

I went past a dock where a tow was holding a convoy steady while tugs weaved in and out putting yet more barges on. It seemed a very messy operation and it made me realise I was not the only one that Old Misery caused problems for. Beside the dock was a floating shop, giving me an idea of the monotony of the rivermen's lives: cigarettes, sweets, and girlie magazines. I would have stopped there myself but didn't have any money.

At 7.45 pm, a marker loomed wearily into sight. It was No. 137. 'Strange,' I muttered, 'no sign of the boys.' At 8.45, I became a little fed up. Inland lay a mass of head-high maize. After half an hour of scratches and curses, I emerged onto a little road. They weren't there.

I started to hitch-hike towards some distant lights, wondering whether such an unshaven and filthy creature as myself would ever be picked up. In the event, it did prove quite a lengthy process, as not a single car passed. 'Strange,' I muttered again, and started to walk resignedly up the hill. The moon wasn't out and a ghostly quiet hung over the place.

Soon I rounded a corner. In front lay two parallel lines of 15-ft electric fencing. In the middle stood a pair of cross-meshed gates, and stretching to a double infinity were watch-towers with searchlights. I retreated down the hill in total confusion.

Taking a different route at random, I finally found proof that a nerve-gas attack hadn't wiped out the entire Western Hemisphere. It might only be the Soviet Supreme Command (Central Missouri), but a workshop was undoubtedly producing humanoid noises. Inside, there was even a man welding.

I exhausted a lungful of air, then tapped him on the shoulder. He jumped like a cat, while I asked him if he could please tell me whether there were any police officers in the immediate vicinity. For some reason, he jumped again, nearly giving me a lethal dose of acetylene. Then he began to eye me coolly. With whitening knuckles he inched the angle of the flame round, while the other hand walked towards a massive adjustable spanner. 'Are you being funny?' he growled. I replied that I didn't feel in the least bit funny. We stared at each other for another while, as he spoke rapidly into a walkie-talkie. 'Farm to central pen. Have alien. Request immediate assistance.'

Wheels skidded, sirens muffled, the door slammed open. Half a dozen heavily-armed policemen frogmarched me into a car as if I'd just blown up the White House. The car speeded up towards a building bathed in an eerie white light. My neighbour muttered into his hand and the gates swung open. I glimpsed a sign marked 'ALGOA STATE PENITENTIARY. NO UNAUTHORIZED PERSONS' and then the gates clanged shut again. It must have been the only prison for miles and miles and I'd had to canoe straight into it – I really was in trouble this time!

A very young lieutenant was doing a very big crossword.

'OK. Let's hear your story.'

I started on the whole lot, but he cut in: 'You guys were on the news one half hour ago! That's quite some trip you's doing. We don't often get Englishmen coming into the Pen. Most often, it's Americans, and they're dying to bust on out!' We were firm friends and a telepathic assistant brought in coffee and sandwiches.

I mentioned the boys, and the lieutenant swung into action. 'No way will they find you!' This time he gave the instructions by phone. Then he took me on a tour. Various famous names were graduates of the place, including 'Pretty Boy' Floyd who had been killed here in a shoot-out with the guards. The radio crackled. 'You won't have to spend tonight in a cell after all.' We drove out from the inner citadel and past the prison farm. Behind yet another line of fencing was the Dodge, basking familiarly in the glare of the spotlights. Tim grinned at me quizzically and pointed at the map. 'OK, you old rogue, you win,' I said. 'In future *you* choose the rendezvous points!'

In the morning, a new set of guards were on the gates. I tried to tell them that my kayak would make an ideal getaway 'vehicle', but they just ushered us into the crowded waiting room. Without fruit or flowers or metal-laden chocolate cakes, we felt very peculiar. After about an hour, we were taken out and searched. Apart from Liam's metal comb, we were judged clean!

A few minutes later, we had found our way through the yellow maze. Prisoner No. 137 was still there, lying forlorn on the mud. Something caught my eye. A baby deer was swimming bravely towards the main current and into the grip of the Missouri. I held my breath and willed the creature on. Finally she was scrabbling shakily up the opposite bank. I tore up my pass, and followed her out towards freedom.

IV

Twenty-four hours later, I came to the solitary hump of Côte Sans Dessein, where the sidewheeler the *Thomas Jefferson* went down. It had ventured onto this part of the river to investigate whether it was navigable by steamboat. Clearly it wasn't!

Soon afterwards, I saw a timber-raft at least 300 feet long being pushed downstream by a tiny tow. I remembered my own tree-felling days in Edinburgh, and then what I'd read about the early lumberjacks on the river. They used to spend most of their time jumping from trunk to trunk – herding the hundreds of thousands of logs – using their long poles to bring strays back in. A moment's inattention, and an Escher-style logjam had developed that only dynamite could heal. It was another mythical moment in the winning of the West, but an unecological one – the floods that have beset the Mississippi-Missouri system ever since are perhaps due to the destruction of the forests.

After lunch, Bill headed off for a marketing marathon in St Louis. Just before that town was the point, only two days ahead now, where the Missouri and the Mississippi finally met; and I felt a bit worried by what I'd read about it. For the Indians, the coming together of the two giants was a mystic union, one which no mortal eye was allowed to see. Black, green, and red monsters floated above the banks, and descended on all desecrators. But more terrible was a roaring demon in the water, whose mouth swallowed up any canoes rash enough to venture near him. Modern anthropologists have argued that the monsters were in fact pictures painted on the cliffs, that the roaring was really the turbulence, and that the demon's mouth was simply the mouth of the Mississippi. But these explanations only partly reassured me, given what I had read elsewhere. Twain, for instance, had talked of the Missouri as 'a torrent of yellow mud boiling and surging: that savage river poured its turbid floods into the bosom of its gentler sister'. Other witnesses had spoken of 'a riot of entire trees, branches and floating reefs', and of 'terrible standing waves, sharp and thrusting'. Whichever way you looked at it, it didn't sound much fun.

To allay my anxiety, I mulled over the explorers on the Upper Mississippi. Perhaps it was just the way Bill had told it, but they seemed comic and ineffectual – as if aware of more serious things going on in the West.

A certain Pike decided he wanted to discover the source of the Mississippi. He got terribly confused in a snowstorm, and had to enlist the help of an anonymous Scotsman and a Frenchman with the implausible name of Rousseau. These gentlemen pointed him in the right direction and after three months he did get to a lake from which some of the water flowed. Leech Lake hit history.

Unfortunately it wasn't the longest branch, and in 1823 an Italian called Beltrami resolved to put his name on the map. But then he realised that there was perhaps an unfortunate rhyme with salami, and so substituted the name of his former girlfriend. (If that didn't bring her back, then nothing would.) Our intrepid explorer caught a steamboat most of the way up. For the last bit, he climbed into a canoe and started paddling. Then he capsized. He was so unnerved that he got out and started walking up the river. 'And when I say up,' said Bill, 'I mean up – and he didn't have any wellies.' To cap it all, it started pouring down, but here he was prepared. Quite soon, the Indians lining the shore saw a very wet man pulling a relatively dry canoe crowned with a magnificent umbrella.

Posterity does not record the Indians' opinion. We are therefore free to surmise that they must have either admired his courage or pitied his wretchedness. Nor do we know whether they provided him with dry socks but they did guide him to his destination, a lake from which some of the water flowed. Lake Julia certainly sounds better than Leech Lake. One wonders, nevertheless, whether Beltrami was doing himself full justice when he compared 'his' discovery to those of Christopher Columbus and Amerigo Vespucci.

It still wasn't quite the longest branch. In 1832, the poet Schoolcraft found a lake. Discovering that it was already known, and called Lake La Biche, he cursed and swore. Still, the name was pretty unpoetic, and, what was more, French. If he couldn't change history, at least he could change the name. Deciding that something Red Indian was called for, he opted for Lake Itasca, from verITAS CAput (Latin for 'the truth head' – I kid you not); for, as everyone knows, the Indians of the day spoke excellent dog-Latin.

This time, it *was* the longest branch. (And thousands of tourists amuse themselves there each year by jumping over the shyly emerging tricklet.) 'But you can't help feeling,' concluded our resident orator, 'that all three could have saved themselves a lot of trouble. The Indians knew where the furthest source was all the time, and were telling anybody who would listen . . . .'

As dusk came down, I paddled into the town of Hermann, a small island of Germanicness in an ocean of Midwest. Everywhere were bierkellers, würst, Gothic capitals, Mercedes, and buxom blondes with pigtails and rosy cheeks. Our morale was high that night. The weather had decided to stop imitating a bald weathercock and had stabilised at an un-Teutonic 90°. Also, we were just coming up to Saint Charles (of French and Lewis and Clark fame). St Louis was just around the corner, and with it, the end of the Missouri – our cursed enemy when throwing surprises at us, but our beloved friend when disappearing into the inland seas . . . .

That was as far as I got before my head started dropping. But as I launched the following morning, I continued assessing the expedition. Affairs were ticking over, I knew, but also wearing down and out. The only idea in all our heads was New Orleans and National Smoke-Out Day, a mere month away. I now thought I could make it but at the same time, I was aware that anything could happen on a river like the Mississippi – her untamed reputation had to come from somewhere.

Stirred Up and Grandmother River must have been jealous, for I suddenly had a desire to answer nature's call. My cup wasn't appropriate, so I came ashore, and fast! I was busying myself behind some meagre shelter, when I heard a soft scraping noise. I peered reluctantly out. *Lochinvar* was creeping off towards Saint Charles and the sea. Springing up as if on a hornets' nest, I started running across the shore. I tripped over my jeans and fell into the Missouri. *Lochinvar* nodded in recognition of the help and proceeded to line herself up with the current. I swam

116

towards her but got nowhere – the jeans again! Then at last I was fixing my teeth firmly on the toggle. Turning on my back, I swam awkwardly towards the shore.

Soon I was a new man. *Lochinvar* was heading south once more; my pants and underpants were drying quickly on the baking hot fibreglass; and my modesty was nicely concealed beneath the spray-jacket. I arrived at Saint Charles much sooner than I had expected. I was horrified to see a small group of elderly people standing beside Liam and Tim, apparently part of an organised outing. Trying hard to pretend not to have seen anything or anybody, I shot straight past and hit shore 200 yards downstream. Liam and Tim soon came rushing along, only just outrunning the octogenarians! A towel and a spare pair of jeans, and the situation and I were saved. But it had been a damned close-run thing.

Three hours later I paddled up to Bellefontaine Bridge, the last one on the Missouri, and only 8 miles from the end. Bill helped me ashore and introduced me to our hosts, a young couple called Diane and Ron Carson.

Soon we were in a red Ford Mustang, roaring towards our first home-cooked dinner for three months. Another stage in my marathon was over. After all those efforts, the unbelievable had happened. The Missouri had bent, and then finally broken.

'St Louis here we come,' I said, as Diane offered me a huge cigar and a lovely smile.

# A Tale of Two Rivers

You an' me, we sweat and strain
Body all achin' an' racked wid pain
Tote dat barge
Lift dat bale
Git a little drunk
An' you lands in jail.
Ah gits weary
An' sick of tryin'
Ah'm tired of livin'
An' skeered of dyin'
But Ol' Man River
He jes' keeps rollin' along.
('Ol' Man River')

## I

First on the agenda was a press conference. We realised I wouldn't be able to do the 20 miles from Bellefontaine into St Louis in time, so Diane drove us down to the waterside about a mile from the centre.

I felt like a heartless bigamist as I surveyed the inexorable flow of the Mississippi. At half a mile, the combined river was only slightly wider than my companion of the last three months. But she was much busier, with dozens of convoys moving steadily up and down, leaving bad-tempered swells behind them.

All of a sudden the view began to look distinctly *déjà vu*-like. I'd stood on this spot in a previous existence . . . it was before I started . . . when we strolled down from the hotel . . . when I'd had all those bad dreams. Seeing it now in the daylight was like seeing a long-forgotten friend in an old negative. That time, I'd been very much overawed: now I was just awed, but ready to take on this new monster and give her everything I had.

I got into *Lochinvar* and nosed gently out from the shore. The current seemed marginally slower than before, and yet I was aware of a terrible strength under those sullen waters. After a few minutes I saw an enormous arch, the famous Gateway to the West. At 600 feet it stood out

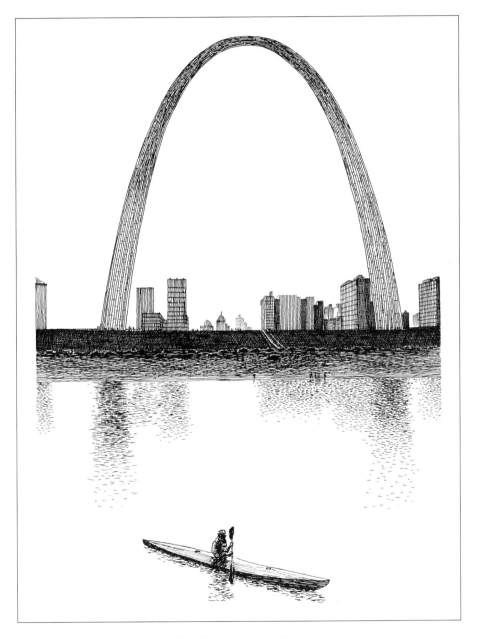

The Gateway to the West.

dramatically against the blazing azure of the sky: two slender aluminium fingers, incandescent as they reached up to form a single arc of reflected light. Soon I went under the contrasting arches of the $1^1/2$-mile-long Eads Bridge: the first bridge to cross the Mississippi-Missouri (1874), and the most Victorian. Next there was a huge sternwheeler, emblazoned S.S. *Admiral* and resplendent in the sunshine; and lastly, a throng of pressmen and a big crowd of bystanders. A sharp surge of guilt came to me: I was going to have to pretend that I'd already beaten the Missouri. Knowing her character, she might want to take revenge – and she still had 8.21 miles to play with.

*Lochinvar* had meanwhile ground to a halt, the cameras were whirring like mad, and an elegant figure in a crisp Savile Row suit was striding up. He wrung me warmly by the hand. 'Mr Nicholas Francis, I presume! Gordon Brown, British Consul-General – welcome to St Louis!'

With these words the show really got off the ground. Liam and Tim, looking very professional in their British Airways gear, carried the boat out of the water and slid her onto the truck – and then did it again facing the cameras. I answered a lot of alert questions from the three main American television networks and endlessly hopped in and out of my canoe, while Bill acted as a one-man information bureau, talking nineteen to the dozen and handing out copy after copy of the press release mark-2.

Finally the famous four were left alone again. Bill announced the next item: a laid-on lunch on a stern-wheeler, with a wily journalist who wanted the *full* story. We groaned and asked where he was from. The *St Louis Post-Dispatch*, came the proud reply. As we walked over, I remarked that, once before, the *Dispatch* had covered nautical affairs; their correspondent had been the first to tell the world about the *Titanic* – from the sinking ship itself. Tim said what a good job this wasn't the season for icebergs!

We ate like wild horses, while answering question after question. Then, still swallowing our just desserts, Bill and I rushed off and thanked Mr Gordon Brown for all his help. In fact, it was only just beginning, for he had an important piece of news. The Prince of Wales was visiting the United States; he was due in town in three days' time. Gordon Brown thought the Prince might like a change from all those civic receptions. Would we like to meet him? Most definitely we would!

Leaving Bill to cope with the incoming calls, I went off to the Missouri branch of the American Cancer Society. I had a quick meeting with their president and then telephoned national headquarters in New York. I told them that, as far as I knew, the Missouri had been kayaked for the first time in recorded history; that we had had several dangerous incidents; that President Ford's and Prince Charles's names were linked with the expedition; and that we'd been plugging cancer research across the whole

North American Continent. In the pause that followed, I added that the deal was on for National Smoke-Out Day – by hook or by crook, I'd be in New Orleans for 17 November. I stopped; and there was a long, contemplative silence. Finally a slow voice came: 'Well, that *is* interesting.' (Another extended pause.) 'Why don't you phone if you make it to New Orleans.' (Click.)

I was left speechless. The A.C.S paid millions of dollars a year for its PR men, their expense accounts, their secretaries, and *their* expense accounts. And here were the four of us, risking our lives 'for free', and they just didn't want to know. As I looked round at the wood-lined office, I conceded that maybe they had been right not to trust a young man fresh from London, England, and travelling very blind. But now that I had done over 2300 miles, I really couldn't believe that a megamillion-dollar society could be so shortsighted.

Time after time newsmen and members of the public had asked how contributions could be given; and time after time we had shamefacedly not been able to answer. But now I decided to test New York's claim that each state branch was autonomous. I went back into the main office, and spoke to the fundraising representative for Missouri, suggesting that we organise a joint appeal. She agreed to take on the organisation, saying she would try and think of some suitable stunt. Next I drove to K.A.D.I. Radio Station. There I gave an interview and recorded an appeal for the American Cancer Society.

Then we all went to City Hall, where the Mayor, Mr Conway, gave us a warm welcome. He also gave us the Freedom of St Louis, as symbolised by blue silk ties covered with tiny silver arches.

For two days we were in a wonderland of excellent company, dry sheets, hot meals, and morning-to-night work in an office with a telephone. 'Why don't we do this all the time?' I asked Bill.

Thursday was yet another full day. Most important for me, Cathy flew down. After a loving reunion at the airport, we went directly to the Hilton. In return for six-course lunches for the crew, I was due to address the assembled businessmen of the Rotary Club.

Silence fell over the conference room as 1000 eyes converged on me. I looked along the rows of captains of industry, thinking of the tons of peanut-butter we had consumed – and felt very much out of place. Then I spotted the sole lady present. Gaining confidence from her smile, I began to speak. (The following is reconstructed from the two lines of notes I scribbled between the soup and the main course.)

'Like the Mississippi, it just keeps rolling along. Let it roll! Let it roll on in full and inexorable benignancy to other lands and better days.' Winston Churchill spoke these ringing words during the darkest days of the Second

World War. He chose the image of the Great American River to describe the bonds of friendship linking the two great English-speaking democracies.

'St Louis would seem an especially appropriate place to celebrate the friendship between the New and the Old Worlds, because of Lindbergh, the first man to fly solo from one to the other. Born and brought up within sight, and smell, of the mighty Mississippi, Charles Lindbergh's first adventures came when swimming in the deceptive swirls of the Father of Waters. Later it was your farsighted and generous predecessors who gave the greatest support to his epoch-making venture. In recognition of their sense of enterprise, he called his plane the *Spirit of St Louis*.

'But, as you know, St Louis was at the forefront of the transport business from the days when a traveller called it just "a smear of dwellings along the greasy banks of the Mississippi". St Louis was where Lewis and Clark rowed west from – and, fortunately, sailed back to. St Louis was where those famous routes to the Pacific, the Oregon and California Trails, ferried precariously across the river.

'Of course, things were a bit slow in those days. When the Spanish acquired *le beau Saint Louis* from the French, it was a couple of years before the town itself knew about it. Forty years later, the French flag went up once more. The day after, it was hauled down again: the St Louisians were no longer Louisianans but had finally become Americans.

'From last outpost of civilisation, to navigational centre of North America, St Louis also became its railway nub. Later, the first directed balloon flight in history occurred at the centenary celebrations of the Louisiana Purchase, otherwise known as the 1904 World Fair. Then, in the 1920s, water-skiing was invented on the Mississippi. The speedboat used didn't prove quite speedy enough, so with typical American enterprise you borrowed a sea-plane – and hauled the first water-skier along at a hair-raising 80 mph!

'Ever since, you have continued your contribution to man's desire to go farther and faster. After water, land, and air, the stage was space. I have no need to tell you that your city is a major aerospatial centre, amongst whose achievements is the building of the first American manned spaceship.

'From raunchy river-vessel to sleek space-vessel in a century and a half. It's not bad going at all. But, while acting as a launchpad for the whole Solar System, your virtue lies in never having lost touch with the past. It is appropriate that the space-rocket boosters left town on that primordial symbol of the American dream, the Mississippi-Missouri. In your beginning was your end.

'You have much to be proud of. And so, by ricochet, I am proud to have been able to speak to you today. In the name of Anglo-American friendship, and in the name of the epic journey that is mankind's, may I ask you, gentlemen, to keep it up: Long Live the Spirit of St Louis!'

II

Straight after lunch, I got a phone call from the local A.C.S. The managers of Phenix Kayaks of Tyner, St Louis, and The Outdoor Store of Belleville, Illinois, were offering us the choice of any kayak in stock. All we had to do was publicise the gift in subsequent news conferences. We were overjoyed, and drove straight to the showroom. We found a fine range of slalom-boats, but no sea-going kayaks at all. The ocean, admittedly, was over 1200 river-miles away but clearly people didn't do much canoeing on the Mississippi-Missouri either! It might have looked churlish, however, to refuse the offer, so Tim and I found one that was a bit longer and slimmer than the others. We posed for the publicity photographs and profusely thanked the management. As we drove back through a most unGallic-looking 'French Quarter', I said that I just wished there were some rapids nearby to try the boat out on. 'We could always go back to Three Forks' came the terrible reply!

Back at the Consulate, I sent a telegram to my brother, asking if he could lend me £100. Next I called into Mr Brown's office. He too had been pretty busy. We were going to meet the Prince of Wales at nine o'clock the next morning. I would have to have a bath (my thoughts – not his words) and excavate the pick-up for a shirt. There was not a moment to lose.

Cathy found a tonne of industrial soap and the preparations got under way. At 8.50 on Friday 20 October, the gorgeous gang assembled in prime place under the Gateway to the West and a perfect blue sky. Tim's kilt was in fine fettle, despite the unfair treatment it had been subjected to. Several times I noticed it drawing the suspicious perusal of a severe posse of Secret Service personnel, and several times, the admiring attention of a whole horde of winsome women. Then disaster struck. My St Louis tie had somehow acquired a big coffee stain.

I asked Liam if I could borrow one of his and Cathy helped me put it on. I realised that it was a Royal Navy Reserve one, and started pulling it off. But Liam gave me a nudge to say that the motorcade was already there so I quickly tightened it up again. The car doors opened, a huge cheer went up, and the Prince of Wales stepped spritely into the sunshine.

Very soon, Gordon Brown presented us to His Royal Highness. He immediately put me at my ease by asking if I sang 'Ol' Man River' when alone in the canoe. Zooming in on my ill-tied tie, he enquired with keen interest which Royal Navy ships I'd served on. How embarrassing! I started telling him about my merchant-seaman days, but then came clean

123

and told him about the coffee-stain. He grinned understandingly, congratulated us on our remarkable progress, and wished me the very best of British luck with the rest of the venture.

The Prince of Wales had an insiders' chat with Liam about the Navy Reserve, and with Tim about navigational problems. Seeing us all spick and span in the blazing sunshine, I'm not sure whether anyone could have guessed just how many hardships we'd been through. But Bill explained what we were trying to do. Then, seeing the interest in the Prince's eyes, he took a gamble and told him about our disastrous episode on far away Fork Peck, complete with sinking sand and rescue plane, leaving the Prince looking suitably astounded and somewhat amused.

And then the Prince left, leaving us all with the impression of a most charming and intelligent man, one who might easily have become a friend – if only he hadn't had so many prior engagements.

III

Bill passed the phone. It was the A.C.S., with news of the fundraising stunt they had arranged – in twenty minutes' time! When we got to City Hall, the road was jammed by a massive fleet of police cars and press vans. We resolved to ask the Mayor what the problem was. Arriving in his office, however, we found it occupied by a stern-looking Chief of Police in the gold-braided dress-uniform of a full colonel. His name was Moran. As we gaped in amazement, he majestically intoned: 'Mayor Conway, Nicholas Francis: you're under arrest. The charge is mopery on the high seas and flying without an airplane.' We had no time to resist, for with a deft click representing decades of experience, he handcuffed us together and led us down to the street. As we walked past the cameras, the Mayor nonchalantly waved his wrist, virtually pulling me off the ground in the process. A taxi screeched to a halt and a head asked 'Hey-y! Is that the *May-yer??*'

'Yeah! He's under arrest!'

'Give him life!' – and the car was rubbering away.

We drove under full flashing and wailing escort to police headquarters. When we got there, a nervous young lieutenant started taking our fingerprints but somebody whispered in his ear. More photographs were taken and then a cell door was closing behind us with a loud clang.

That same evening, in the middle of a dinner party, a disc-jockey phoned from a truckers' radio station. Having informed me that we were on the air from coast to coast, he asked me what my prison cell was like. I said it was quite comfortable really, but the porridge was sometimes a bit lumpy, and the rats occasionally bothersome. Also, the Mayor snored.

The only worry was that I had a rendezvous with the Mississippi in thirty-six hours. Listeners could help me make it by sending bail-money to the American Cancer Society, at the following address . . . . The disc-jockey lent his enthusiastic support, the jingles came on, and I went back to the smoked salmon and social chitchat. I just had to hope that this stunt would bring the funds pouring in to the A.C.S.'s coffers.

On Saturday, knowing that the river was going to come between us, Cathy and I were inseparable. In the afternoon, we set off to visit the remains of a major Indian town, just 6 miles from St Louis. The taxi swept us over a big brown river, but we hardly noticed, so much did we have to say to each other. At the site, we were guided through broad avenues, but we had eyes only for one other, and hardly took in the twelfth-century artefacts found there: bracelets from the Great Lakes, lead and iron implements from the Upper Mississippi, carved sea shells from the Gulf of Mexico. Only several days later did I glance at the guidebook Cathy had bought me, and realise that we must have walked past a huge terraced pyramid with the remains of a sun-temple on the top. Somewhere as well, we probably saw a 400-ft-wide circle used for calculating the winter and summer solstices. But I have no memory of it at all, just a vision of Cathy's sparkling blue eyes . . . .

At dawn the following day, I drove with Cathy to the airport. I thought back to our first meeting in the discotheque, and then how devotedly she had come down to visit me. But now the Mississippi-Missouri was tearing up apart, pushing us towards the opposite ends of the country. We talked for a moment about our times together. And then we kissed a long farewell.

In a daze, I watched as the aircraft hurled itself along the tarmac and climbed towards the sky, heading towards a town which had become but a shadow in my mind. Then Cathy was gone, leaving me walking unhappily through the departure lounge.


## IV

We drove back through depressed suburbs to the bridge at Bellefontaine. The Missouri was still where we had left her. She seemed strangely docile now, as if in atonement for all she had thrown at me.

An hour and a half later the banks began to move further apart. Ahead of me lay a vast expanse of water, bisected by the magical line where the Missouri and the Mississippi finally met. To my relief, there was little sign of coloured monsters, river-demons, or floating reefs – just a nasty-looking gash of angry water and an air of savage significance that hung over the water like a flock of pregnant vultures.

Wishing to savour the moment, I pulled my paddles inboard and let the current take me where she would. I was still on the Missouri, and yet already under the influence of the Mississippi. My mind began to range back through the sensations that Smoky Water would always conjure up for me: the Gates of the Mountains, the Missouri Breaks, Cassidy's Hole-in-the-Wall; Sakakawea, Oahe, an aluminium War-Chief; joy and despair, loneliness and laughter, and now, perhaps strangest of all, nostalgia – nostalgia for my age-long voyage across the northern and western tracts of this great land. With a shock, I realised that a whole part of my life was about to disappear for ever.

A new, firmer current began to tug at the bow and I drifted over the line, into another state, and onto a new river. After all those years of waiting, I had finally fulfilled my dream of 'sliding down' the Mississippi. And it felt mighty good.

Still in a sort of trance, I narrowly missed being mowed down by a huge tow. As it skewed past me, I read its name: *'Nouvelle France – Québec'*. A bit puzzled, I got my maps out. I eventually deduced that it must have come down through the St Lawrence Seaway, then Lakes Ontario, Erie, Huron, and Michigan, a connecting canal, the Illinois River, and finally the Mississippi. Its journey perfectly mirrored the Missouri's, in both direction and distance. And like the Wild Mizoo, it was a trip down a French memory lane: Prairie du Chien, Dubuque, La Crosse; Le Claire, Saint Paul, Saint Cloud; the Illinois, Détroit, Montréal, and Trois Rivières. For a long moment, I was in a North American continent that had remained true to its French history.

Then I looked ahead again. The line between the brown Missouri and the yellow Mississippi was still clearly visible. I was glad that my former companion had grabbed about two thirds of the common bed – I only hoped *I* wouldn't end up on the floor. I continued to think about the twin rivers and their longstanding rivalry.

I finally began to realise just what a bad deal the Missouri has had and just how overrated the Mississippi's reputation has been. The Mississippi flows awkwardly north-south, and so got in the way of the early explorers; whereas the Missouri flows generally to the southeast and was therefore useful to them. At the confluence, the Mississippi can compete for size with the Missouri – but that's only because it hasn't come across the thirsty plains. The Mississippi's catchment area is 160,000 square miles – hardly the size of France – whereas the Missouri's is a round half million. The biggest lake on the Mississippi is $3/4$ mile wide and 22 miles long, while the Missouri itself is as wide and Lake Oahe is eleven times as long. The Mississippi alone breaks no records; at 1100 miles, it is about the thirtieth longest river in the world and less than half as long as the Missouri.

Looking at it objectively, I thought, as I picked up my paddles and moved back onto the brown part, two rivers come together just above St Louis. And it's the shorter of the two, the paler, the less turbulent, the less historic, which transfers its name to all the water. The reason for the lacklustre Mississippi's success, I slowly deduced, must be that it lay further east, and was thus able to grab the world's attention first. But what an indignity for the longest river of the continent to be abolished at two thirds of its struggle to the sea. It's as if the Seine stopped at Paris or the Nile at Khartoum! All those people tripping to the piddling foothills of Minnesota would be much better off climbing to a distant source high in the Rockies. There and then, I challenged the world to find one really interesting fact about the Upper Mississippi.

I could see my sceptical back-up team asking what *I* would call the two branches. It *was* all a bit tricky. Were I world dictator, I mused, I would decree that the main river, from Three Forks down to the Gulf, should be called the Missouri, and that the name Mississippi be restricted to the tributary. But I reluctantly recognised that it was perhaps a bit late for such drastic measures. I decided, nevertheless, that I would continue to speak of the Mississippi-Missouri whenever possible. The Mississippi was just about acceptable for the lower river, I conceded, so long as you were aware of the inverted commas hovering over the name like a poorly-maintained guillotine. It was certainly *not* acceptable, however, to follow the Collins Dictionary, which listed the Missouri as 'the longest river in North America; chief tributary of the Mississippi'. A mapless Martian would be driven hairless trying to sort that lot out!

At this point, I had to stop by my bemused musing, as the towboats were all slyly sloping off towards the left bank. A US Army sign read 'CHAIN OF ROCKS DAM. ALL VESSELS *MUST* ENTER THE CANAL'. I hesitated for a moment. Using an artificial cut-off seemed like cheating, but I was also only too aware of the pleasure that beating one last dam would give me.

I felt good as I hauled the kayak laboriously round (no back-up team to do all the hard work this time). Then I saw the reason for the canal: the Chain of Rocks, a vicious line of half-submerged teeth reaching across most of the river.

As the water rushed me past the Chain, I remained a little apprehensive but I got through with only a couple of bursts of manic side-paddling. Then I got back to the serious business. For a long time, something had been nagging insidiously at the back of my mind. In fact, it had been there since those weeks at the library. The lists of books on the rivers of the world had overawed me – there had been more than a hundred on the Missouri or the Mississippi alone. But even without reading them I had

had a feeling that they all missed something essential. I could now feel the two hemispheres of my tired brain throbbing together round the core of the problem, like clotted cream around a walnut.

Then suddenly the two halves stuck together and a tremendous discovery shot out. All those dusty catalogues had listed more books than you could use on the Missouri *or* the Mississippi, but not a single one on *both*! Not a single slim fascicule in any language. The river I was on just didn't have a recognised name. From the official point of view, it didn't exist.

So that was why the idea had so much trouble getting off the ground at the beginning . . . . By saying that I planned to canoe the Mississippi-Missouri, I had seemed boastful ('Who is this guy? Isn't *one* river enough for him?'). And I had put people on the spot, since they weren't sure which river was which, whether I wanted to canoe the whole or both, and why I wasn't talking about the Missouri-Mississippi.

This last question *was* a pretty good one. But I had no time to answer it, for I was already in the centre of St Louis. I pulled into the same causeway, felt *déjà déjà vu*, and ate a bar of chocolate to calm me down. Ten minutes later, a shiny new Phenix powered into the farewell press conference. I said all the right things, and thanked Gordon Brown again for his tremendous

Slidin' down the Mississippi.

assistance. As a last gesture, he fixed a Union Jack on the bow. Then I rowed off again with the little flag waving in the wind.

I went over the last week. It made quite a list. In seven short days, I had conquered my fear of the Mississippi, beaten the Missouri, received the Freedom of the City, fallen back in love, dined at the Hilton, been given a free kayak, met the Prince of Wales, been arrested and imprisoned, beaten the last dam, and discovered a river that nobody else knew about.

'Not bad going,' I thought to myself.

# *A Name I Will Remember*

> The object of the game was not to win, but not to lose. The only rule was to stay in the game.
>
> (From the film *Scorpio*.)

## I

Over the next week, the slogging reality of long-distance canoeing came back to me. The air was very hot and humid, and despite a faster current, the effort of every stroke hit me like a wet face-flannel. In my mind, St Louis had represented the real goal, and I had borne all the Missouri's thwarting and battering by thinking of better days to come. I had now done over two-thirds of the distance, but that still only meant reaching the Steppes – India, alias New Orleans, was nowhere in sight.

The Illinois countryside was also very monotonous: a few farms, all identical, some low hills in the distance, and that was it. Most of the time, I couldn't even see *that*, hemmed in as I was between rocky bluffs and reinforced levees. As I fought my way on, I had too much time to think about various other problems which had been eclipsed only temporarily by the delights of St Louis.

First came the river's treacherous tendencies, which were legion. The whirlpools were usually easy to avoid, especially as they tended to occur on the lee of obstacles. But the seemingly most placid stretches of water sometimes revealed themselves to be 'boils' – violent mushrooms of upsurging water making an eerie hissing noise and thrusting the kayak bossily aside. I saw a thirty-barge tow go over one and quiver as if in delirium tremens. Thereafter I had no qualms at all about giving them a very wide berth – when I could spot them in advance. Another problem was the foreign bodies in the water. Most were pretty harmless but once in a while there appeared a 100-ft tree-trunk, with branches bigger than my

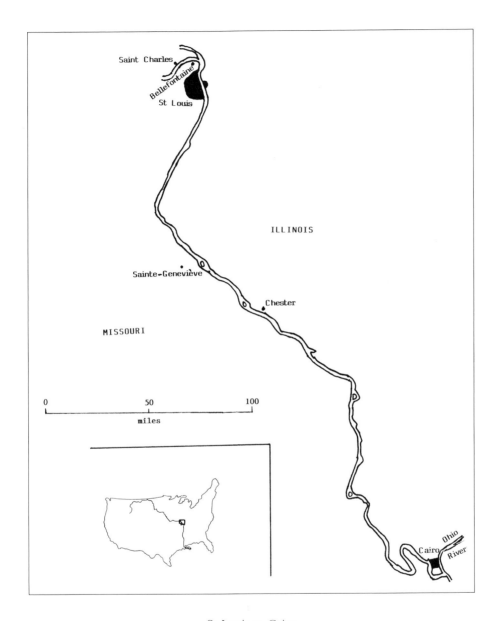

St Louis to Cairo.

canoe flailing like drowning men. It was spectacular, but, once again, could normally be avoided. Only when a tree-trunk was stuck on the bottom – technical name, a 'sawyer' – did I have the occasional bad fright. I would be canoeing over a boringly average stretch of river when a branch would suddenly stick sharply out of the water. Then it would disappear again, like Excalibur in the lake, leaving my nerves a jangling mess. I

131

simply had to hope that one wouldn't pop up directly below me. Yet another hazard was the pile-dykes: the relatively benign wooden wing-dams had now given way to these vicious-looking lines of sharp rocks. Also, *Lochinvar* herself was getting pretty worn out – the forward hatch hardly worked, odd leaks kept developing, and she didn't manoeuvre half as smoothly as before.

Off-water wasn't much better either. I was used to the pathetic penury by now, and the problems produced by the petty penny-pinching. But I had another worry, Bill. Like the others, he had come out 'for the summer'. Once already, he had obtained permission from the authorities at the Universities of London and Paris to stay on for seven weeks longer. But now they were adamant. Even a transatlantic phone call and personal plea by the Consul-General hadn't moved them. Bill just had to be in Paris for 15 November.

But most worrying of all was the apparent lack of impact back home. We hadn't had a single press-cutting from Britain since leaving. As a result, the fundraising drive was doing very badly. Colin MacKenzie's letters had apparently received very few positive responses and, without publicity, it didn't seem at all likely that the situation could get any better.

Another day passed under heavy rain. At one stage in the late afternoon I saw a solitary barge washed up on the bank. It was trailing the broken shreds of massive steel cables: obviously one that had got away, I reflected, and vowed to give the boils an even wider berth.

That evening I was expecting to go past Brackenridge's Sainte-Geneviève, but when I got there, there were just walls of rich, black soil. I looked at the maps more carefully, and got a shock. The Mississippi had moved Sainte-Geneviève two miles bodily inland, and there was nothing but a pathetic 'Front Street' to remind it of its watery past. *'Sic transit,'* I murmured melancholically to myself, wondering whether New Orleans would still be on the Gulf when I got there.

At Chester, I pulled the canoe right up onto the 25-ft levee, as I'd been told the river could rise several feet in a few hours. After much searching, I eventually found Liam in a bar several hundred yards away, chatting to the editor of the local newspaper. A hamburger arrived, but the questions never stopped and by the time I got to it, it was stone cold. But then the editor offered to book us into a motel. The eternity of hungry interrogation seemed worthwhile after all.

The whole of the next two days it rained hard. Then it stopped – and I realised what kayaking at 27°N was like. The sun just hung in the sky, motionless and sweltering. Sweat stung my eyes, and the dazzle from the shimmering surface sneaked in under my hat. I could feel my whole face contorted trying to keep it out. As the afternoon wore on, I knew the sun had to turn. It did, but so did the Mississippi.

Those long, hot miles did give me plenty of opportunity to think about Cairo, Illinois, just above the confluence with the Ohio. This was the point where the lower Mississippi and the Southern United States are generally considered to start. It was also where the infamous Mason-Dixon Line, the frontier between the free and the slave states, left the river and cut away towards the Atlantic.

In the South, I had always imagined balmy afternoons with water like glass; perhaps because of the conjunction of the names Memphis and Cairo (even when pronounced Cay-ro). True, the Corps of Engineers had warned me that there had been one steamboat wreck *every mile* on this stretch, that the 'gradient' would only be about 1 in 8000, and that there would be swampy bayous and alligators and snakes. The alligators liked stagnant waters, and I didn't, so I was sure we could come to some arrangement. But the copperheads and water-mocassins were apparently something else. Both are much more poisonous than the mere rattlesnake – their bites are normally fatal within a few hours. And, above all, they both spend most of their time in the water.

But my imagination didn't have time to get really worked up, for two successive bends arrived and I saw Cairo Railroad Bridge in the hazy distance. A slight breeze began to blow up but it still took me ninety minutes of agony to get there. I had canoed a record of 66 miles.

Bill had hitched down from St Louis and was waiting with a letter. My brother had sent a cheque for £200, twice what I had asked for, and told me to regard it as a gift. I was very touched. Then a very pretty reporter arrived. I opened my heart and told her all about our problems on the expedition. When she had gone, the boys led me up a small hill. To my amazement, I saw a river that looked exactly like the Mississippi, only bigger: the Ohio.

Over a crackling fire, we admired the awe-inspiring sight in front of us: two rivers grappling and groping, deadly rivals but undergoing a forced union. On our right, the Mississippi-Missouri, already the disdainful receiver of a thousand lesser rivers, flowing with confidence and majesty towards that last rendezvous. On our left the mighty Ohio, no longer the Belle Rivière of the explorers, but powering her effluence here from most of the Eastern United States: from Indiana, Ohio, West Virginia, and Pennsylvania; New York, Maryland, Virginia, and North Carolina; Kentucky, Tennessee, and Mississippi; and even from Georgia and Alabama.

Liam reminded us that the Ohio featured in *Uncle Tom's Cabin*: the Black heroines found freedom by fleeing north across its ice. He also claimed that this river was pushing a quarter of a million cubic feet of water past us each and every second – three times as much as the Nile at its mouth. I seized this golden opportunity to turn the subject round. Feeling I was stating the terribly obvious, I began to tell my friends about the Mississippi-Missouri.

But Bill's eyes soon lit up: 'I've never looked at it that way. It's absolutely amazing. The longest river in known history, and everybody's been blinded by mere names.' A long silence, and then suddenly he asked me question after question about the US Corps of Engineers, Twain, Lewis and Clark, Coronado, and lots of people I'd never even heard of. I couldn't understand what he was getting at, until he burst out abruptly, 'Don't you see? Nobody has ever canoed the Mississippi-Missouri before, that's fairly obvious. But nobody seems to have even *navigated* it, powered or unpowered. Not since time began. The upper bits were too small for big boats and the lower too big for small ones. But above all, nobody had the idea of the Mississippi-Missouri. (The hyphen was clearly audible.) It stands out like a male member of a croquet club for nubile nudists, but nobody ever noticed. The double-barrelled name fooled everybody. To think that a $1^1/2$-ft wide vessel, with a laden weight of eleven stone and peak-power of $1/5$ horse power . . .' ('Thanks a lot!') '. . . will be the first one ever to navigate the river!'

There were still two rivers 'laying' noisily in the dim darkness, but for me everything had changed. The M-M was no longer a gruelling accumulation of day-long slogs but an authentic whole. Townsend, Fort Benton, Mobridge, Omaha, St Louis – Cairo, Memphis, Vicksburg, Baton Rouge, New Orleans – they were all just stations on the way. The soaring Rockies and the gleaming Gulf were now intimately connected; the two limits of Louis XIV's empire had found a perfect harmony. After four months of trying, the river had finally become The River.


## II

I slept fitfully that night, impatient to be back on the water. A furious, blustering wind was blowing – blowing, as I quickly confirmed, directly upriver. Goodbye, balmy afternoons!

I cautiously moved out into the tortured waters. It was then that the full force of the wind hit me, blowing me backwards despite the current. Mercifully, we had arranged a midday rendezvous at Columbus, only 17 miles away.

After only a few strokes, I reached the confluence with the Ohio. There was a man chopping wood on the far bank: the sound arrived a full four seconds after the fall of the axe and it was then that I finally understood just how big the Mississippi-Missouri really was.

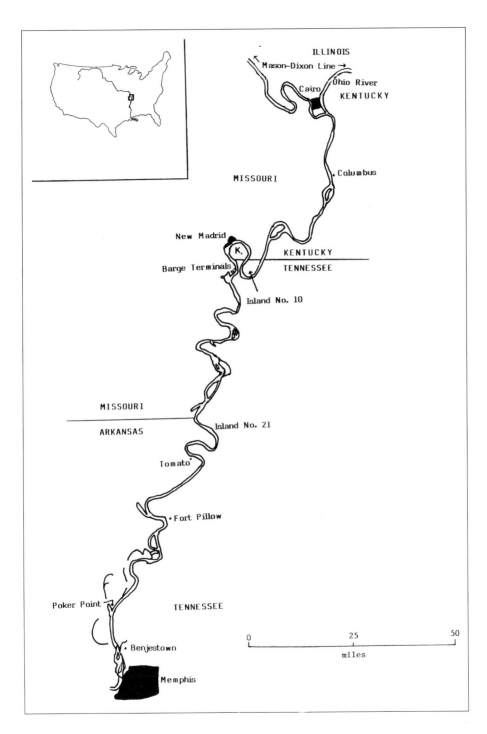

Cairo to Memphis.

Paddling hard to stay level with a submerged log, I calculated the speed of the current – just about 2 mph. I was very disappointed, as modern writers have talked about much greater speeds. Jonathan Raban, for example, reports seeing tows go down some sections of this stretch backwards so that their engines can slow them down, in a description curiously identical to one of Twain's. He also recounts how he tried to go up one of them in his 15 mph powerboat, and couldn't! If only some of those unbelievable 15 mph sections would come my way, I muttered sourly to myself.

When midday came, it found me a ridiculous 7 miles on. It was then that I remembered Twain's 'you feel mighty free and easy and comfortable' on the river. I personally felt mighty uncomfortable and difficult and cramped. Envying the wild geese winging south, I wondered if the continental winter mightn't catch me still struggling pitifully. Minutes before dark, I inched round a heaving headland. I had just made it to my lunch-time rendezvous!

In the morning the Mississippi was lying femininely there, as if yesterday had never existed. Over Liam's fine six-egg breakfast, I mused out loud about the strange name Columbus, stranded 1040 river-miles from the Gulf. Bill pointed out that, according to the *Encyclopedia Americana*, Columbus may have sighted the mouth of the Mississippi-Missouri, for something very like it is indicated on his map of 1507. We were all a bit dubious. But the image was certainly a powerful one: halberds, muskets, and pipes of peace, travel-stained Spanish sailing-ships surrounded by gaudy Indian canoes . . . .

After another 40 miles, I studied the maps one last time, looking for terrestrial short-cuts across all those 270° meanders. But my friends, perhaps wisely, had fixed the rendezvous at the end of the biggest loop. Something caught my eye. The land on the right was called Island No. 10 – but it wasn't an island. Curious. I did another double-take. Island No. 10 was in Tennessee. I'd left Kentucky behind before even realising it was there. Such a nice place too. A real United State (1792), as distinct from those upstart colonies further north.

Nevertheless, I thought as I paddled on, its horse-racing, fried-chicken and Blue-Mountain easy-goingness hid dark doings, for it was the first slave state east of the Mississippi. This simple geographical fact caused Twain all sorts of problems in *Huckleberry Finn*. Certainly the river down to Cairo was a superb escape-route for a slave – a raft 'doan' make *no* track'. But then there were slave states on both sides. The author does his level best to keep Jim and Huck on his beloved river as long as possible. They miss the biggest tributary in the Northern Hemisphere under cover of a thick fog. They feel too embarrassed to ask where they are (Kansas

City again, I suppose). The journey is then bravely spun out as far as 'Pikesville' (Tennessee?). But Twain has to eventually let his characters ashore – at which point the novel falls apart. (I may be a little biased.)

Meanwhile I had got round to the other side of the 'island' and was able to enjoy the same scenery inside out. I now remembered that this same piece of land – in its island days – was the site of a major battle in the Civil War.

The Unionists' response to the secession was to blockade the whole coast, from the St Lawrence down to the Rio Grande, forcing the Confederates to bring their imports in via Mexico, Texas and the Mississippi. Most of their strongholds were in fact on the river: Island No. 10, Memphis, Vicksburg, Port Hudson, New Orleans, and Fort Jackson. The Unionists' objective was thus clear. They assembled a fleet, sailed it round Florida, and then up the Mississippi. They fought their way as far as Tennessee. When Island No. 10 fell after a long siege, it was the turning point of the whole war.

At nightfall, I was only about 5 miles from New Madrid. All around, I could see the red forward lights of the tows. A long way away, pretending they were nothing to do with their tell-tale friends, were the white searchlights – restlessly revolving, probing along 1000-yd shafts of sudden, searing light, searching for unseen dangers. I carried on for a while, keeping well out of harm's way. Finally I saw the twinkle of street-lights far ahead. I now had quite a problem; I had to make a mile-and-a-half oblique crossing of the busy lanes.

I was about halfway across when roving lightbeams told me that two towboats were forging upstream, as well as one heading down. I knew that the downstream tow would be gaining a few knots – that was the one to watch. But suddenly the right-hand light gave birth to twins – there had been two tows there all the time and one was closing the distance fast. For a moment, I dithered: should I try and get clear across? Or should I try to steer *between* the two closest tows? The increasing throb of the downstream tow made up my mind: rather than throw myself under his bows, I would stay in the middle. After all, the two opposing tows *had* to leave some sort of gap between them.

I quickly turned my 16 feet around and headed back the way I had just come. Behind my left shoulder, I could dimly hear, feel, and even smell the first barge, but my mind was fully concentrated on the upstream one. I only hoped that I was invisible to his radar, otherwise my movements would undoubtedly be interpreted as a suicide mission. He might even think I was trying to cross his path, and steer still closer to barge number one. Trembling at the thought, I drifted to a halt. Although the metallic din and shuddering vibrations of the two boats had completely blended together by now, I could still only see number two ploughing upstream at full power. He was big, and growing bigger all the time. His red light was twinkling, only 100 yards to my right and way above me – twinkling and moving almost imperceptibly along the looming silhouette. 'The bastard's turning!' I yelled with triumph, but my cry was drowned by the spuming wash. Although he was still bearing down on me, I craned my neck round and saw with horror that the downstream tow had blotted out the shore behind me. He was only $1^1/2$ kayak lengths away. I'd judged it dangerously fine – but then again I'd had to. The wash from number one arrived, swept the back of the kayak into the air, and surfed us forwards at a frightening speed. I leaned back as much as I could, and back-paddled with all my strength. Number two had also crept up and I was moving into him much too fast. In front was *his* wash. With a mixture of terrible fear and relief, I remember thinking better perhaps two monsters than one – there's always a chance that the two will devour each other.

We arrived with great majesty. For a moment there came white water fore and aft with me somewhere below. Then buoyancy reasserted itself and the waves moved on. Not a moment too soon, for my vision was now totally blocked out by high metal walls. Fighting the claustrophobia of this terrible vibrating corridor with its ominously flat, upsurging floor, I had to force myself to just sit there and think of England. Seconds later, I twisted my head round again, waiting for the secondary wash to arrive from the stern of the 'downstream' barge – by now all sense of direction had vanished. For some reason it was the other barge's wash that hit me first. But I had seen it coming, and deftly resisted its assault, glad at the sweat shaken off my face. Next the other, as if in a well-rehearsed sequence, and then the river had come back and I was breathing fresh air again. To my amazement the other two barges had hardly moved.

I headed sharply across the water, and a quarter of an hour later, the team were helping me out. I swore then that I would never again paddle at night.


### III

On the Saturday, I awoke to a sizzling sound, a sausagey smell, and a strange sensation. Behind the hissing, there was a deathly calm. I peered out to discover that the Mississippi had completely disappeared behind a swirling swathe of fog. Then I heard the resonant boom of foghorns. The tows were clearly too busy to stop.

After breakfast, the fog hadn't moved, so I decided to wait for a bit. Tim told us about one of the early legends. In bygone days, he told us, the slaves believed that the river took the form of a huge alligator called Old

Devil River or Old Al, who used to create the currents with his tail and move the sandbanks around at will. Al used to smoke an immense pipe, and it was the smoke from this that produced the fogs – and thus stopped all work. So, to give Al the wherewithal to do his stuff, the slaves used to throw quantities of tobacco onto the water.

We debated the validity of non-rational conceptions of the universe for a while, and then I lifted the tent flap again. The blanket had begun to move, and visibility was now about 50 yards. It wasn't really enough for total safety, but then again, I thought, conditions on Old Devil River very seldom were.

We arranged to meet at the first of a series of terminals on the right-hand bank. Having checked my canoe for poisonous guests, and as the smoky ghosts on the bank floated out of sight, I remembered Twain's remark: 'Nothing don't look natural nor sound natural in the fog.' He was dead right. The water was glass-smooth (at last!), and as I paddled, spectral wreaths of mist would shift, revealing tempting tunnels of water.

After a few minutes, however, a light headwind blew up and the cover began to lift. I swung over towards the left and into the current. Then I saw a sign saying 'Kentucky Point Bar'. This couldn't be right. At breakfast, I'd been in Tennessee. True, I'd had a desire to go back and see what Kentucky was really like, and true, I could have got confused in the fog. I was so worried that I balanced the paddles on my lap and got the charts out.

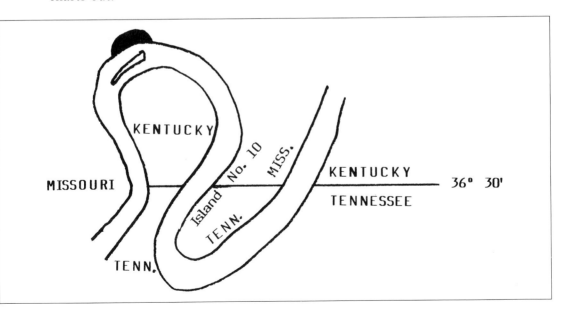

Kentucky Point.

At first it only made things worse but after a few more minutes, I began to understand. The bit to the 'west' of the river constituted inalienable Missouri territory; the bits below 36° 30' and not already grabbed by Missouri were Tennessee; and Kentucky got the rest. Presumably some bureaucrat in Paris, Madrid, or Washington had insisted that his weird instructions were carried out to the letter; unless the river had been playing its cut-off tricks again. In the days when No. 10 was an insular island, might the two bits of Kentucky have been connected? Yes, that was it. I was glad to have solved the mystery – and to be in easy-going Kentucky once more.

Two hours later I came to a barge terminal. There was no sign of a Dodge with red and orange kayaks, so I continued on towards a second terminal, about a mile downstream. Meanwhile, the sun threw aside the last corner of the fog and started impersonating a fiery furnace. But nobody was at the second terminal either. For the second time in twenty-four hours, I found myself hesitating. Afraid of retreating again, I carried on to a third terminal. Another blank. Why did you have to be so keen? I growled to myself.

I tied the kayak up, patted its rump, and started walking. There was a high fence and a high padlocked gate so I cut back to the river and found a lone tow about to cast off. Remembering our encyclopedic friend, I asked if I could have a lift. A deep Deep-Southern 'OK,' so I climbed down forty corroded rungs and jumped aboard.

Feeling very dynamic, I thanked the skipper and alighted at the first terminal. Still no sign of Liam and Tim. Arriving at a workman's shack, I peered in and asked for news. No news. At the gate, the security men wanted to know how I'd got in — Algoa all over again.

I finally located the boys beside the *second* terminal. They'd arrived there five minutes after I'd paddled forlornly past. Five minutes that had cost us $2^1/2$ hours.

The following day my destination was Tomato. In the afternoon, I entered Arkansas and soon went past Island No. 21, mentioned by Twain as, like its younger sister, having 'retired from business as an Island'. A few miles on, I saw evidence of the Corps of Engineers' attempts to tame the river. Massive slabs of reinforced concrete were being laid along the bank and tied together with steel cables as thick as telegraph poles. That'll hold him down, I thought with grim satisfaction.

I rounded the next bend and saw the same set-up after Old Al had passed by. The cables were in shreds, and the slabs were like a half-completed jigsaw for seven-year-olds. I decided it was possibly best not to count on the Engineers any more.

The river kept on going into massive meanders and I felt that I was being led a merry paddle. I had in fact been trying for several weeks to find a sound scientific basis for my choice of route. I had eventually decided that there were four basic possibilities: the middle of the river, the channel, the current, and the shortest route. But I had also concluded that the four routes crossed each other whenever possible, like Mexican desperadoes going through a bad patch or a knock-kneed haggis's sword-dance. But in any case, the real question was which cocktail of permutations and combinations of routes was the best.

One thing seemed certain: the current and the channel deliberately took the long way round every time a short-cut presented itself. I then belatedly realised that there was one additional factor: the tows! I not only had to keep out of their actual path, but also *any* path they might choose to take. This meant that, when more than one tow was in view, at most 2 per cent of the river remained mine to have and to hold. Much of the time, in short, I was keeping near the outside — where it was also less stagnant and snaky. I reckoned I was doing at least 15 per cent more than the official distance.

At one stage that afternoon I had somehow spun off into a mini-Sargasso Sea. On one of the side-channels I spotted a broken tree supporting a whole squadron of snapper turtles. Since the first one on Lake Katonah I had become used to these primitive reptiles with their sheepish group dynamics, and had got into the bad habit of testing the speed of their reactions. Not able to resist doing so once more, I smacked satisfyingly down on the yellow scum. With great obedience, alacrity, and regularity, the snappers started to dive into the water, like paratroopers from an aeroplane. Eventually there was just one brown reptile gamely holding his position. I paddled closer and smacked the water with all my strength.

This time there was a reaction. It was awful. First the head and then the body began to slowly uncoil and straighten out. It became a copperhead. It was about 4 feet away from me, but all I could see were the unwinking eyes and the flattened diamond-shaped head. I watched, frozen with morbid fascination, as it slithered shiftily along towards the end of the trunk and dropped, gracefully and horribly, into the slime below. Then it glided off, leaving a perfect ripple-wake. Back-paddling like I had 100 horsepower under the cockpit, I spun the kayak round in a single telemark. I would never play games with the snappers again. I didn't like the company they kept.

Soon afterwards, I came to the site of Fort Prudhomme, generally reckoned to be about where the French-Canadian explorers Jolliet and Marquette had ended up in 1673. They had performed the amazing feat of canoeing here from Quebec across Lake Michigan and down the

Wisconsin and the 'Conception River' (the Mississippi). Having reached the Ohio, they spent two more weeks paddling 'through a solitude unrelieved by the faintest trace of man'. For whatever reason they turned round somewhere near here, and headed slowly back to Quebec.

When I got there, Tomato proved to be little more than a shack selling everything from peanuts to shotgun shells, but sadly no tomatoes. The owner's son said he knew where Liam was and offered me a ride to the campsite. Only too late did I realise that his 'vehicle' was a chopper motorbike, and his style, Steve McQueen combined with *Deathrace 2000*. I died at least two thousand deaths before we bounded over an exposed root and found Liam, calmly reading amongst the cottonwood trees!

I was exhausted, and after dinner went straight to bed.

IV

The next day was one of the worst I was ever to experience on the Mississippi-Missouri. It started badly, for I awoke with a problem that had been growing during the gruelling descent. The interminable weeks of living together under a few square feet of tent were exacting an ever-heavier toll on all of us. Tempers (and the canvas) were fraying and impatience mounting. After the 'high' in St Louis had come a prolonged sense of frustrated anti-climax and lethargy, exacerbating major character differences between Liam and Tim on the one hand and Bill and myself on the other.

Liam pointed out that the river was quite fast here, and announced that he would meet me at Memphis itself.

'I can't possibly paddle that distance by nightfall.'

He stared at the charts and said it would have to be Benjestown then, 60 miles away. This was the site of one of the worst steamboat disasters on the river, so I tried: 'With a mid-afternoon rendezvous in case of problems?' Liam said he had a lot of things to arrange in Memphis, and he thought we were losing too much time.

'Twelve hours alone on the river can do strange things to your mind. A meeting would be much safer,' I said.

'Bill's putting us up at Memphis University. Imagine. Sheets and a bath. That should keep you going!'

The temptation proved too strong — crafty Liam! In my heart, I knew that had I been in his position, saddled with the unglamorous and monotonous task of organising camp routine, I too would have demanded an all-out push for Memphis. I gave up, heading back out into the sultry, shifting world of the Mississippi. The consequences of my capitulation nearly proved fatal.

After a while, I went past Fort Pillow, another famous Civil War site —

142

Twain says that it was doubtless the only massacre in Anglo-Saxon history since Richard Coeur de Lion (but what about Glencoe and Wounded Knee?). I was hit in the face by the southerly wind, and my speed went right down. An hour passed as the wind increased. Crouching low, I was making about 3 knots — in a 3-knot current. It began to rain.

As three and then four o'clock passed, I realised that I would be paddling through the darkness again. Deep inside, I knew that anybody who kayaked on the Mississippi at night was an idiot. New Orleans was now almost in sight. The circle begun in a darkened library a decade before was nearly complete; but I was feeling less and less brave. I didn't want to fight the river-lord any more. I just wanted to sleep.

The wind fell but so did the darkness. I began weaving carefully across the Mississippi, hoping to avoid an action replay of the towboat roulette. Stopping for a rest, I stayed drifting in the kayak to gain distance. On the near bank appeared the lights of Poker Point. I felt very tempted to head over, but knew I'd have to come back across the river to get to Benjestown.

I decided to play cautious for the last stretch and to keep well to the left of the main channel. After a couple more miles, a headland loomed out. I cleared it and saw the long-awaited fire winking in the distance. My heart gave a leap as I pushed *Lochinvar*'s bow through the gloom towards warmth, companionship, and shelter.

Then, almost imperceptibly, something changed in the rhythm of the river's moving silence. The relentless calm gave way to a whisper and the murmur to a roar. Seeing about 300 feet of rocks piled across the water ahead, I dug down into a right-hand telemark. The river began to snarl. The current was dragging at the bow now — pulling us towards the teeth of the rocks. I tried to ignore the din, and stabbed for the smooth curve at the end of the dyke. The current was still dragging us broadside to catastrophe, as I stabbed even harder. In another life, we might have made it — but not in this one. I spun the bow back parallel, resolving to go into whatever was waiting for me head-on.

*Lochinvar* shot forward like a greyhound unleashed. There *was* a small gap, and the current unerringly sucked me towards it. Then we were there with a crunch, plunging sickeningly through half a metre of oblivion towards surging white waters. We came out of the nosedive, but before I could start to swing the bow towards the main channel, another dam was upon me. With a couple of sharp turns and side-strokes, I managed to avoid some preliminary rocks. Then the current was aiming me straight at the jagged line. Once again I had to hope there would be a hole. There was, and we rushed through with room to spare.

Yet another dam had sprung out of the water ahead of me. 'What *is* this, a canoe-race with hurdles?' I screamed, knowing that I was entirely at the mercy of the fates. I cursed the rendezvous that hadn't been and prayed that, somehow, we would make it. This one had no hole and we didn't. An upthrusting cradle of rocks seized the keel like an electric tin-opener. We hung suspended on empty air for half a second as momentum and friction fought for control. Then the stern kicked crazily at my back, gravity and water slewed treacherously sideways, and we were humped ignominiously into the churned-up water below.

I felt the grind of fibreglass being violated by invisible rocks, sharp and thrusting. For a moment everything went black and surprisingly cold. Water was flooding painfully into my nostrils, telling me to do something. I did. Nearly kicking a hole in my boat, I jerked down and out. Then, gasping for air to dilute my red-hot lungs, I broke surface.

My poor boat seemed to be hardly moving, floating back up in the water like a fluorescent whale. I tried to swim over to her but the paddles kept wanting to twist my arm. At last I seized the forward toggle. Wedging the paddles firmly in the inverted cockpit, I turned on my back. With the sharp-tasting toggle in my mouth, I started swimming back to the dam, the only fixed point in a black, swirling universe. After every three or four strokes I was forced to slow down to catch my breath, and each time, the eager surging bow travelled on and hit me in the face. I gritted my teeth and swam and swam but the dam didn't come an inch closer. This was certainly poker, I thought, but the cards were way too high and wild.

When I had used up all my strength and still not got there, I became very frightened. Clutching the side of the kayak as if about to meet St Peter, I began to shout for Liam with all the strength I could muster. I started trembling with cold, and my hands began to slip. Turning over, I struck out for the dam again. Still it wasn't getting any closer.

At last I understood. I had completely forgotten about the current! It couldn't have been more than half a knot in the lee of the dam, but it was enough to destroy my exhausted attempts. Since I couldn't go back, I now told myself, I would just have to go on.

I tried to right the boat. On the third attempt, she came halfway, and water began to fill the cockpit. Another hard heave, with my legs desperately kicking on nothing, and I got her completely over – whereupon the paddles popped out. Jamming them back in, I heaved myself onto the bucking rear-end and tried to slither towards the centre of gravity. As I edged tremblingly forward, I caught sight of the flames again, mocking me from the safety of the distant bank. They even flared up as I landed noisily back in the water.

I tried again, got the same result, and wondered if I would ever see Memphis. I rolled onto my back and masticated the sharp toggle once more. I began to swim pitifully slowly in the direction of the bank, unable

144

to see where I was going – if anywhere at all – and all the time, *Lochinvar* continued to beat her music on my face. I swam for twenty minutes, not really knowing if I was staying with *Lochinvar* to save her or to save me. Then I put my legs down. Nothing. After ten more minutes, I tried again – and felt soft, squelching mud.

Together we stumbled and crawled out. I looked across the dark waters, beginning to shake uncontrollably. My legs folded like pieces of perished rubber and I dropped onto the soft ground, thinking about those dry sheets. I must have lost consciousness.

After a while, I reluctantly opened my eyes. Careful not to break her back, I turned the kayak over – and watched grimly as three or four gallons flooded out. With horror, I discovered two savage cuts in the rear. Then I surveyed the surrounding 'countryside'. It consisted of nothing but swampy floodland – just the sort of area the cottonmouths liked. That way out was simply too dangerous to try. I gradually persuaded myself that I could bring my craft the half-mile to camp.

Listening for tell-tale noises in the water, I eased my aching frame into the damp cockpit. Aiming the bow on a diagonal course, I was soon well away from the shore – and hidden from the fire.

I had only paddled about 400 yards when I heard another roar in front of me. I craned my head forward, scanning the moving darkness for rocks, for snarled timber, for any sort of clue. There was nothing – just the din of tortured water. Then the surface began dipping ahead, dipping and spinning. 'A bloody whirlpool,' I thought grimly. If it's spinning clockwise, you swing the bow to the left, following it round. Spinning otherwise, you do otherwise. Mentally spinning a coin, I telemarked into the right-hand darkness, praying to God that I'd got it right. I hadn't and it wasn't. The bow veered towards the left-hand paddle like a divining rod, and a giant hand gave me a shove in the back. Then we were well and truly in it, racing across yards of curving water. Switching my weight, I tried to paddle out from the sloping centre. The rear end was awash and didn't seem to respond at all. Not knowing what else to do, I struck out as hard as I could – and capsized.

I search my mind to remember what happened next. It's all a bit of a blur. I think the kayak swung me further into the whirlpool. I must have kicked out of her and grabbed at the toggle, trying to save her. All I remember is a mighty wrench on my arm, forcing me to let go. With all my strength, I swam away. The current was pulling at my legs. It got my right shoe but that was all. Suddenly the roar began dying behind me and I was drifting in slack water.

As I twisted onto my back, I saw *Lochinvar*'s bow swaying at a crazy angle, like an unsteady headstone. She wobbled again, as if still fighting, and slowly sank into the vortex. Then she was gone, as completely as if she had never been. I was left alone, staring insanely at the scene of her last desperate battle.

I reached the shore, God knows how, and found a high eroded bluff. Clutching a muddy root, I didn't even feel relief at my escape, only emptiness. After half an hour of numbed inaction, I wearily struggled up between gnarled trees and Spanish moss and met a mesh of tangled brushwood.

Then it hit me: 'It's finished . . . it's all over.' I'd lost my only sea-boat, my paddles, and, maybe worst of all, any wish to see New Orleans. All I wanted was a nice long sleep, so I curled up in the undergrowth. But the mosquitoes soon objected and several massed attacks later, I got shakily to my feet and ploughed on.

Eventually I came to a steep bayou. Knowing that the swamp was probably crawling with cottonmouths, I started shouting like a madman and ran through the sodden vegetation with all the finesse of a wounded elephant. Something moved as I hit it with my shoe, but it might have been just a stick. I plunged on anyway. The water went waist deep, then relented. I was through.

At the top of the hill, I saw a track and some houses. Soon I was in dry clothing, and the wave of despair which had submerged me began to die. As my benefactors drove me into town, I thought about the events I had been through – and began to grow up. On too many occasions, I had told too many people that I was going to conquer the river but now Benjestown had taught me that you can't beat the North Wall of the Eiger, nor the Pacific in a sailing boat, nor the Mississippi-Missouri in a kayak. One avalanche, one storm at sea, or one misjudged whirlpool, and there's nothing more to be said. Some words flashed through my mind: 'The object is not to win, but not to lose. The only rule is to stay in the game.' I hadn't conquered the river and I never would. But so far I *had* managed to stay in the game – and that was enough to be going on with.

Five minutes later, I was thanking my hosts. I went inside a Hall of Residence and soon lost myself amongst well-dressed students; pretty girls, bustling young men. I had only one shoe but didn't give a damn. They were from a different culture but that didn't matter either. And then I caught sight of Liam, Tim, and Bill. They looked at me, and knew that I had been through a hard time. I looked at them, and knew that I was home.

# *Memphis Blues*

As I was going down an impassive river
I realised the men on shore weren't pulling any more
Loud Redskins had taken careful aim
And naked fixed them to the sacred totem-poles.
(Arthur Rimbaud, *Le Bateau ivre*)

## I

Early next morning – 2 November – Liam and I had it out. He told me he had waited hours at Benjestown – until well after dark. He had then reasoned, erroneously but understandably, that I must have pulled in further upstream so had piled wood on the fire and driven off to meet Bill and Tim in Memphis. At this point, I became livid, my anger perhaps fuelled by the secret knowledge that I had been beaten by the water. I had screamed for Liam but he hadn't heard. 'Your duty,' I shouted, 'is to wait until I come in, whatever time of night or day it is. Otherwise, why the hell have a back-up team?'

'Nick!' he bellowed back. 'You promised you'd get to New Orleans in eight weeks! Your team's stuck by you for *eighteen* weeks. And it's still not finished.'

'Liam, last night, I very nearly blew it, and you weren't there,' I said tiredly. And so it went on, the two old friends slugging it out until they were almost eating each other and all the time the MMCRSKE was steadily disintegrating. The thousands of miles had also taken their toll on Tim. He had but one idea – New Orleans or bust! Bust it might very well be, I thought resignedly.

I walked to the bank of the Mississippi and looked out over the shimmering, mocking expanse. My mind was a wall. I felt nothing, just emptiness, disillusionment, and apathy. And then slowly, in the mirror of

147

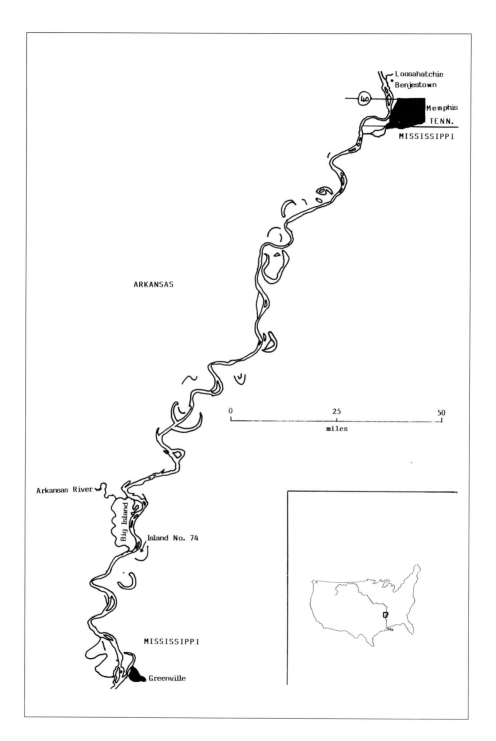

Memphis to Greenville.

the water, I saw recognition. After long minutes, I began to understand the cruel game she was playing. Divide and rule! She was wearing us down, turning us against each other, breeding fatigue and distrust amongst us all. 'New Orleans is only a few hundred miles away. Just a couple of weeks. I'll keep that rendezvous whatever happens . . . if need be alone.' I thought back to Liam's words of comfort during the inland seas. Our team had dwindled since then. As I looked back for Liam, I found him beside me staring out across the great river. The rendezvous at New Orleans . . . but at what price, the price of losing one of my oldest friends and companions-in-arms? We walked back from the river's edge in silence, each I think numbed by the price the M-M was exacting.

Only Bill seemed as eager as ever but then he had been spared the wearing weeks before the expedition properly began. Ironically, he would have provided back-up until the very end, but just had to be in Paris for the 15th. For the last few days, the six would be three. I had a chat with Bill. He offered to stay until the 14th and to prepare the reception in New Orleans in the style to which we were accustomed. But perhaps there was a silver lining? Where our liaison was shakiest was in New York and London – and Bill could be in those two cities at the right time. We finally agreed that he would leave on about the 9th.

Meanwhile, more immediate problems were pressing. I now had no craft fit for the Mississippi – or indeed for an untimely press conference. In the end, we took the Phenix off the truck almost within sight of the journalists. As I paddled unsteadily towards the cameras, I decided to broadcast a suitably hangdog appeal to the people of Memphis requesting aquatic help in a last shot at locating *Lochinvar*. With the appeal out of the way and hangdog back in his kennel, I was asked by one of the journalists for the ninety-ninth time what had made me want to canoe the Mississippi-Missouri. For the ninety-ninth time, I replied that I didn't want to wake up at the age of forty, and realise that I had wasted my youth. 'As Bertrand Russell said, "Youth is a wonderful thing. It's a tragedy it's squandered on the young!"' The journalist's next words cut right through my shield: 'Wasn't it George Bernard Shaw?!'

Afterwards, we read our mail. The first item was an article from the pretty reporter I had met at Cairo. She compared the MMCRSKE to another British canoe expedition in the Americas, currently going down part of the Orinoco River. Fascinated by the news, I made a mental promise that, one day, I would meet its leader, a man called Mike Jones, and compare notes. Sadly I was never to keep it, for he was to die in the Himalayas a few months later while canoeing to rescue one of his team.

The last letter was from the C.R.C., with a cheque for £500 – and the news of a complete publicity blank in Britain. We were very glad for the money but very disappointed at the news. Nevertheless, Bill had been up to something for ages. It was a nightmare trying to communicate across 4000 miles when we had no fixed abode and couldn't afford telephone calls, telegrams, or express letters. That very afternoon, however, he'd scheduled a 'phone-in' for the British media. We drove to the local A.C.S., and I made a quick call to the A.C.S. in New York, telling them that New Orleans for 17 November was now a dead cert.; but they didn't seem very interested. Then Bill and I sat beside the two phones, and waited. And waited . . . . Suddenly, the Atlantic was buzzing with radios, newspapers, and televisions. Bill fielded as many as he could, while I was batting for all I was worth with journalist after journalist. It went on for about twenty-five minutes. Then, just as suddenly, it all stopped and we could breathe again. Never had I spoken so many words in so few minutes and never did I want to do so again!

The rest of the day was time off. We drove to the mansion called Graceland where Elvis Presley had lived, and died, only weeks before. Scores of beautiful girls were keeping vigil in front of the high gates. Through the shrubbery we caught a glimpse of a colonial-style house with white pillars but that was enough for me. Any more would have killed a whole part of my youth. Songs like 'Heartbreak Hotel', 'Blue Suede Shoes', or 'Jailhouse Rock' had been part of my under-the-bedclothes universe for so long that exposure to reality might have done them irreparable harm. In the evening we were also made conscious of the musical heritage of Memphis. Bill had met a lovely girl called Debbie Matkin. She kindly invited us to a blues concert in Beale Street. As we were waiting, she told us about Memphis, Tennessee, the intersection of so many myths and dreams. In 1795, it was the site of a battle between the Spanish owners and the United States, over navigation rights on the Mississippi; the Americans triumphed again and gained access down to the Gulf. In the early nineteenth century, it was the point where the notorious El Paso trail crossed the river. In Twain's day, it became a major railway centre, with a rosary of six trunk lines leading to all parts of the country. At the beginning of this century, it was the home of W.S. Handy, the 'Father of the Blues' – the first man to write down the five-note blues scale using the seven-note 'Western' system, and the author of such classics as 'St Louis Blues', 'Memphis Blues', and 'Beale Street Blues'. And in 1968, it was the place where Dr Martin Luther King, Nobel prizewinner, was callously shot down.

Bill asked about the Mississippi, and Debbie ran off a whole string of titles, including 'Deep River', 'Rollin' down the River', 'Roll on, Mississippi', 'Moonlight on the River', and 'Darkness on the Delta'. She pointed out that even that wrong-side-of-the-blanket third cousin of the blues, Bing Crosby, sang his 'Mississippi Mud'.

I asked what the Deep South was really like, knowing that if Cairo is the geographical gateway to the South, Memphis is usually considered the historical frontier town. Debbie told us that from here on, we would be in Ku Klux Klan country. Until very recently, school manuals talked of the 'superiority of the White race'.

'I remember when the first non-White student went to the University of Oxford [Mississippi]. It was under Kennedy, and they had to send the storm-troopers in! In the South, 'The War' is not the '42–'45 one, nor the '17–'18 one, but the Civil War. Abraham Lincoln is still disliked; and because he was a Republican, many Whites still vote Democrat . . . .' The music had begun, and we really began to soak up the atmosphere, trying to spin out the beers Debbie had bought us. Only too soon, it was all over. We thanked Debbie, and she and Bill went off hand in hand, leaving Liam, Tim, and me feeling very much like gooseberries.

Feeling very lonely, I phoned Cathy in Nebraska. The connection was bad and it was as if we were talking across a million miles. I didn't mention Benjestown or the difficult time I was going through. But I felt glad just to talk to her.

The following morning, I started to pluck up courage to use the Phenix again. I couldn't help thinking that, instead of raising the expedition from the fire, it might just plunge it down into the depths. In any case, my speed would be seriously reduced . . . . The phone rang and I gratefully put off the moment of truth. A kind gentleman called George was offering to help look for *Lochinvar*.

We passed a huge road sign with the incredible message, 'SHOOTING IS ILLEGAL ON THE HIGHWAY'. After launching on a little river called the Loosahatchie, we zoomed up and down rather at random, scouring every backwater, channel, and mudbank. Eventually we headed back up to the three pile dikes – in the sparkling sun they looked quite ordinary – then downstream again. We found two islands I hadn't even seen in the dark, went past the rendezvous point and carried on a long way down; then started up again. The straw of hope now seemed too slight for even a drowning man to grasp; and even the sunshine seemed grey.

Suddenly lynx-eyed Liam gave a cry and pointed towards the far-away shore. Some sort of browny-orange object was barely visible in the reeds. I thought at first that it was just a fibreglass shard but at 300 yards I knew that it was *Lochinvar*, lying darkly under the water.

My eyes went out of focus, as I felt a lump rising in my throat. We had found my old companion, perhaps terribly wounded, but still in the land of the living. Tim and I dropped into the water, and carefully freed her from the evil-smelling growth. Emptying several gallons out, we laid her across the back of the powerboat. The rear hatch had been pulled off, but was still hanging by its cord – the launching spot had proved incredibly prophetic! The two 4-inch gashes at the back were still there but that seemed to be the only significant damage.

We spent another hour combing the marshes for the paddles; but they seemed to be lost for ever. Fortunately we had a spare pair – they were quite a bit heavier but I too had become quite a bit stronger. We took one last look at the desolate reeds and turned in a large circle. I asked Liam and Tim to repair the kayak straight away, so that it could dry during the night. Then relief and exhaustion caught up with me and, after an obligatory half-hour recording, I fell gratefully asleep.

Too soon came an unmistakeable knock on the door and before long we were heading back to Benjestown. As the canoe was unloaded, I glanced at the repair work. It gave me a nasty shock. The unbearable Southern humidity had prevented the resin from setting properly. The coats of fibreglass had lifted from one of the gashes, leaving just a razor-thin covering that let the light through. The boat was completely unseaworthy.

On the spot, I applied another coat myself and then we settled down, waiting for it to dry. At 3 pm we were still waiting. We sank all ideas of a launch that day and drove hell-for-leather into Memphis, trying to give vent to the frustration which was rapidly becoming terminal. Bill went off to see Debbie. The rest of us passed the time trying not to think about them.


## II

Early the following morning, I headed for Benjestown for the fourth time but now with a canoe that would float. Very cautiously, I paddled down an estuary and into the long-exposure world of the Mississippi. But I needn't have worried. *Lochinvar* had completely forgotten the nightmarish events – or if she hadn't, she was too proud to say so. As I paddled into Memphis itself, I was touched to see Bill and Debbie waving from the Hernando de Soto Bridge.

Then Interstate 40 and Tennessee were behind me and I was in Mississippi State. I looked at the map, encouraging myself that it went all the way down to the Gulf of Mexico, although it has to leave the river to do so. In fact, I realised, the Mississippi never really goes into Mississippi, but just creeps along the edge.

As I paddled on, I saw increasing signs of segregation and poverty. There were dozens of 'shanty-boats' under the cottonwood trees: miserable shacks on platforms, with a door, two windows, a tin smokestack, and barefoot children playing everywhere. The only visible

The faithful old Dodge.

difference from Uncle Tom's Cabin was the leaky skiffs for Saturday-night sorties.

About a dozen miles later, I came to the site of one of the worst steamboat disasters: 1050 people had died. This whole stretch of river was in fact notorious for its disasters, with 5000 people killed on it in the fifty years following 1811 (when the first steamboat went down from Pittsburgh to New Orleans, via an earthquake which opened up the banks). After a catastrophe the replacement boat inherited the name of its defunct companion, and so it continued with each new boat, down to *Zebulon Pike 7* – not the best of advertisements, you would have thought. Charles Dickens insisted on having a cabin at the very front, as far away from the boilers as possible but such caution was the exception. Passengers continued to flow recklessly onto the 'palaces on paddle-wheels', the 'floating wedding-cakes', the 'swimming volcanoes', as if positively stimulated by the danger.

153

One of the reasons why the boats didn't last long was that men were frequently paid to sit on the safety valves to make them go faster. But the main reason was that they were racing against each other. Boats that won races attracted passengers; ones that didn't, didn't.

The most famous race was between the *Lee* and the *Natchez* from New Orleans to St Louis. The *Lee*'s captain spent weeks beforehand, stripping down doors and rigging, and lining up refuelling points so he could touch and go. He won in the incredibly short time of 3 days 18 hours and 14 minutes.

Also on this stretch was a field where a local farmer was supposed to have ploughed a rich furrow. One day in 1891, his plough hit a piece of wood. He dug deeper, and found it was the top of a mast. According to the story, digging at night, he then secretly discovered a whole ship, the *Drennan White*, as well as its safe, which had contained $100,000 in the 1850s. He apparently went away to get help to open it – and came back to a flood. Everything had gone. The mischievous Mississippi had struck again.

Some time later, I got to the bank where the Mississippi-Missouri was first seen by a White man, Hernando de Soto, and my mind went reeling back.

It was 1541, only fifty years after Columbus had sailed off into the blue unknown. Amazing rumours were coming out of the new land. They included a persistent tale about a place in the north where even the plates were made of gold. De Soto was quite inclined to believe them for the very good reason that he'd already found one El Dorado. Then he had been under Pisarro's infamous orders; now he wanted to find one for himself.

He also had another aim: to find a short-cut from Europe to Cathay (China). This was probably not quite so stupid as it seems today, since the information at his disposal was in fact pretty mixed. From Magellan's story of a strait in South America, the academic geographers had deduced that there just *had* to be a strait in North America as well. Other sources of 'knowledge' included maps showing camels, ostriches, and a giraffe; not forgetting the accounts of an Alfonso Alvarez de Pineda and a Cabeza de Vaca. Alfonso claimed to have discovered a major river on the Gulf of Mexico, which he called the Rio del Espiritu Santo (River of the Holy Ghost). He'd sailed up it for about 20 miles, observing a rich, beautiful and healthy countryside, dotted with forty fine towns. Cabeza, for his part, had been sailing on the Gulf, and had somehow discovered that the water was good to drink. Amazed, he traced the water back to its origin at the mouth of a huge river. History doesn't record what de Soto made of their accounts, with their pleasant countryside and drinkable water, but from my own experience, I thought that they were both fibbers!

154

De Soto landed in Florida in 1539 with 515 men and 237 horses. After several days of hacking and pushing into the virgin forests, they found a group of semi-naked savages, who all fled, except one. This man threw himself on the ground, shouting unintelligible words – and crossing himself! At first the patrol thought there'd been a Second Coming in the New World. Only slowly did they realise that the man was actually a fellow Spaniard, who had got lost from a previous expedition. Perhaps Alfonso had been telling the truth after all.

After recounting all the latest news, the army set to again. They struggled through swamps, over deserts, across rivers, over mountains, through forests. After two years of trying, all they had found was a river bigger than any yet recorded by a White man. Some two miles wide, its dirty chocolate waters formed a chaos of whirlpools, floating tree-trunks, and crumbling banks. Only one name was possible for such a disaster: the Rio Grande!

Six weeks later, they had built barges, and were able to ferry across. They struggled on again, through forests, over mountains, across rivers, and so on . . . . By this time they had crossed Arkansas and most of Kansas. De Soto crossed Coronado's path somewhere in the wilds and thus narrowly missed depriving Stanley and Livingstone of one of their best lines!

Still there was no gold, and no China either. In the end, they decided they might as well just go home. But de Soto caught 'fever' (malaria?) and, after muttering 'Cathay! Cathay!' (Cathy? Cathy?), expired on the very banks of the Rio Grande. His companions laid him to rest in the water itself. The discoverer and the river were united for ever.

Moscoso, the new leader, decided to put the brown monstrosity to good use. The only problem was that they didn't know whether it went down to the Atlantic or through the back of beyond to the Sea of Cathay (where, fickly, they no longer wanted to go). They decided to risk it anyway and spent the winter building more boats. In March (1543), the Rio Grande became grander still, flooding the whole countryside. Then they were attacked by Indians. They finally got away on 2 July, in a motley collection of coracles, rafts, and dugouts. Although they were afraid of cataracts, they could do nothing except keep their fingers crossed and their ears open.

In fact it was again the Indians who caused problems. Resenting this foreign intrusion, they sent 200 nifty war-canoes at them, each one with a row of archers, a row of rowers, and a man who alternately shouted 'Heave-ho!' and 'On the count of three . . . .' Moscoso sent out his quickest dugouts. The Indians were amazed by their coats-of-armour but soon retaliated: they simply capsized the dugouts, reuniting the unfortunate

Spaniards with their leader on the bottom. After that, Moscoso left as quickly as he could.

They carried on down, despite various other problems: they lacked fresh food as the banks were often impenetrable for days on end; their hands had blisters on the blisters; their mosquito bites were so bad that they didn't recognise each other in full daylight; men deserted and were never heard of again; they had nothing to wear; and they were tortured by thirst. This last fact may seem surprising on the biggest river in the known world but the problem was, they had to wait hours for the silt to settle – 'even then, the lukewarm liquid was gritty and foul to the taste'.

In the end, after four years and 1800 miles, less than half the expedition got back alive. As I surveyed the turgid flood all around me, I sympathised with their problems. I wouldn't even have tried to wash myself in it.

I got to camp at nightfall, which was just as well, since a heavy fog was coming down. Meanwhile, Liam and Tim had nearly been shot in a valiant rearguard action against an irate landowner. He had been swearing and brandishing his loaded shotgun for ages but Liam had been bravely gaining time by explaining, in deliberately lengthy Irish fashion, that they *had* spent a long time looking for the mansion-house, but since it was *such* a large plantation . . . . For the first time, we were in the presence of an authentic Southern accent but somehow it didn't seem as melodious or as slow as the guidebooks said. With no other choice, we backtracked out of the forbidden land and went to pick up Bill, who had hitched down from Memphis. Then back to the pea-soup world, where the boys had to put up the tent once more. They were rewarded, however, by Bill's news. The man he'd got a lift from shared a monthly feast with his business colleagues; it was tonight and we were invited!

A rough shave, a rougher track, and soon we were standing in front of a typical Southern house, all wrought-iron balconies and authentically knotty vegetation. There was a huge door, and an immaculate table. Sixty eyes fixed on us. Bill scanned the faces anxiously. No sign of his friend. A hurried explanation followed. 'Hey! That's Jack for you. Always late. Make yourselves at home boys. It's a maaghty pleasure to meet y'awl!' It was great to be in the slow and melodious land of Southern hospitality. We told them about Guy Fawkes and had a riotous evening.


### III

The morrow brought a splitting hangover and a troubled conscience. I was 5 miles downstream from my landing point, but since there was a shotgun between me and my manifest destiny, I simply launched from the campsite.

156

What bothered me more was another piece of Bill's news. A.C.S. Memphis had insisted on being paid for the call I had made to A.C.S. New York! The sum was pretty insignificant, two or three dollars, but that made the principle even more ridiculous. Since Kansas City, our publicity for cancer research had spread from coast to coast – all of it high-impact and at peak viewing-times. It would have cost them a fortune to attempt to do it themselves. I only hoped that the actual treatment financed by the A.C.S. wasn't run in such a constipated fashion – otherwise I really pitied the people who got cancer in America. Poking frustratedly at the water, I paddled glumly on.

Soon it was time for lunch and I climbed up the levee, looking for the boys. I found myself on the edge of my first cotton-field – rows of little round bushes covered with little round balls, just like in my faded school-books. I began singing the well-known song:

> . . . in them old cotton-fields back home.
> It was down in Louisiana
> Just about a mile from Texarkana . . . .

Looking at my map, I discovered that the songwriter's geographical sense was even worse than mine: Texarkana manages to be in both Texas and Arkansas but nowhere near Louisiana. Still, I asked myself, what else does rhyme?

As I paddled meditatively on, the water was chewed up ahead of me and two rifle-shots rang out. Maybe shooting wasn't illegal on the waterway? I whipped my head around – and saw with great relief that it was Tim. He said he'd been shouting at me for ages and had 'hit on this as the only way of catching my eye' . . . !

That evening, I had another bad fright. A towboat came forging into sight, only about 100 yards from 'my' bank. By this time, I could judge speeds pretty well, so I nipped across his bows and hugged the dark shore while waiting for him to pass. But the mass of juddering iron just ploughed nearer, with his revolving, luminous eyes shining high above me. He was almost on top of me now and, incredibly, closing the distance all the time. 'They always keep near the edge,' I muttered nervously into my life jacket. 'But he'll turn pretty soon.'

The massive craft thundered alongside me, shutting out half the world. He was so close that I couldn't even see the superstructure. Suddenly, the water began to churn and rise below my keel as the juggernaut lurched bodily sideways, squeezing the water from the river. In a second I had rammed the kayak onto the rocks. While still dragging it out, I was hit by a wave of water and then the ghastly, grinding noise of metal on stone. The massive engines shuddered to a lugubrious halt, a deafening stillness hit the Mississippi.

A few shaky minutes later, I clambered along to survey the damage. The towboat was stuck on the rocks – stuck pretty fast. I heard low voices and saw two red glows way above me. Shouting up, I asked as casually as I could if there was any particular reason for their presence. The left-hand glow was joined by a flashlight who eventually picked me out. Soon all was made dazzlingly clear. The skipper had come in to allow room for another tow.

'But why did he hit the shore?'

'Oh, that's normal,' explained the other glow, which was expanding and contracting like a sea-anemone on heat. 'That way, the rocks hold the tow in place, and we save power. Them barges sure can take it. They's as tough as hell!' The cigarettes had other things to do. Thanking the darkness above me, I headed back to the long-suffering *Lochinvar*.

As I paddled out the following morning the river seemed to continually show off, first a left turn, then a right, then a left, all in perfect rhythm. Twain had called it 'the crookedest river in the world,' 'a long, pliant apple paring'. For my part, the river made me think of a ski-instructor demonstrating Stenmarks. I was very glad to see that, like all show-offs, she was occasionally hoisted with her own petard: several times she had tried to turn too sharply and ended up in a demeaning ox-bow lake. Twain also discusses the cut-offs on the Lower Mississippi, pointing out that between 1722 and 1883 they had shortened her by 207 miles. If this carries on, he wrote, any fool 'can see that 742 years from now, the Lower Mississippi will be only $1^3/4$ miles long, and Cairo and New Orleans will have joined their streets together, and be plodding comfortably along under a single mayor'!

At eleven o'clock, I came to two more landmarks. First there was 'Island' No. 74, another of Twain's border anomalies. As he told it, Arkansas claimed 'up to the centre of the river', Mississippi, 'to the channel'. In between was 74 that paid no taxes at all. I suppose it was lucky it didn't declare independence and war on Mexico at the same time! It was now situated on Napoleon Bend – all that was left of the proud town of Napoleon, swept away one night by the river. *La Grande Rivière* taking her revenge for the sale of Louisiana, I mused . . . .

But I was immediately interrupted by the mouth of the Arkansas River. Getting out the map, I marvelled at the wide connections it had. It had come down from Arkansas, Oklahoma, Colorado, and Kansas. It had competed for the melting snow of the Central Rockies with the Colorado and the Rio Grande (the little one). It brought water down from the

'Canadian River' and from Las Vegas, New Mexico. Its closest neighbours had names like Santa Fe and Los Alamos. I realised that I had invented a new method of studying American geography – by placing every town and state in relation to my friend and foe.

I would never be able to watch a Western again without a map beside me.


## IV

That evening I was exhausted once more. I started telling Tim about my ski-instructor idea, but as he explained: 'The alluvial plain here is 50 miles wide. So the river has more room to mess around in than is good for it.' The boys had met two members of the Corps of Engineers, who'd told them some pretty horrifying stories about floods on the Mississippi. I surreptitiously switched on the tape-recorder, as my three friends outdid each other offering up their own flood of statistics, literary references, human anecdotes, and corrosive comments.

The Mississippi River was low at the moment, a mere half-million cubic feet a second, but in the past, it hadn't always been so amenable. Especially disastrous years were 1858, 1862, 1867, 1882, 1884, 1890, 1897, 1903, 1912, 1913, 1922, 1927, 1937, 1951, and 1972. After each new catastrophe, the Engineers had built the levees still higher, promising that, this time, there was absolutely no danger. Nevertheless, the inhabitants of New Orleans continued to build their cemeteries on the highest ground. And in fact, each time Twain's prognosis had proved correct: 'Ten thousand River Commissions, with the mines of the world at their back, cannot tame that lawless stream.' The levees had merely spaced out the fiascos – but then, when it did flood, you really knew about it!

The 1927 flood was a particularly bad one. After heavy rain – 240 cubic miles, or 40 million million cubic feet – the Mississippi rose 30 feet. It flowed up most of its tributaries, including the Ohio. But life carried on pretty much as usual, with the huge steamboats suspended 20 ft above the ground, like teatrays in the sky.

Then the Mississippi rose another 20 feet.

'Crevasses' began to spout in the levees, despite desperate sandbagging by tens of thousands of men. Some of them happened naturally, but some were made by farmers on the opposite side from their own land. They were impossible to stop once started; and like Topsy, they just grew and grew. Many of them made deep growls like packs of wild animals. Such was their awesome power that they gouged out huge 'blue holes' (or 'blew holes') – lunar craters where soil, trees, concrete, tempered steel – everything – was swept away like straws in the wind.

When the Mississippi-Missouri had spent its anger, it had become a sluggishly moving sea, 90 miles wide and 1000 miles long – a swathe that would have stretched from London to Africa. To get a real impression of the awful size, it is perhaps best to read Twain's description of his travel over an earlier flood: 'League after league, and still league after league, it pours its chocolate tide along [. . .]; and so the day goes, the night comes, and again the day [. . .] majestic, unchanging sameness of serenity, repose, tranquility, lethargy, vacancy – symbol of eternity.'

Two hundred and forty-six people had lost their lives, 700,000 their homes, and New Orleans itself was saved only by dynamiting the levees further up. President Hoover called the flood 'the greatest economic catastrophe in the history of the United States'.

The flood found echoes in Bessie Smith's 'Backwater Blues' and 'Muddy Water (A Mississippi Moan)'. Even T.S. Eliot speaks of 'a strong brown god – sullen, untamed and intractable', 'almost forgotten by the dwellers in the cities – ever, however, implacable, keeping his seasons and rages, destroyer, reminder of what men choose to forget'. He was also a local and seems to have known what he was talking about.

The following day the river was still going into its impossible meanders, making the choice of route a constant problem. Sometimes I followed the outside round with the tows bigger than supertankers, feeling stupid, and sometimes I cut through the sullen bayous, feeling scared.

I was extremely glad to get to camp by dusk. This was Bill's last night and he served a superb dinner. Then, well into the night, he and I discussed co-ordination plans. First, we talked finances but here we were very brief, as there just weren't any. Bill would have to pay the publicity and living expenses out of his own pocket, together with the fare from Paris to London and back again. Also, Tuttle hadn't produced the wages he owed Bill – I cursed the man then for his refusal to pay up.

We also talked about the end. It may seem a bit surprising but I still hadn't decided where I was going – where the expedition would finish! Since St Louis, New Orleans had been my only goal, the mental machinery that I used to get me through to the next stroke. Only slowly had the realisation come that the river continued after that, for another inexorable 110 miles. We discussed the Delta. It was one of the most dangerous regions of North America, with swamps, snakes, alligators, and fast-moving ocean liners. Bill said it would be tricky taking a canoe through America's busiest shipping lanes.

There was possibly one let-out, he continued, or rather outlet: some of the water went directly from New Orleans into the ocean, avoiding the Delta altogether. I looked at the maps and saw that it was a man-made canal. I told Bill that cutting corners in this way might cause me sleepless

160

nights in twelve years' time, with haunting visions of a canoeless Delta.

But Bill had another card up his sleeve: the strange case of the Atchafalaya. Just before Baton Rouge, some of the Mississippi left the mainstream and cut its own impatient way down to the Gulf, saving 40 miles in the process. If it could, why couldn't I? The outlet was entirely natural this time. In 100 years, *all* the water would be going that way.

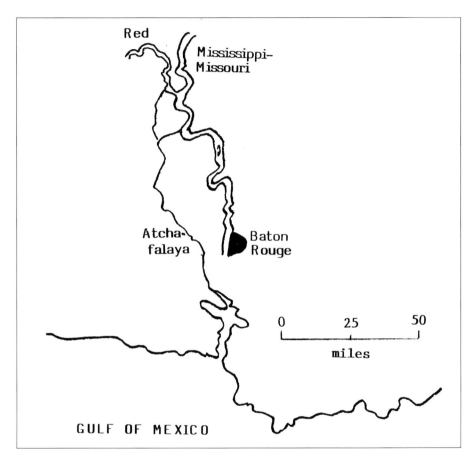

The Strange Case of the Atchafalaya.

I told my friend I couldn't put my objection in words, except that it *couldn't* be put into words. 'Nick Francis, on behalf of N.B.C., were you the first man to canoe the Mississippi?'

'Well, er, no, actually. I did the Missouri-Mississippi-Atchafalaya.'

'Bless you!'

No self-respecting canoeist could possibly let such tongue-twisters loose on the poor public.

161

In the end, we decided that, for the media – and the A.C.S. – the official end would be in New Orleans. But for my own satisfaction, to have come down from the Rockies and never see the Gulf of Mexico . . . . I swore I would try everything this side of suicide to see the Mississippi-Missouri through to its end.

We took a last stroll down beside the river and turned in. A few hours later, Bill said how much he would have liked to stay, and wished me the very best of luck for the last few days. As we said goodbye, I knew it was going to be very different without him. He had become almost indispensable as researcher and Publicity Agent. But he was also my companion and confidant.

And then I was alone on the Mississippi, a feeling of emptiness welling up inside me. Three images flashed across my mind: the meal when we had demolished the two girls' left-overs; the aeroplane zooming in over the hills with a familiar smile in the window; and the rapids where, the day after his arrival, my friend had unhesitatingly dived into the maelstrom. Bill and I had shared a great deal.

I would miss him in the French Quarter at New Orleans.

# *Journey to New Orleans*

Never, perhaps, in the records of nations, was there such
unvarying and unmitigated crime as the history of the
turbulent and bloodstained Mississippi.
(Capt. Frederick Marryat, R.N.)

## I

That morning, 9 November, I was only 450 miles from New Orleans. Just
before lunch time, a good wind pushed me towards a very large island,
and I took my usual sneaky route along the inside. The water died, the
maps came out, and I realised that lunch was on the other side. There was
nothing that could be done, so I just headed for the 'fail-safe' rendezvous
(a recent innovation). By the time I got there, I was eating my kayak.

In the evening, Tim stayed very quiet, running over the pages of his
diary again and again. Suddenly he looked up and announced: 'We've
eaten mince and tatties twenty-eight times since Three Forks.' There and
then, we resolved never to again. Liam pointed out that our diet of eggs,
peanut butter, and bread was enough to put white hairs on a teenage
health-freak's head. But, surprisingly, there was not a day's illness between
the lot of us. Not even the toothache that is meant to plague every
expedition. We all looked tanned, lean, and hungry.

In my case, however, not everything was what it seemed. From my waist
up, it did appear that I'd followed a whole string of Charles Atlas courses.
But from my belt down, an undernourished grasshopper would have
looked better. Also, the two end fingers of my left hand were increasingly
painful and that whole side of my hand was white through lack of use,
threatening to go the way of the orang-outang's tail.

I was back in the water again before dawn. As the light came up, it
revealed a surreal world. Away from the brushwood of the bank, the

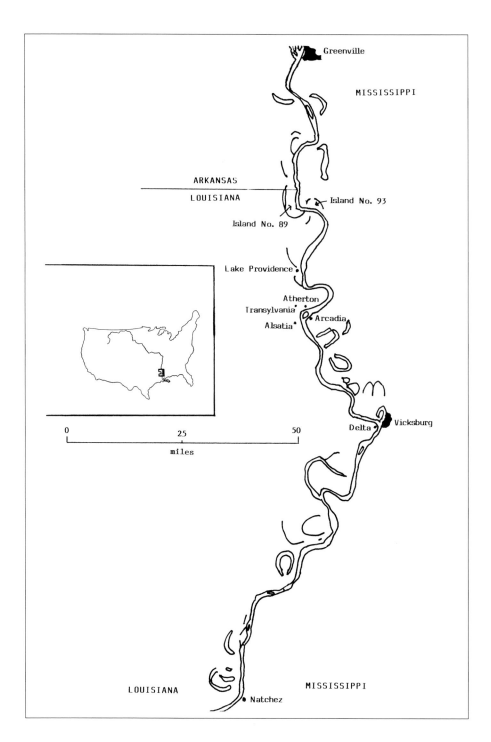

Greenville to Natchez.

164

Mississippi lay in a silent blanket of mist. Everything was blurred like an old film. There was no metallic hum, and no mechanical vibration, just the soft water-sound of the kayak. I inhaled the peace that nature was offering, until it lay deep inside me. For that long moment, I belonged to the Mississippi, and she belonged to me.

I paddled reluctantly on, but soon a headwind began to wake the river up. As the last wreath danced away, I went past 'Island' No. 89 and then No. 93. The errors in the numbering system were on my side now, I decided with glee – not like those horrid highways. Nevertheless, I felt a bit disappointed not to have seen No. 92, as it had been a favourite in my Twain-reading days. No. 92 was situated in Arkansas, where no liquor taxes were paid, but where trade was very slow. A farsighted man opened a whisky-shop on it, it jumped over the river to nestle snugly beside Mississippi, and he became a very rich man.

Suddenly I jumped as well. 'Island No. 89 (Arkansas–Louisiana– Mississippi)'! I'd been in Louisiana and never noticed. I'd had a glimpse of paradise and then the river had whipped it away from under my nose. I seriously considered turning round, but before I could make up my mind, my beloved, my exquisite, my infinitely sought-after Louisiana came flooding back. The countryside, to be honest, didn't look much different but the name alone was powerful enough to set off in my mind a seething collection of memories and hopes, dreams and desires. For a long while, I was a loyal subject of Louis XIV.

After eleven hours, I started looking for Atherton. I reached the next bend but the boys weren't there – nor at the next. My paddling slowed right down, as doubt entered my mind. I decided that Atherton must have been that rather grotty-looking village on the right bank. I turned dejectedly round and started rowing doggedly against the current. (At least the wind was on my side now.)

After a desultory and darkening half-hour, I heard the sound of a big powerboat. Twisting round, I started waving my paddles like a wild man. The occupant roared over and asked if I was in trouble, or just plumb crazy. I enquired in turn if he had seen my friends.

'No. I'll give you a lift up to Providence though. It's only fifteen minutes away.'

'Are you sure?'

'Yeah, it's not more than 5 miles – look for yourself.' I was horrified. I'd turned round 13 miles short. What a mistake to make!

Lake Providence proved to be a long lean bayou, cunningly hidden from any canoeists in the mainstream. As I looked at the cold dank backwater with its motley collection of soggy boats, I remembered Twain's words: 'Lake Providence is the first distinctly Southern-looking town you come to

[with its] shade-trees hung with venerable grey-beards of Spanish moss.'
Who was he trying to kid?

I thanked my friend, ran over to a man trying to escape in a pick-up, and asked if he was heading downriver. He was only too happy if I joined him. For over an hour, we criss-crossed a maze of interlocking levees. At last a Dodge appeared silhouetted against the starlit backcloth of the Mississippi. After a progressively more Schlitz-y hour he left us to mincemeat and potatoes – our resolution hadn't lasted long! Then it started to pour. We played catch-the-drip and imagine-we-were-in-Gerard's-mobile-home.

I remarked that we were camped exactly halfway between Alsatia and Transylvania. Liam, not to be outdone, replied that Arcadia, directly opposite, was where two callous mass-murderers were blown to bits in 1943 – their names were Bonnie and Clyde! As a result, I spent a distinctly un-Arcadian night. I dreamed of wet German shepherds rising from the sodden grave only to be attacked by their sheepdog-vampires, fangs dripping.

In the morning, I was driven straight back upriver. When I got into camp again, delicious Liam-inspired sausages and eggs were waiting for me. What made me feel even better was the realisation that we were only 30 miles from Vicksburg and 368 miles from New Orleans. We were going to win!

An hour or two later, I came ashore for a quick rest on the sand. I hadn't been there long when I noticed a pair of tracks leading to the water's edge. Strolling over, I examined them more closely. They were about as wide as a motorbike tyre, but smooth and shallow, and gently undulating. I sprinted along to my boat, and took off at a rate of knots. The tracks were those of water snakes, either copperheads or cottonmouths – the exact species was unimportant.

Much later I went past a hamlet called Delta. Twain claims that it used to be 3 miles below Vicksburg but was now 2 miles above. Then Vicksburg itself arrived, and was gone in a mere flash. I felt very sad, as the name had meant so much to me for so long. The siege of Vicksburg itself had come to bore me a little – in the last week alone, two different windbags had refought it for my benefit. What interested me more were Grant's previous attempts to get his fleet past the city.

At first, he had tried digging a by-pass canal, but floods had washed away his weeks of effort. He had then loaded his gunboats to the gunwales, and tried to work his way round – via the bayous! Swamps, tree trunks, and rampant vegetation slowed him down to less than 1 mph. After a few days, he found it all just too sticky, and decided to turn round. The problem was, he couldn't. In the end, the proud ocean-going fleet had to reverse awkwardly out, sweating and swearing, and Grant was almost relieved of his command.

As dusk came down, I gave thanks that I at least had a reliable reverse gear.

II

That evening, the rain poured and poured – even inside the tent. We left it to its Chinese-torture rhythms, and drove back into Vicksburg. I wanted to visit the huge model of the Mississippi-Missouri system built by the Corps of Engineers for testing changes. It was closed. To console ourselves, we booked into a cheap hotel. Then we went out for a cheap meal, with cheap wine. It nearly broke us, but it was probably worth it in gained mileage the following morning.

Much of this was spent on the inside of an island which then decided it might prefer to be a promontory. I'd forgotten my maps and, after two further miles of rainy and current-less paddling, wasn't sure whether I'd ever see the Mississippi again. Climbing onto the bank confused me more, so I climbed back down. Then I spotted two long black snakes gliding in hideous harmony through the stagnant water beside me. Water-mocassins. I paddled cautiously on.

Soon, however, I detected a very slight current. The bayou's banks came to a disagreement, turned their backs on each other, and went their indifferent ways. Minutes later, I was back in the bosom of the Mississippi – pockmarked and wrinkled, but I was glad to be there all the same.

I had come out opposite another big island; meaning that it was too late to go outside it. In any case, the inside had quite a fast current. I soon found out that there was a pile-dyke all the way across. Undeterred, I pulled up and did a quick recce. The rocks were completely covered. Fixing a spot where the drop was less than a foot, I headed for it. A big splash and I had shot the dyke. If only it was always this easy.

Deciding to take no more short cuts, I soon began to gobble up the miles. I was about halfway through Piaf when I passed two ordinary-looking logs drifting lazily with the current. Then I heard a most extraordinary noise. Unbelievably, incredibly, my music was being answered by the increasingly tinkly notes of a honky-tonk piano. Then, trundling rapidly into view, came the *Delta Queen*, perhaps the most famous paddleboat ever to plough the M-M. I watched in fascination as the ancient sternwheeler came towards me, her yards and yards of copper shining in the sunlight. A couple of hundred people were lining the side and waving.

The black and yellow funnel let off a couple of friendly blasts and then

167

Resplendent *Delta Queen* on Lower Mississippi.

she was on her way up to St Louis and St Paul. I swivelled round. Above the paddlewheel was the pianist, resplendent in a red jacket, but now I could hear nothing but the steady thresh-thresh.

The boat was now about opposite the logs. Suddenly with a violent splash they up-ended and then were gone. I was in a state of shock. That was as close to a pair of alligators as I was ever likely to get.

I rowed on, humming the Creedence Clearwater Revival song:

Cleaned a lot of plates in Memphis,
Humped a lot of dames down in New Orleans,
But I never saw the good side of the city
Till I hitched a ride on the *Riverboat Queen*.

Two hours later, night fell over the Mississippi like a big blue blanket. My rendezvous was meant to be at Natchez, only 8 miles away, but I was feeling more and more worn out. With New Orleans only 270 miles away, I didn't want to blow it.

I drifted in. On the other side of the levee was a floodlit cotton-field, with scores of men working beside a huge machine that seemed half vacuum cleaner, half combine harvester. Keeping well away from the operating end, which was sucking in everything in sight, I asked the driver when they planned to finish. He was Black, like everybody else in the field. 'Heh man! We're-a-finishin' in two minutes' tahm!' he said, giving the proboscis a tremendous yank. 'It'd be a maaghty big pleasure t' take you

168

into Natchez!' My grin became nearly as wide as his.

Soon we were squashed into a twenty-year-old Chevvie pick-up. To the accompaniment of mad whoops and cries of 'C-r-razy, man' we bumped our springy way across an unlit maze. 'Heh Nick,' said Earl, 'why don't Aa take you back fer lil Southern Comfort.' Soon we pulled up beside an enormous caravan, where he proudly showed me snapshots of his wife and daughters. The Southern Comfort turned into a large steak washed down by bourbon. Earl then insisted on driving me back into Natchez, even though he'd put in a twelve-hour day ('Aa said Aa would, 'n' Aa will').

We drove past pompous mansion after pompous mansion, all gleaming columns and neoclassical friezes. Helped by the alcohol, I could envisage the interiors: fragile porcelain and stern top-hatted gentlemen devouring fragile beauties playing 'uptight' pianos. But Earl was saying, 'There y'are Nick. Good ol' Natchez Bridge,' and my vision was gone with the wind. I gave him all my thanks for his company and generosity, and then he drove off into the river of headlights. I was left with the realisation that, at the age of twenty-five, I had never been in the home of a Black person before.

There was no sign of Liam or Tim, so I went into the Ramada Inn and phoned the Police Department. They promised to look out for my friends. Next I phoned Bill in New York. He had been traipsing round the newspaper offices with lots of press-releases, a few photographs, and Mississippi mud still on his jeans. He said there was something big in the offing (more he wouldn't say). Just as I thanked him, the receptionist announced a call on the other line. Feeling important, I took it: it was the Police Department – ever efficient, they'd found my friends.

While waiting, I suddenly thought of my old friend Ewen Macleod. Since Argyll, he'd fallen in love with an American girl called Debbie, married her, and settled in Williamsburg, Virginia. I told the receptionist everything I knew, and five minutes later he was on the line! It was just like old times. On the spot, he decided to drive halfway down the country and meet me in New Orleans. A lot of water had flowed under the bridge since that long hot summer.

Liam and Tim had still not arrived, and my mind began to wander off. I had read about Natchez being a major staging-post for the hardbitten keelboatmen sailing and floating their boats downriver. Once here, they had to laboriously haul them back up again, or else sell them for scrap and take the Natchez Trail back up via Nashville, Tennessee. So hardbitten were they in fact, that Twain, not normally a puritan, condemned the 'moral sties like the Natchez-under-the-Hill of that day'. Taking a quick walk, I was disappointed to find that downtown didn't contain many moral sties any more.

Long before the keelboatmen, however, Natchez was a major Indian settlement, the centre of a highly organised civilisation called Mississippian Culture. It stretched up to Memphis and St Louis, and – as shown by the pyramid-shaped burial mounds – was almost certainly influenced by the Aztecs. Down here there was no birch-bark to make canoes with. Most commonly, round wicker boats covered with buffalo skins were used instead, or else giant dugouts holding up to fifty warriors. But before the French arrived, something had broken and the civilisation was already in terminal decline. All they had time to do was record – and accelerate – the decline and dispersal of the Natchez Nation. By 1730, Mississippian Culture had disappeared from the face of the earth.

Just as I was going to phone the police again, four familiar feet staggered in. I was weak with hunger and exhaustion and so were they. We revived a little over the camp-fire, as they told me that after an anxious hour peering into the gloom in search of a battered piece of fibreglass they had decided to drive along the bank, flashing their headlamps to guide me in. The road ran out, and my friends trudged further along the bank. After a couple of hours of head-high Indian corn and mosquitoes, they headed back for civilisation and flagged down a police car which was already looking for them. I started to tell them about the Natchez Indians but realised that now wasn't really the moment. Very soon, we pushed the embers into the river and watched the sparks mistily floating away.


### III

We awoke early. It was the 13th and Liam was going to hitch into New Orleans. As well as arranging accommodation and contacting the media, I wanted him to organise some eleventh-hour fundraising with the Louisiana A.C.S.

As I set off, the Mississippi was bathed in sunlight, with the arches of Natchez Bridge gleaming 8 miles ahead of me. The town itself was set high on a green hill, its windows twinkling like bright topazes on an emerald base – and all the time the copper ball of fire was hanging in the sky.

I was just passing the Glasscock Cutoff, thinking what an extraordinary name it was, when a familiar feeling came to me. I was sandwiched between an upstream tow and a downstream one. The river had got much narrower since Cairo and was now only 1000 yards wide. Over the past few weeks, however, I'd been practising my towboat negotiation and so managed to avoid both of them in a rather elegant fashion. My complacency was soon shattered however by a metallic voice echoing three-dimensionally off the banks: 'H-o-o-o! Who's that crazy bastard in the middle of the Mississippi in a tinpot kay-yak? H-o-o-o-o! Any crazy bastard like that must be half-cayned!' Dramatically spinning the

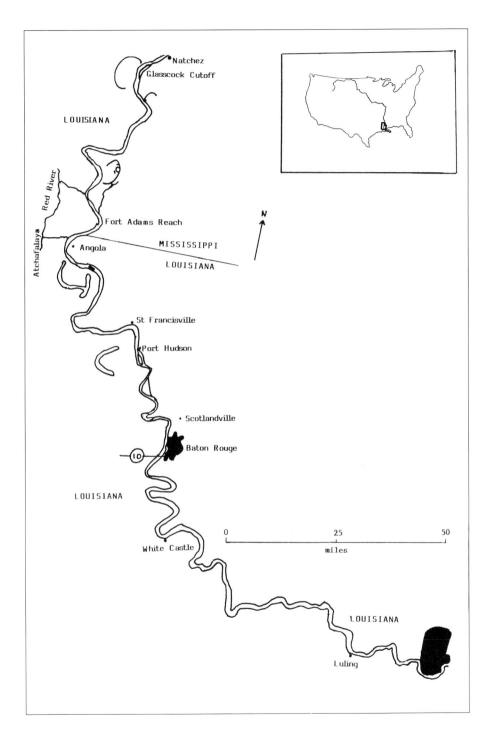

Natchez to New Orleans.

aforesaid kayak on a dime, I glared up at the bridge. But the word-perfect syllogiser was invisible behind smoked glass, and so I had nothing to swear back at but the churning waves.

After dinner, Tim said it looked as if some sort of party was afoot at a house about a mile away. We found a huge Gothic mansion straight out of Gormenghast. So, to judge from the jeeps, had half the US Army transport corps. We knocked apprehensively at the front door. It opened, we said we'd come down from the Rockies, and could we please use the telephone? We *could* have, they told us, but there wasn't one! Bourbon had been thrust into our hands. Our hosts explained what they were doing out here but I only caught about one word in four – hunting season, Orleans, bayous.

'We're Cajuns!' came the proud explanation.

'Come again?'

*'Nous sommes Acadiens.'* (I couldn't believe my ears.) *'Nous parlons le vieux français. Nous venons du Canada – Québec, Nouveau Brunswick, et Nouvelle Ecosse. Expulsés par les Anglais au début du dix-huitième siècle.'* All this was mixed with modern American and gallons of 'Twenty-per-Cent' wine – which tasted stronger than most sherries!

'My mother's French,' I tentatively confessed.

'Heh! That makes you an honorary Coonass!' came back the crazy chorus. We were treated like Bourbon Kings. Our friends served us a huge meal of jambalaya – ham, prawns, wine, rice and spices – and regaled us with stories of their adventures in the forests of Louisiana.

When I asked about New Orleans, they told us about the Civil War! As a last-ditch attempt to save the city from the Unionist fleet, the Confederates set the river on fire – literally – by sending 35,000 burning cotton-bales towards the ships. It didn't work, and a terrible repression followed, under the notorious Butler.

There was a skidding noise outside and another four Acadians rushed in. They'd brought several pails of goodies all the way from the Delta. Minutes later, we were tucking into a shoal of floured oysters, dunked in boiling oil.

Tim asked about the showboats. 'Hey Charlie, *viens nous parler de ton vieux Armstrong!'* No second prompting was needed. The roots of jazz, he told us, went very deep: African music, the blues, ragtime, working songs, French Creole music, sexual undertones.

Fate Marable had developed his showboats from about 1916. He himself played the calliope (steam organ) and used to take jazz bands upriver from 'Orleans'. As well as Armstrong himself, such famous names as Joe (King) Oliver and the Dodds Brothers made their debuts on board 'the Conservatory'. 'And why did it all start in Orleans, and why did it become so commercial when it left? Because,' he said proudly, 'this was the only place where Black and White, French and Spanish, wetbacks and Yankees could mix. Those was some days!'

I enquired again about the place I had dreamed of for so long that it didn't seem right to be getting near. To find its soul, our friends replied, you had to ignore Bourbon Street, with its nightclubs and antiseptic jazz, its striptease and massage parlours. You had to shun the American interlopers and make contact with the Villarés, the Grimats and the Delarauds – the old French Creole 'aristocracy'. You had to like red wine, rich cooking and dancing in the streets ('You'll do O.K. I reckon').

But if you wanted to speak French, you might as well give up. Mr Average New Orleans didn't understand two words. In some towns and villages around, there were people who still spoke Cajun, valiantly resisting the melting pot. But for how long? Almost nobody could write French any more. It was a miracle, said Charles, that it had lasted this long. We had another drink, *'A la belle langue de la Louisiane'*. Then the musicians came on. For two hours, we were in the slow, rhythmic, absorbing world of Cajun music, singing of *'le grand dérangement'*, *'shauvages'* and *'gaillardes'*. Only at 2 am with our eyes irresistibly closing, did we bid our *'Coonass amis'* farewell, and stagger back to the faithful Dodge.


## IV

Soon after a dawn start, I arrived at a huge and messy complex. This was where the Red River, 'down' from Texas, joined the Mississippi, and where the Atchafalaya, off to the Gulf, left it – sometimes in that order, sometimes not.

I remembered my discussion with Bill, feeling a virtuous glow at my decision to stay with the M-M. But meanwhile, water-courses continued to come and go, making me understand why the mapmakers had been so mean with the arrows. It was up to the man-on-the-spot to decide which way things were going. I resolved to lay down the guidelines of a learned monograph on the subject and began straight away.

Decisive point number one: the arrows couldn't all go the same way round, unless someone had invented perpetual motion and not told me. *Et voilà*. One for Nicky. Decisive point number two: to understand what was going on, you had to adopt the points of view of the actors themselves. The Red River was really making coy advances towards the Mississippi. She had never completely made the plunge, however, and man had had to come to the rescue of the reluctant couple. That neatly explained the sign warning that commerce between the two rivers was regulated by a system of locks and sluice-gates. In fact the Mississippi was also pretty standoffish – only deputing tiny offshoots of herself for the meeting, like an executive sending his secretary's secretaries. The two *had* shared banks and current accounts for a while, and at one stage, with arms and mouths everywhere, it wasn't even clear where the bed was. But then they had run into liquidity problems, and had had to separate. The Red, a scarlet woman, had been obliged to conceal her blushing identity under an unpronounceable name.

'Perhaps monographs aren't really my genre?' I thought, as I paddled over the distinctly pinkish water. A huge sign suddenly said 'Tows, powerboats, dinghies, etc. should navigate as close to the left descending bank as safety will permit.' Honoured that somebody had taken my existence into account, even as a small-bit extra, I scuttled to the far side like a lame Manx cat. No sign of a descending bank, however.

As usual, everything had come and gone quicker than I could register. First, somewhere in all the flesh-coloured confusion, I had gone down the Fort Adams Reach. Twain claimed that the Mississippi was so fast here that three steamboat watches went by before they got up and out of it. According to my own evidence, and with the greatest reluctance, I am obliged to say he may have been fibbing a little. Secondly, I had crossed the line of 31°N – about the same as the temperature in degrees centigrade. And finally, Mississippi State had run off along that same line towards the Gulf: both banks were now Louisiana territory. All those white cotton-fields had given way to exotic-looking bayous, with oblique tree trunks and coloured flowers everywhere.

By the time I had caught up, I was well past the hothouse vegetation of 'Angola' and coming to a pleasantly-wooded island. As I cut across its lower tip, something green, red, and orange caught the corner of my eye – 400 yards upstream!

After twenty minutes' hard paddling, I made it back to the island. I grabbed hold of the sinewy bushes and worked my way up, hand over hand, until I was opposite. My loudest shouts and signals went unnoticed. If only I dared use Tim's favourite way of getting attention . . . . Then forty northbound barges swam valiantly past. I cut across the choppy water, pulled in, fought my way through the dense undergrowth – and found an empty mug. But Tim soon reappeared and all was well.

We decided to meet again at St Francisville. (My surname had certainly been promoted since South Dakota; from a windswept lake to a French county-town and from a Case to a Sainthood. The only problem was that most saints were dead.) That afternoon, I felt very tired. The river seemed to be getting stickier and stickier and I was convinced that it was slowing me down. Also, the decisions about which course to take were a constant drag on my mental resources. I cursed the Mississippi then, for her

174

promiscuity with every water-course for hundreds of miles around.

Even the landscape was getting industrialised. It must have changed a lot, I thought, since the nineteenth-century artist Henry Lewis resolved to immortalise it. He considered that previous painters hadn't taken sufficient account of the size of the Mississippi. His painting was 12 feet high and 2 miles long! Somewhere along the line, a careless posterity has mislaid the artistic achievement itself but Lewis's name survives for all time in the *Guinness Book of Records*.

Over dinner, I told a sympathetic Tim about the terrible stickiness. He consoled me by describing an attempt to swim the Mississippi. Apparently the brave man did about 200 miles, before complaining that his skin felt a bit funny. When they pulled him out, his whole body was covered with boils and sores. (Just like the Mississippi itself.) And that, said a triumphant Tim, was on the Upper River!

I was only 35 miles from Baton Rouge. By now I knew that I was about as likely to find a red totem-pole there as a circumflex accent on the word Baton. But it did lie within spitting distance of the finish, and that made up for a lot.

All that morning, I felt that my quest was at last coming to an end. First I went past Port Hudson, the last Confederate fort on the Mississippi to fall; next a U-bend, complete with the unmentionable detritus of a whole state; then a nostalgic 'Scotlandville'; and finally civilisation, in the shape of the fourth biggest port in the United States.

Mile after mile of docks and cranes stretched to a wavering infinity. Anchored at the wharves or queuing in midriver were a huge variety of vessels – tiny coasters and tugs, Gulf oil-supply ships, and 20,000-ton ore carriers. The river had chosen this precise point to become narrower than anywhere this side of St Louis: a mere 800 yards. I knew that it had also got a lot deeper, but this hardly consoled me.

I weaved cautiously through the rows and rows of shipping – none of which, on closer inspection, seemed that small, and all of which, without exception, ignored me completely. Very slowly, a massive highway bridge came into view: Interstate 10 (at last). Florida to Mobile to El Paso, all once Spanish, but all three completely American. In the shadow of the frenetic dinky-cars was some waste-ground, and on it I spotted Tim with two journalists. I was relieved there were so few, but even so, I didn't want to stop.

I could smell the sea.

V

The meet-the-press was soon over. 'Why don't you stay at our place and head out tomorrow?' our new friends asked.

We spent the afternoon at C.B.S., watching as the evening news was put together. Suddenly our friend rushed in: 'Hey, c'm' *ahn* you guys. Fire in the tire dee-pot. 'S go check it out?' His car was already moving, and we were flying down Main Street, overheating the siren and burning every light. I had got through a whole string of Hail Mary's and half a very Imperfect Act of Contrition, when we smelt burning rubber. Our tyres or theirs, I wondered philosophically. When we arrived, we saw dense smoke, but no flames whatsoever. But the drive had made it all worthwhile.

I was up very early on the 15th. A mile or two on, the Mississippi gradually filled up with sea-going ships. It was like the English Channel and as I continued my death-race through the shipping-lanes, I felt on very familiar territory.

Even at 9 am the heat of the sun was unbearable – thank God I hadn't been here in September . . . . After only 20 miles, I came ashore feeling like an old man. I lay down on the sand and waves of weariness flooded over me. I realised that, after all the thousands of miles of slogging, the expedition's time was running out – that this way of life was soon going to come to an end. At once a feeling of disorientation and unfathomable sadness descended on me. I just couldn't imagine a life without the M-M.

At midday, I arrived at a town called White Castle. Tim and I had a quick hamburger in a bar full of young Black boys who were clearly dying to have a go at us. Then I was off again, still feeling very weak and dispirited. My old friend, the headwind, had come back, and though it kept the heat just tolerable, it made me feel as if I was hardly moving. I was so nearly there that all my willpower had flowed out of me like a tide on the ebb.

The shipping was also still causing me problems. The closer I got to New Orleans, the bigger the remaining tows became. The largest I saw was pushing forty-eight barges, wired together six across and eight down. This crossword was 1000 feet long: bigger than an aircraft-carrier. The liners were going twice as fast as the tows – up to 25 knots – and with my pathetic maximum of 6 knots, I felt very unsafe. My Cajun friends had told me that New Orleans was where one Scotsman with a French connection had already taken a nasty fall, and I hoped it wasn't an omen.

John Law was his name, and he had first worked his way up to become Comptroller-General (Minister of Finances) of the Kingdom of France (1717). He had then set up the farsighted 'Mississippi Scheme', whereby money was put up for the development of New Orleans and French North America. But in the end, he proved just a bit too farsighted. Wild speculation began to spread like fever, and in the end the whole idea just collapsed. So *that* was what Jim had meant by the 'Mississippi Bubble'. I thought back to my own 'scheme', with all its financial juggling. There and then, I gave solemn thanks to Lady Luck – and the back-up team – that the holes had held together despite everything.

About 10 miles short of my rendezvous, it began to get dark very quickly. After a few more shore-hugging miles, I made out the stationary outline of five parallel barges. Ten feet separated them from the shore; easy enough for the sleek *Lochinvar* and the bag of bones within it to negotiate – provided a certain incident didn't repeat itself.

Having sneaked along the length of three barges, I was just congratulating myself when a searchlight clicked exasperatingly on, and slowly began to revolve. The water began to eddy and froth under my keel as far-away engines throbbed into reluctant life. With a mounting feeling of *déjà vu*, I pulled *Lochinvar* onto the bank, turned her round, and dropped her back in. With my heart in my mouth, I raced back to the front of the beast. Deciding that I'd wait until he moved, I became even more annoyed when he didn't.

I was now back to square one. I had a choice of being crushed against the shore or else mowed down by a ship passing in the night. After five minutes of dithering, I paddled 300 yards upstream, swivelled round, and paddled directly at the centre of the Mississippi. The current pushed me towards the barge, but the phantom captain was a gentleman, patiently sitting there in the darkness. I cleared the sharp overhanging corner of the outermost barge with 7 feet and a $^1/_4$ oz of nerve to spare. There wasn't another vessel in sight. But I didn't really mind.

After a quick meal, Tim and I drove into a tiny village. We soon found the only bar, where Tim sipped an insipid beer, while I telephoned the rest of the world and Liam in particular. I told him we were only 30 miles from New Orleans and that we'd be there tomorrow. He said that was great, but he sounded pretty fed up. He had had a dreadful time battling against the local A.C.S. – they seemed to know very little about what we were doing, and care even less. But he did have one good piece of news. Bill had phoned from Kennedy: his coup had come off, and the *Sunday Times* wanted to know about our trip. One of their roving reporters was flying over from the Bahamas. He wanted to see me tomorrow. (Good job I'd phoned!)

Then I phoned A.C.S. New York, reminding them of their own suggestion about National Smoke-Out Day but I couldn't get anything out of them at all. I felt very bitter, remembering the 3000 miles I had done since Williston, North Dakota, to meet their rendezvous.

Up at six the next morning, I couldn't find my wallet. Asking Tim to retrace the spoor of our (non-existent) revelry, I headed out again into the horizontal-hold world of the Mississippi.

I was very aware suddenly that Louisiana had been on my mind for so many months and years and that I was at last there, at the climax of my adventure.

I paddled on for several hours, conscious of growing excitement. Every detail of that last journey towards the capital of French America became sublimely nostalgic. It all seemed diffused with a heavenly light and it set off reaction after reaction within me.

I rejoiced at the few tows that remained, for their very scarcity meant that the river was coming to an end. I rejoiced at the rusty ships and off-white seagulls, because they were a sign that I was getting near the ocean. I rejoiced at the factories and chemical installations, since these made up the arteries of the city that had meant so much to me for so long. I rejoiced at the sweltering heat of the sub-tropical sun, for I knew that on this day, 16 November, it would normally be snowing at Three Forks, Montana – and at a certain boarding school in Scotland. And I rejoiced at my own numbed and sweaty weariness, because it represented the result of all those miles of effort – something nobody could ever take away from me now.

Towards the middle of that euphoric morning, I arrived at Luling. Only a few years before, I had seen the television film about a dreadful fogbound night here. A ferry, crammed with passengers, had collided in midstream with a massive tow that had burst upon it from a wall of fog.

I hated the treacherous Mississippi then. This river, which seemed so calm, could turn like a viper to engulf scores of people in an unmarked and watery grave. Twain had called her the crookedest river in the world; and Lord Roberts had said, 'She demands respect, and she better damned well get it, or she can be awful uppity.' The two men had been writing a hundred years ago, but their descriptions still held true. The Mississippi would never change.

I paddled swiftly away from the site of the horror. At exactly 12.30, I pulled up at the rendezvous point. Tim and Liam were nowhere to be seen. After twenty minutes, I felt pretty wretched and stuck a wavering thumb towards the glowering sky.

The first vehicle to pass was an old pick-up. The second was a black and gold Ford Capri with a journalist from a small island 3000 miles to the east.

I spent most of the afternoon under the harsh glare of the camera. At last our friend was satisfied. We were free.

The first thing I did was phone Britain. After an interminable wait, I was overjoyed to hear my parents' voices, faint across the thousands of miles. I told them my news. For them too, the months of worrying and waiting were at last over. Reluctantly replacing the receiver, I finally

178

realised the full weight of the burden they had had to carry.

We carefully carried *Lochinvar* to the pick-up, and slid her onto her familiar slot at the top. We stowed the paddles amongst the mouldering rubbish on the bottom. And then we drove fast and noisily into the centre of New Orleans. A decade ago it had all been a dream. Now it was hard reality.

That night, we went to a little jambalaya restaurant in the French Quarter. I was in a complete daze. I was sitting opposite a pretty girl from the American Cancer Society, but I hardly saw her. Ewen and Debbie had come down from Virginia but they scarcely registered in my fuddled brain. Bill phoned his congratulations 'on your first river!', but I gave him largely incoherent thanks.

All that time, I was thousands of miles away. There was a tiny hamlet surrounded by snow-capped mountains. In the cold light, I could see two very clean-looking men carrying a shiny boat down to a jetty, and a third, climbing awkwardly in. The M-M was nothing like he thought it would be. The Gates of the Mountains, the Missouri Breaks, and the Badlands – Fort Peck, Sakakawea, and Oahe. The end of a river – a river born anew. Arrowheads in the dust and bobbing sawyers. Wing-dams and a whirlpool, orange groves on a green hillside. Black cottonmouths, white cotton-fields, Indians and Acadians. Fear and joy, betrayal and love, tears, sweat, and blood. A journey against a scourge, a journey for self-discovery. The Mississippi-Missouri was everything I had dreamed it would be.

The following morning, Liam and Tim carried the kayak down to the water one last time. Rounding the final bend, I saw a huge bridge stretching across the river. There was a sign hanging from one of its arches: 'The Crescent City Welcomes British Kayaker'. Two fire-fending boats were anchored near the shore, shooting an arch of coloured drops a hundred feet into the shining sky. There came the uncanny skirl of 'Scotland the Brave'. A burning wind blew in my face, bringing a musky tropical smell. My Journey to New Orleans was over.

Slowly turning *Lochinvar* under the cool arch, I paddled towards the people waiting on that beckoning shore.

# And Quiet Flows the Mississippi

Dere's an ol' man called de Mississippi
Dats de ol' man I like to be
What does he care if de world's got troubles
What does he care if de land aint free?
Ol' Man River
Dat Ol' Man River
He mus' know sumpin'
But don't say nothin'
He jes' keeps rollin'
He keeps on rollin' along.
He don't plant taters,
He don't plant cotton,
An' dem dat plants 'em
Is soon forgotten,
But Ol' Man River
He jes' keeps rollin' along.

('Ol' Man River')

## I

As far as the rest of the world was concerned, I had canoed the Mississippi-Missouri and achieved my life's ambition. For two or three days I concurred, enjoying the good life in the least puritanical city in America.

But deep within me there was still an absence, one which became more apparent over the long, sunny afternoons. At the beginning, it was just a set of disconnected reminiscences; but then they started to line themselves up.

I remembered the sighting of the Mississippi-Missouri by Columbus – probably a mere myth, but an incomparable image of the meeting of two worlds. I remembered the once-overwhelming French influence in

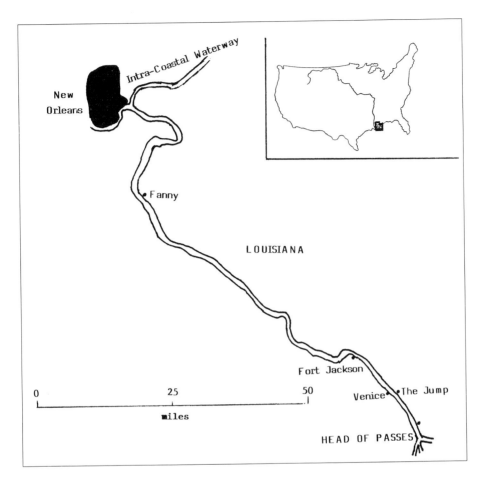

New Orleans to the Gulf of Mexico.

Louisiana, and wondered whether more authentic traces remained than fries, knickers, and discotheques. I remembered the anti-slave forces of the North, and their long voyage past Florida and Alabama before fighting their way up the river. I remembered my last evening with Bill, and our amusement at the vagaries of Old Al and the Atchafalaya. And I remembered the circle, opened so many light-years ago, but in which I thought I could still detect the faintest of cracks.

My mind was made up. I was not going to abandon my faithful friend. I longed to share her relief when she finally gave herself up to the infinite ocean. I felt in some way like the childhood companion who is sincerely glad to give the bride away because he has participated in all her disappointments and knows that this is what she wants more than anything else in the world.

181

The Mississippi was calling with all her might; but I was the only one who could hear. Liam and Tim elected to stay in New Orleans and sell off the equipment. Part of the reason, I knew, was the aftermath of the ticker-tape welcome. A.C.S. Louisiana had shared the excitement of our Honorary Citizenship and our final press conference, and then abandoned us outside their head office – funds $15, and nowhere to go. They could do no more 'because of the Tutankhamen Exhibition and the football game'. Some National Smoke-Out Day! I lit a cigarette and decided to go into the Delta alone.

The Coastguard had told me that for the first 80 miles, the main danger was man-made: impatient captains and overcrowded shipping lanes. But for the last 30, the land gave up altogether, replaced by treacherous, water-logged vegetation. There were carnivorous orchids, mosquitoes, and copperheads in profusion but precious little else. The region was also notorious for its tropical hurricanes – similar to the tornadoes further north, but with the bonus of lashing rain. In all that open space, there was only one haven – a small island with a shop and a bar for mariners dying for contact with a world outside the menacing, drowned Delta.

For all these reasons, the Coastguard had forbidden me to attempt it alone, saying 'we can't answer for the consequences' – which did wonders for my self-confidence! But I told them I was absolutely desperate to finish the Mississippi-Missouri, and would go into the Delta with or without them. Finally they had agreed to escort me out of New Orleans. But from then on, they warned me, I would be on my own.

And thus it was that on the 24th, a slightly embarrassed young man could be seen carrying a long orange object through the early-morning shoppers. 'Whoops, Ma'am; I'm really most awfully sorry. If only you hadn't stopped so suddenly. We'll soon get this sorted out . . . .'

Then Canal Street, and a solitary, furtive launch, under the efficient eyes of my gleaming white escort. Feeling very strange, and more than a little nervous, I moved slowly out into the mainstream.

After a few hundred yards, a sign said 'INTRA-COASTAL WATERWAY. CAPE COD 2000 MILES', but I wasn't to be tempted. Another sign read 'MISSISSIPPI RIVER OUTLET: GULF OF MEXICO 70 MILES' – but I didn't waver for a second. Then the city limit hoved into view, and the cruiser surged frothily off. As they had warned me, I was now alone – bar a couple of dozen ocean-going ships.

It took me about 2000 paddle-strokes to calm down and take an interest in the scenery. But I soon realised that, if there was any, I couldn't see it. My whole world consisted of the river and its twin levees, richer and blacker than ever.

As I carried on through that roofless black tunnel, I found the water more and more awkward. Perhaps there had been a storm in the Gulf, or the tide had changed? Perhaps it was the effect of long-gone liners? Or perhaps I was just off form? What made things worse was knowing that if I did overturn I probably wouldn't be able to get back in. I would just have to drift forlornly along the greasy wall for miles and miles. The proud Maserati was now down to the bare and bumpy rim, carefully observing every exit before venturing fearfully on.

In the late afternoon, I limped past Fanny. My lewd and poetic imagination immediately started looking for wisps of brushwood or other tell-tale signs; but honesty compels me to admit that I couldn't see any. At precisely the same point, I crossed the line 90°W, the exact middle of the Western Hemisphere – and the same latitude as the Sahara.

Just before dark I pulled in. Again feeling a bit strange, I proceeded to set up a solitary 'camp': a sleeping bag, a tarpaulin, and a fire. Dinner was sausages, toasted with a burning fork. I'd salted them that morning but they still tasted funny so I smothered them in blackened bread, and took the taste away with a bar of runny chocolate. Then, with the Mississippi-Missouri breathing heavily in the background, I was quickly asleep.

I was very glad to have got through my first day alone.


## II

Just before sunrise, I set off on the last stretch of my journey. I wanted to get the 52 miles over as soon as possible. A couple of hurried miles later, the left-hand levee stopped. Everywhere lay low-lying clumps of dirty green vegetation, separated by winding channels of clearish water. Occasionally, gnarled, bent-over trees were visible, huddling blackly on brown islands. In the distance were dozens of gaily-coloured pipelines, carrying gas and petroleum from the Gulf.

This part of the Delta was, I knew, where the French buccaneers, Jean and Pierre Lafitte, had hung out at the beginning of the nineteenth century. They and their followers lived completely outside the laws of the land, emerging on only one occasion: to help defeat the British at the Battle of New Orleans (1815). Stories still existed about their treasure, buried in long-lost bayous, and as I contemplated that terrible desolation, I could quite believe them.

Huddling now against the shelter of the one remaining levee, I pushed exhaustedly on. I went past Fort Jackson, the site of the first Unionist engagement on the river. The Confederates had constructed a mile-long dam here, using scuttled ships, tree-trunks, bicycles, and anything else that came to hand. With their scores of cannon raking the dam from both sides, they considered it totally impregnable. But one dark night, the Mississippi felt slightly restless, and upped and brushed away the entire construction. The Unionists camouflaged their ships with layers of gumbo, gave the pathetic remains a wide berth, and got by with minimal losses. Then they headed on for New Orleans and victory.

At 3 pm, I got to a most un-Italianate Venice. The remaining levee gave up, and soon the grey, lonely sky was there all around me. I tried to comfort myself with the charm of the French names – Bay Denesse, Bay Pomme d'Or, Bay Jacques, Bayou Grand Liart, Bayou Baptiste Collette. But my mind kept coming back to the end of the levee: it was called The Jump, and I wanted to know why. Also, the maps kept saying, again and again, 'Line of demarcation between salt and fresh marsh not determined.' This lack of tidemarks seemed disturbing – was it high tide now?

A 20,000-ton liner doing 20 knots directly at my kayak made me zoom off towards the edge. It took the bend very fine, forcing me into the swampy mess. By the time the wash had subsided, a slow brown drift had pushed me past where I came in. I could have gone back but I wanted to explore the Delta bayous one last time. 'The Gulf can wait,' I thought, and pointing *Lochinvar* at an angle, I started threading my way obliquely back towards the river, through a whole wonderland of branching channels. Very soon I was back in my early childhood, marvelling at the self-confident courses the water took on the pavement – sometimes happily following the cracks, sometimes rushing off at an enthusiastic tangent, sometimes stopping dead in its tracks. I weaved and wandered with the best of it.

I was abruptly brought back to Louisiana and the mainstream by the sight of the most gigantic frog I had ever seen. It was sitting on the soft mud, puffing its throat in and out in a desperate attempt to look prince-like; and it seemed nearly as big as a football. I kept looking at it, then away again, but I couldn't make it appear an inch smaller.

III

My meanderings and frog-like encounter must have shaken something loose in my head, for as I carried on towards the mouth, my mind started to glow hot and cold. Then it began racing back over the whole trip. For some reason, it highlighted all the things the M-M had ever been called, in love or in anger: turbulent, majestic, magnificent, fickle; Father of Waters, Big Muddy, Wild Mizoo, Old Misery, Graveyard for Steamboats, Queen of Rivers, River Road, Great Common Sewer of the West. But the names it really focused on were the Indian ones Leah had told us about: Boundary Between Two Pieces of Land, Smoky Water, Navigable Stream

Full of Dirt, Stirred Up and Grandmother River.

While my mind continued to turn over, it seem to slip gear. It started sifting and shuffling the disparate elements, until they all fell into place with a loud click. At the junction with the Ohio, I had sensed that the river possessed some sort of overriding unity; now I *knew* that it really was one, in some transcendentally deeper way.

Then, with the shore still drifting dreamily past, a real brainstorm invaded my exhausted skull. It touched down initially on Mark Twain's words: a steamboat pilot had been the only totally independent human being on earth. But Twain had let the machinery isolate him from the water, he had let the technical aspects of his craft destroy the magic of the Mississippi. My original, ambitious, aim had been to put the magic back in. I had wanted to travel back beyond Twain's era: to a time when a man, a boat, and a river formed a perfect universe.

Since then, I had learned a great deal. I had found that the Mississippi really did wander all over the land, and that keeping your boat on the water was not as easy as all that. I had been lucky enough however to avoid Twain's trap. My aching arms and sticky skin told me, in no uncertain terms, that I was neither too much cut off from the water nor too technically competent. I had fulfilled my dream of not just 'floating' the river but being immersed in its very substance – much more satisfying than I had any right to expect.

I had also discovered the bitter dregs of the American dream. More perhaps than anything else, I had always known the Mississippi-Missouri embodied that dream at its clearest and purest. The river had always been the stamping-ground of desperado individualists, of loners in search of themselves, of seekers after total union. But somewhere between the top of Montana and the bottom of Louisiana, my desire for the primitive, backwoods experience had been more than exorcised – the hard way.

I now understood that it was attempting an impossible purity to try to face the wilderness alone and as if the twentieth century had never existed. Without a back-up team, and without fibreglass, matches, and maps, I didn't know what would have happened to me. Or rather, I did, when I looked at the fate of de Soto, Marquette, and La Salle. All three had in fact lost their lives because of the river, their river. I now knew that the M-M would never be my river in that all-embracing sense. I had become too attached to life to want to become totally one with it.

Not all the magic, though, had run out. I had found that plenty of poetry was still there, if you were prepared to get close enough. But I had also discovered that the pearl I had been looking for was flawed in its very core – that the beauty of the river was inseparable from its terrible violence. T.S. Eliot had said, 'On a halcyon day it is merely a monument;

in navigable weather it is always a seamark to lay a course by; but in the sombre season of the sudden fury, it is what it always was.' The strong brown god's primeval, savage force was still there, to be experienced by a man desperate enough. You just had to know when to stop.

And stop, for the moment, I had to as I had just arrived at Pilottown. I hadn't been expecting much, but even so I felt disappointed to see nothing but two white buildings and a cluster of stilt-houses. Pretty much the same as in Twain's day. I went into the bar, ostensibly in search of information about the tide and the last few miles. But the only client was dead drunk and the barman wouldn't give me a glass of water. 'Forget it,' I said, and strode bitterly out. The final cut from a changeable river.

## IV

I got into *Lochinvar* for the last time in my life and headed slowly downstream again. I knew little about the two or three miles ahead of me. The maps did show that, at the Head of Passes, the mileage was '0.0', and that three branches formed a brackish no-man's-land suspended uneasily between the Mississippi and the Atlantic. I also knew that the river dumped about 400 million tons of mud into the Gulf each year, together with as much water as the twenty biggest European rivers put together. But lastly, in my haphazard reading of the nineteenth-century travellers, I had retained two particular descriptions.

One was a Mrs Trollope's: 'I never beheld a scene so utterly desolate as this entrance of the Mississippi' – she claimed that it needed a second Dante to paint 'its horrors'. The other was Parkman's, and not much more encouraging: 'The low and marshy shores drew apart, the brackish water changed to brine, and the breeze grew fresh with the salt breath of the sea. Then we came to the broad bosom of the great Gulf [. . .] tossing its restless billows, limitless, voiceless, lonely as when born of chaos.'

Mulling it all over, I continued towards the sea, helped on by some grey clouds moving glumly south. I began to consider my situation very seriously indeed. Behind me, as well as half a million cubic feet each second, were: possibly a rushing, oceanic tide; probably a 30 mph wind; and without doubt a pitch-black night. One monster I could handle, two I might risk, but three or four seemed to me too much. Very reluctantly, I decided that to venture out into the Gulf in such desperate conditions would be unmitigated madness. What was good enough for the mileage-markers was good enough for me. 'Mile 0.0' would be my Interstate 00, my *ultima Thule*, my restless journeying's final end. If I didn't find at least a bit of peace there, I knew I probably never would.

Knowing that I was at last getting there, I slowed my paddles, and then pulled them completely inboard. Drifting steadily with the chocolate-brown waste, I contemplated the circular green horizon, wondering how it possibly held in all those miles of convex water. The sky, meanwhile, was cavorting giddily around, playing some sort of sublime symphony, but not bothering to tell the rest of the world about it. As Parkman had warned, it *was* all a bit lonely and voiceless. For the moment, however, I couldn't see any of Mrs Trollope's horrors.

I thought back again to La Salle, the first White man to navigate the Mississippi and the first to see the scene before my eyes. He had stopped here, it came to me. He had even erected a column in the marsh. On it was inscribed the name of his King, Louis XIV of France, and his claim to half a continent: the land between here, the highest Rockies, and Western Greenland. Since then, there had been one or two changes. The Empire had passed; and I couldn't see any sign of a column either. But perhaps I wasn't looking in the right place . . . .

As I continued to scan the shore, my flow of French nostalgia was suddenly interrupted by a cross-current of electric intensity. It refused to state its exact business straight away, but proceeded to make repeated declarations of self-importance. It was something to do with the Rocky Mountains and the three passes now clearly in view . . . to do with the Chain of Rocks and the spit of land below Cairo . . . rivers that come together, rivers that fork . . . . Then it came to me, in a sudden, searing flash: *Three Forks!* The Mississippi-Missouri sprang from three forks, and it returned to three forks. Tridents at both ends and the Chain of Rocks as a pivot. The missing rhyme for Louisiana was Montana. In its beginning was its end. Now the river really was one.

I could feel the hairs prickling all over my body. I couldn't wait to tell Bill about this one! Then another brainstorm began to invade my poor skull: none of the myriad books we had read had noticed this blatant fact, because no-one had thought of it as a single river before. No-one had noticed it, above all, because no-one had ever gone from one end of it to the other or, it seemed, even just visited both ends.

And then the inexorable drift had brought me to the very end of my dream. The point where the river unloaded all her sticky frustrations and passionately embraced the sub-tropical sea. I scooped up a handful of the blue-brown water, careful not to let it all trickle out, and I tasted it. It was both silty and salty, a bit like buffalo soup might be.

Without warning, the sky went translucent and let forth a flurry of heavy drops. I stretched out a hand and, to my surprise, felt that they were warm. Then I knew. The circle was complete. I was there.

With gallons of joy pumping into my heart, I turned *Lochinvar* round. Then, together, we headed back for New Orleans.

# Mothers, Tell Your Children?

That night on them banks I'd lie awake
And pull her close just to feel every breath she'd take.
Now those memories come back to haunt me
They haunt me like a curse,
Is a dream a lie if it don't come true
Or is it something worse
That sends me down to the River
But I know the River is dry.
That sends me down to the River tonight
Down to the River
My baby and I
Oh down to the River
We'd ride.

(Bruce Springsteen, 'The River')

## I

It was raining, then, when it ended. I was caught between America and the deep blue sea.

Safely back in New Orleans, thanks to a kindly towboat captain, I learned that Tim and Liam had sent $400 to Rogers, Arkansas – the Dodge-owner must have got the shock of his life! They were going to set off for South America and a round-the-world tour. I thanked them for all their support, wished them the very best of luck, and headed back to my only haven.

Cathy was very, very glad to see me. For five days, I slept or just sat in her kind company. Like a golden-wedding couple, she took me for slow walks in the parks, holding me whenever my spindly legs would go no further. We went to the cinema, and we went for long, sunny drives.

Our idyll was interrupted by a middle-of-the-night phone call from the

188

Old World. Mr MacKenzie wanted to see me. I groaned, and went back to sleep. This hero was tired, he simply couldn't be bothered any more. The Mississippi-Missouri had broken something deep inside him, and he didn't know if it would ever mend. He wasn't sure if he even wanted it to.

Several hours later, Cathy brought in some hot, milky coffee and reality had to be faced up to again.

I left Omaha with my heart breaking. As if reliving earlier reincarnations, I flew to New York and to London, where I was kindly met by Randal Sadleir and my parents.

In his office in Edinburgh, Colin MacKenzie asked me for the accounts. I said there weren't any; and no funds either. It was just the way things had worked out, and it could have been much worse. But on his side, things *were* much worse. What he said gave me a very nasty shock. The total amount of money his office had raised was £1500. Or rather not even that. My fundraising dream was irrevocably shattered. We'd have been better busking.

A civic reception given by the Lord Provost of Edinburgh did bring me a moment of cheer, for Bill flew in from Paris and I was able to publicly express my debt to my parents. When the last champagne toast had been made, I was a free man. Without a penny to my name, the only proof I hadn't dreamed it all was a pile of muddy maps, ten C90 cassettes, and a metronome in my head. That, and a bruised and beaten orange friend.

*Lochinvar* found a permanent home in the Royal Scottish Museum, and her faithful companion a home-from-home at Mrs Kay Butcher's. And then I started writing up our American adventure – or rather just *writing* it, as I soon found out. The main problem, I realised, was not lack of material, but making what I had into an interesting and coherent narrative.

I began to read the books of various other expeditions on the globe. Most of them gave admirable general accounts, but very few, I discovered, gave the why as well as the how. I realised I was back at the beginning: wondering how I could begin to distinguish myself from the 4,000,000,000 other human beings on earth.

One of the things I had been trying to avoid was the air of complacency I detected in so many people. Unwilling – or unable – to fight them on their own self-satisfied terms, I had been attempting a radical cock-a-snook. I had wanted to say: 'You sat in an office, and played with figures. I canoed a river for cancer.' But now it was over. I no longer wished to say such things to Messrs Smug and Commercial. All they would say was: 'Gee! How wonderful! All those alligators and things! Weren't you ever frightened?', with Mrs Smug and Commercial smirking in time, and looking too hard at my rapidly-vanishing biceps. But for those who did understand, I wanted to recount what I had learned from the river and from Twain: the real that sets off the dream.

As I continued my search through the masses of manuscripts, I thought back again to the role of the official organisations, especially the American Cancer Society. What better place to collect money, we had naively thought, than North America, where the cancer rates are amongst the highest in the world? In our innocent way, we had skimped far beyond what was reasonable on food and safety. Costs to cancer research amounted to the ridiculously small sum of £4500. This covered equipment, food, accommodation, and travel over seven months and 20,000 miles for four and a half men. For the same amount of work, *each* man on the expedition could have earned twice this total – and avoided many pre-dawn attempts to start damp and windy fires. £4500 was about a tenth of the cost of most expeditions, and about a hundredth of the cost of some. For that price, the cancer organisations got several world records. They also got hundreds of newspaper articles and radio programmes, and scores of hours of prime T.V. viewing time.

As I considered the A.C.S.'s behaviour, I grew more and more amazed. Our contribution was publicly praised by President Ford and the Prince of Wales, but apparently overlooked by those who worked to promote the same cause. I was well aware that the fundraising potential of the Mississippi-Missouri Expedition was never realised and that I would always feel a sense of disappointment. If a fundraising dinner can raise $500,000 in two hours, what could have been made of the first journey down America's primordial artery? If a two-week bicycle ride from Eastbourne to Istanbul can raise hundreds of thousands of pounds, what could have been made of nearly 4000 miles of mud and misery?

All these ideas – and many more, about myself, the river, and the book – now had to be put down on the white sheets of paper, in all their naked vulnerability. If my Journey to New Orleans was a hard fact, my journey of self-discovery still had a long, long way to go. But at least there was now a starting point.

In the event, I again took a roundabout route to my destination. I got a managerial job at a four-star hotel in Scotland, thus ensuring a secure future for myself. There was room for two cars beside my double living-room.

But ultimately this way of life was not designed for restless souls like myself. It was too impersonal, too stifling. After weeks of hesitation, I handed in my notice, put my maps and papers into ten string-bound plastic bags, and landed on long-suffering Jeannie's doorstep. We were going to Paris for a weekend together. I was also planning to look for my roots – I was perhaps going to stay in France for quite a while.

Bill was waiting at the Gare du Nord, with his girlfriend, Nicole. That night, the four of us went out for a meal in a small restaurant in the Latin Quarter and talked until very late. The day after, Bill found me a small but independent room on the Left Bank, only 200 yards from the Seine.

Now another of my dreams had been exorcised. I fell in love with Paris, and knew that it would be a very long time before I moved from here. I found myself a job as a barman in Les Halles on the Right Bank, and in my spare time I settled down to write in my garret-style room. And so it was that a draft appeared. I passed the manuscript over to Bill and the whole process began again, resulting eventually in a *Mississippi Madness* . . . .

The last question that the writing of the book raised was the classic one: would I do it again? Would I let my children do it? Older now, but not feeling any wiser, two replies are possible. If I could have known that Fort Peck, the tornado, the towboats, and Benjestown were waiting, the answer has to be a definite 'no' – only a fool would knowingly risk his life to such an extent. But what if I possessed some sort of magic amulet guaranteeing safe passage? The answer must now be a deafening 'yes'. The Mississippi-Missouri was precious little pleasure at the time but must count as the greatest experience of all our lives.

We have our shared memories, and a legitimate pride. But we also have our regrets: regrets that financial straits hampered all our operations, regrets about the photographer, regrets about the fundraising, and regrets about the wasted dinner-date . . . .

Yes, if we were to do it all again, everything would be very different . . . . Or would it?

# *Appendix 1: Records*

From all the information we have been able to find, it seems that five records were broken with this expedition.

***Navigation of the Mississippi-Missouri.*** Exhaustive research of literature reveals no mention of any attempt before 1977 to navigate the M-M, powered or unpowered. (In Montana, we did speak to several people who had met canoeists attempting to cover the whole river before 1977, and even found a carved inscription in a riverside hut, but nothing further concerning these attempts has apparently been recorded.)

***Canoeing of the Mississippi-Missouri.*** See above. Since 1977, the M-M has been canoed by at least two other teams.

***Longest solo trip by canoe on a river.*** This record apparently still stands.

***Longest river trip by canoe.*** At 3810 miles (figure given by the *Guinness Book of Records*), the M-M trip was at the time the longest recorded river trip by canoe. Jean Laporte's expedition (1953–4) missed out at least 800 miles of the Nile, meaning that the distance covered was below 3400 miles. Similarly, the American Amazon descent of 1970 involved at most 3400 miles. In 1983, a descent of the Amazon was achieved by Alan Holman – but the distance claimed was only 3800 miles. (The sole source of information for this last record is *Paddler's World*, February 1983, p.12.) The *Guinness Book of Records* also reports Steve Bezuk's 3800 miles on the Amazon.

**Longest solo trip by canoe on a single stretch of water.** By November 1977, no longer solo trip on a single stretch of water had apparently been recorded.

Percy Blandford, in his book *An Illustrated History of Small Boats* (1974), argues that the 'belief that an Eskimo from Greenland arrived in his kayak on the West Coast of Scotland' has 'no proof'. (In any case, the distance would have been at most 2000 miles.) He also quotes the claim for Frank Romer's trip in 1938, from Lisbon, via Las Palmas (Canary Islands) and St Thomas (Virgin Islands), towards Santo Domingo, a claim made posthumously by the Klepper canoe company as being 6199 km (3852 miles). But the claim is not fully substantiated, the straight-line distance is at most 3000 miles, and above all sails were used. Again, Dr Hannes Lindemann twice crossed from Las Palmas to the West Indies (1955, 1956), but again sails were used each time, and the straight-line distance was at most 2500 miles. The *Guinness Book of Records* in fact gives the longest 'open sea' voyage by canoe to be one from Venezuela to Miami (2710 miles).

*NB* An appeal for information in *Paddler's World* produced no substantive information about longer trips in any of these categories but the authors would be pleased to receive any further information about these records.

# Appendix 2: Expedition Chronology

The following is a list of places on the river mentioned in the text, with dates. The states listed are those adjoining the river at each point and not necessarily those to which the localities listed belong.

### Chapter IV

| | | |
|---|---|---|
| Three Forks (mile 0) | Montana | 12–13 July 1977 |
| Townsend | Montana | 14–16 |
| Canyon Ferry Dam | Montana | 17 |
| Hauser Dam | Montana | 17 |
| Gates of the Mountains | Montana | 18 |
| Holter Dam | Montana | 18 |
| Craig (mile 120) | Montana | 18–20 |

### Chapter V

| | | |
|---|---|---|
| Craig | Montana | 20 July |
| Ulm | Montana | 21 |
| Great Falls | Montana | 22 |
| Fort Benton | Montana | 23 |
| Missouri Breaks | Montana | 24–26 |
| Fred Robinson Bridge (mile 395) | Montana | 28 July–1 August |

### Chapter VI

| | | |
|---|---|---|
| Fred Robinson Bridge | Montana | 1 August |
| Soda Creek Bay | Montana | 2–3–4 |
| Musselshell Creek | Montana | 3 |
| Devil's Creek | Montana | 3 |
| Hell Creek | Montana | 6–7 |
| Fort Peck Dam | Montana | 7 |
| Milk River | Montana | 9 |

| | | |
|---|---|---|
| Wolf Point | Montana | 10 |
| Poplar (R.) | Montana | 11–12–13 |
| Brockton (mile 466) | Montana | 12 |

### Chapter VII

| | | |
|---|---|---|
| Brockton | Montana | 13 August |
| Culbertson | Montana | 13 |
| Fort Union | Montana | 14 |
| Yellowstone River | North Dakota | 16 |
| Williston | North Dakota | 16–17 |
| Little Missouri | North Dakota | 21 |
| Garrison Dam (end of Lake Sakakawea) | North Dakota | 22 |
| Fort Mandan | North Dakota | 23 |
| Interstate 94 | North Dakota | 24 |
| Bismarck | North Dakota | 24–25 |
| Cannonball | North Dakota | 25–26 |
| Mobridge (mile 1022) | South Dakota | 27–29 |

### Chapter VIII

| | | |
|---|---|---|
| Mobridge | South Dakota | 29 August |
| Moreau Inlet | South Dakota | 29–30 |
| Cheyenne River | South Dakota | 1 September |
| Okobojo | South Dakota | 1 |
| Oahe Dam | South Dakota | 2–3 |
| Pierre | South Dakota | 3 |
| Bad River | South Dakota | 3 |
| Medicine Creek | South Dakota | 3–5 |
| DeGrey | South Dakota | 3–5 |
| Chamberlain | South Dakota | 6 |
| Middle of Lake Francis Case (mile 1400) | South Dakota | 9–10 |

### Chapter IX

| | | |
|---|---|---|
| Middle of Lake Francis Case | South Dakota | 10 September |
| Dam at end of Francis Case | South Dakota | 12 |
| Gavin's Point Dam | S. Dakota/Nebraska | 14–15 |
| Yankton | S. Dakota/Nebraska | 15 |
| James River | S. Dak./Iowa/Nebr. | 15 |
| Vermillion | Iowa/Nebraska | 16 |
| Sioux City | Iowa/Nebraska | 17–18 |
| Lighthouse Marina | Iowa/Nebraska | 18–19 |

195

| | | |
|---|---|---|
| Interstate 80 | Iowa/Nebraska | 19 |
| Omaha | Iowa/Nebraska | 20 Sept.–2 Oct. |
| Bellevue | Iowa/Nebraska | 20 |
| Platte River | Iowa/Nebraska | 2 October |
| Rocky Bluff | Iowa/Nebraska | 2–3 |
| Kansas Border (mile 1828) | Missouri/Nebr./Kansas | 5 |

**Chapter X**

| | | |
|---|---|---|
| Kansas Border | Missouri/Nebr./Kansas | 5 October |
| St Joseph | Missouri/Kansas | 8–9 |
| Fort Leavenworth | Missouri/Kansas | 10 |
| Kansas City | Missouri/Kansas | 11 |
| Lexington | Missouri | 12 |
| Interstate 70 | Missouri | 13 |
| Boone County | Missouri | 13 |
| Jefferson City | Missouri | 13–14 |
| Ewing Landing | Missouri | 14–15 |
| Côte Sans Dessein | Missouri | 15 |
| Hermann | Missouri | 15–16 |
| Saint Charles | Missouri | 17 |
| Bellefontaine | Missouri | 17 |
| St Louis (mile 2316) | Missouri/Illinois | 17–23 |

**Chapter XI**

| | | |
|---|---|---|
| St Louis | Missouri/Illinois | 17–23 October |
| Mississippi River | Missouri/Illinois | 23 |
| Chain of Rocks | Missouri/Illinois | 23 |

**Chapter XII**

| | | |
|---|---|---|
| St Louis | Missouri/Illinois | 23 October |
| Sainte-Geneviève | Missouri/Illinois | 25 |
| Chester | Missouri/Illinois | 25–26 |
| Cairo | Missouri/Illinois | 27–28 |
| Mason-Dixon Line | Missouri/Ill./Kentucky | 28 |
| Columbus | Missouri/Kentucky | 28 |
| Island No. 10 | Missouri/Kent./Tennessee | 28 |
| New Madrid | Missouri/Kentucky | 28–29 |
| Barge Terminals | Missouri/Tennessee | 30 |
| Island No. 21 | Tennessee/Arkansas | 31 |
| Tomato | Tennessee/Arkansas | 31 Oct.–1 Nov. |
| Fort Pillow | Tennessee/Arkansas | 1 |
| Poker Point | Tennessee/Arkansas | 1 |
| Benjestown | Tennessee/Arkansas | 1-2-3-4 |
| Memphis (mile 3075) | Tennessee/Arkansas | 1–4 |

## Chapter XIII

| | | |
|---|---|---|
| Memphis | Tennessee/Arkansas | 4 Nov. |
| Arkansas River | Arkansas/Mississippi | 7 |
| Big Island | Arkansas/Mississippi | 7 |
| Island No. 74 | Arkansas/Mississippi | 7 |
| Greenville (mile 3250) | Arkansas/Mississippi | 9 |

## Chapter XIV

| | | |
|---|---|---|
| Greenville | Ark./Louisiana/Miss. | 9 Nov. |
| Island No. 89 | Ark./Louisiana/Miss. | 10 |
| Island No. 93 | Miss./Louisiana | 10 |
| Lake Providence | Miss./Louisiana | 10–11 |
| Atherton | Miss./Louisiana | 10–11 |
| Arcadia | Miss./Louisiana | 10–11 |
| Delta | Miss./Louisiana | 11 |
| Vicksburg | Miss./Louisiana | 11–12 |
| Natchez | Miss./Louisiana | 12–13 |
| Glasscock Cutoff | Miss./Louisiana | 13 |
| Red River and Atchafalaya R. | Miss./Louisiana | 13 |
| Fort Adams Reach | Louisiana | 13 |
| Angola | Louisiana | 13 |
| St Francisville | Louisiana | 13–14 |
| Port Hudson | Louisiana | 14 |
| Scotlandville | Louisiana | 14 |
| Baton Rouge | Louisiana | 14–15 |
| Interstate 10 | Louisiana | 15 |
| White Castle | Louisiana | 15 |
| Luling | Louisiana | 16 |
| New Orleans (mile 3700) | Louisiana | 17–24 |

## Chapter XV

| | | |
|---|---|---|
| New Orleans | Louisiana | 24 Nov. |
| Intra-coastal Waterway | Louisiana | 24 |
| Fanny | Louisiana | 24 |
| Fort Jackson | Louisiana | 25 |
| Venice | Louisiana | 25 |
| The Jump | Louisiana | 25 |
| Pilottown | Louisiana | 25 |
| Head of Passes (mile 3810) | Louisiana | 25 Nov. |